POSTCOLONIALISM

POSTCOLONIALISM: SOUTH/AFRICAN PERSPECTIVES

Edited by

Michael Chapman

Cambridge Scholars Publishing

Postcolonialism: South/African Perspectives, Edited by Michael Chapman

This book first published 2008 by

Cambridge Scholars Publishing

15 Angerton Gardens, Newcastle, NE5 2JA, UK

British Library Cataloguing in Publication Data
A catalogue record for this book is available from the British Library

ISBN (10): 1-84718-599-1, ISBN (13): 9781847185990

CONTENTS

Preface and Acknowledgements vii

Introduction
Postcolonialism: A Literary Turn
Michael Chapman 1

Unsettling Settler Identity:
Thomas Pringle's Troubled Landscapes
Matthew Shum 16

Indigenous Gardening, Belonging, and Bewilderment:
On Becoming South African
Sally-Ann Murray 40

Revolutionaries or Sell-Outs? African Intellectuals and the *Voice of Africa*
Corinne Sandwith 61

Self-translation, Untranslatability:
the Autobiographies of Mpho Nthunya and Agnes Lottering
M.J. Daymond 84

Waiting for the Russians:
Coetzee's *The Master of Petersburg* and the Logic of Late Postcolonialism
Monica Popescu 106

Deplorations: Coetzee, Costello and Doubling the N
Michael Green 125

"Which World? Whose World?": Postcolonialising Gordimer
Ileana Dimitriu 149

Barbara Adair's *In Tangier We Killed the Blue Parrot:*
A Queer Reading
Cheryl Stobie 171

Living in the World of 'Others':
Interview with Robert J.C. Young in South Africa
Michael Chapman 189

Contributors 197

Index 199

Preface and Acknowledgements

This collection of essays is concerned, explicitly and implicitly, with two particular issues in postcolonial studies: first, the shaping by northern institutions of a field located experientially and materially in the South of the world; second, a tendency of postcolonial studies to elevate theory or, at least, symptomatic analysis over and above attention to the subjective expression—the literary expression—of people's actual lives.

The essays focus on South Africa in relation to both Africa and the West. It is suggested that a global epoch in the new millennium requires not the binary oppositions of empires writing back to the centre (Rushdie's formulation), but more complicated interactions of South and North. We are reminded that Said's *Orientalism* (1978)—the text marked by the North as the beginning of postcolonial studies—was anticipated by several critical contributions from the peripheries including Achebe's attack on racial stereotyping in Conrad's *Heart of Darkness*.

With a literary turn lending coherence to South/African perspectives the essays, which are summarised in the Introduction, range from the difficulties and challenges of settler identity, through the emergence of independent (or compromised?) African and diasporic voices, to the 'postcolonialising' of Nobel laureates Nadine Gordimer and J.M. Coetzee.

Apart from Popescu's essay, which appeared in *Current Writing* (19.1.2007), the other essays—some with slightly different titles—originally appeared in *English in Africa* (19.1.2006). Acknowledgment is accorded both journals.

Introduction

Postcolonialism: A Literary Turn

Michael Chapman

Is there a role for literature—or, to be specific, imaginative literature, or the literary—in postcolonial studies? And where may one locate South Africa in a field delineated by northern institutional purposes, practices, paradigms and, more pragmatically, career/publishing opportunities? Such questions, provoked by a project on postcolonialism from South/African perspectives, have eventuated in this selection of essays.

Having developed as a set of conceptual and perceptual resources for the study of the effects on people's lives of colonial modernity—from its Renaissance expansions to contemporary manifestations of global capital—postcolonialism has come to describe heterogeneous, though linked, groupings of critical enterprises: a critique of Western totalising narratives; a revision of the Marxian class project; utilisation of both poststructural enquiry (the displaced linguistic subject) and postmodern pursuit (scepticism of the truth claims of Cartesian individualism); the condition of both nativist longing for independence from the metropolitan power and recognition of the failure of the decolonisation trajectory; a marker for voices of pronouncement by non-resident, 'Third-World' intellectual cadres in 'First-World' universities. More positively from the perspective of the South—if, indeed, postcolonialism, as Robert J.C. Young has it, is a mark of "the West's own undoing" (2001: 65)—there is a focusing of the ethical and imaginative lens on expression, writing, and testimony outside of, or in tangential relation to, the metropolitan centre-space. Such a focus, in curricular design, involves new selections of texts and revised reading practices prompted by what was earlier called Commonwealth literature or, more recently, new literatures in English or, simply, the new englishes.

I refer lastly in the above list to literary matters. For postcolonialism identifies its priorities not as literary, but as political or ideological. Again

to quote Young, who visited South Africa under the auspices of this
project:

> The assumption of postcolonial studies is that many of the wrongs, if not
> crimes, against humanity are a product of the economic dominance of the
> north over the south. In this way, the historical role of Marxism in the
> history of anti-colonial resistance remains paramount as a fundamental
> framework of postcolonial thinking. Postcolonial theory operates within
> the historical legacy of Marxist critique...which it simultaneously
> transforms according to the precedent of the greatest tricontinental anti-
> colonial intellectual politicians. (2001:6)

With tricontinental referring here to Africa, Asia, and Latin America, it is
indeed political figures, or at least philosophical spokespersons, not
literary people, who feature most prominently in Young's monumental
Postcolonialism: An Historical Introduction (2001), from which the
above passage is taken.

There is seemingly a paradox here. For postcolonialism has sought to
accord value to the personal or human dimension—the effects on people's
lives—of asymmetrical power relations between North and South. The
field—however mixed in its material and cultural presuppositions—has
struck, continues to strike, a chord in literature departments which, as
Young has noted, constitute the "solitary space within academic
institutions where subjective forms of knowledge were taken seriously"
(2001: 64). Yet a literary turn—my qualifier to the title of this Introduction—
requires defence not only because of its marginalisation in postcolonial
political mapping and revisionism, but also because of its status in the field
as handmaiden to theory. In its discursive categorisations—its Foucauldian
acts of enunciation by which the postcolonial formulates the condition of
its own possibility (see Foucault 1970)—postcolonial theory predominates
as sense-maker, or event-maker, over and above the experiential terrain to
which its theory directs its diagnostic or emblematic or, too often, its
obscurantist pronouncements. After twenty-five years of northern
institutional postcolonialism—its beginning is usually tied to the
publication of Edward W. Said's entirely lucid study, *Orientalism* (1978)—
we encounter a repetitious opposition between the 'framework ideas',
principally, of Said, Spivak and Bhabha, designated compositely as the
linguistic-cultural or poststructural turn, and the 'conflict ideas' of a
persistent Marxist materialism in, among others, Ahmad and San Juan Jr.[1]
In what too often is reminiscent of binary argument, the theory or
methodology stands the danger of replicating the very power positions

it wishes to challenge: "the West and the rest of us".[2]

The ordering of the questions, in consequence, has led to scepticisms emanating from those of 'South' identity. Such scepticisms are summarised in Kwame Anthony Appiah's wicked parody—does he, ensconced in the northern university, include himself in his parody?—of postcoloniality as "the condition of a relatively small western-style, western-trained group of writers and thinkers, who mediate the trade in cultural commodities of world capitalism at the periphery" (1992: 63). What constitutes a nation; what, an ethnic group; what, the new world order; what may oppose the hegemony of US imperialism? These questions characterise the utopian agenda of postcolonialism: the aim being a just social or, more precisely, a socialist world, in which class is again granted significant explanatory power, and in which the issues of race, gender, and the translation of cultures are posited upon the value of difference. In such an agenda, difference, or *différance* (see Derrida 1978), does not confirm division, but transforms 'othering' from negative to positive premise.

The utopian model, however, may be as totalising in its configuration as the narrative of Enlightenment-modernity against which, in almost mantra-like reaction (race, class, the unfinished business of gender), postcolonialism regularly pits its opposition. Its cultural materialist tendency seeks to resurrect a Leftish programme of social action in the wake of Thatcherism and, now, in reaction to US capitalist and military adventurism.[3] The emphasis on difference opposes what in neo-liberal global-speak is termed the convergence of markets. That the study of postcolonial literature has not in itself pushed the boundaries, to quote Tariq Ali (1993), of "market realism"—a preference for the elite work in English that is not entirely alien to the suppositions and conventions of Western modernist or postmodernist genre or style—represents an irony of an anti-metropole endeavour located within the corridors of the metropolitan institution.

Where or how do critics of literature position themselves in a project which elevates sociological or economic analysis, or the discourses of philosophy or politics, over and above literary intervention, and in which literature, when it does engage attention, is subjected to issue-driven interpretation. As E. San Juan Jr phrases it, literature is regarded as "an instance of concrete political practice which reflects the dynamic process of the national democratic revolution in the developing countries" (1998: 254).

This formulation promises little more than a return to earlier economistic base/superstructure rigidity. To which a critic of the linguistic turn—Homi

K. Bhabha, for example—might respond that, no, the literary text, indeed the subject in its subjectivity, is characterised not simply as materialist reflection, but as rhetorical, performative act. Accordingly, meaning emerges in the textual palimpsest, deconstructively, or against the grain of full intent, in the slippages, in the "in-between", the "liminal", or "Third Space". It is here that coloniser and colonised interact: not in the binary oppositions of master and slave, but in more intricate, more devious sparrings. In the "sly civilities" of the hybridised encounter—we are told, following Heidegger's insight that a boundary is not where matters stop, but where newness is possible—new social and cultural forms of resistance, or even exchange, find their "presencing" (Bhabha 1994). If the subaltern, as Gayatri Chakravorty Spivak (1985) maintains, cannot speak, she or he can at least mimic the coloniser, ridicule and thus undermine the authoritarian substance and manner. To which the cynic might retort, or simply confirm the coloniser's view that the colonial babu in his wheedling and winking remains—well!—a babu.

Here is a conundrum. It is a conundrum that for the last decade or more has characterised post- debate. Our investment in a common human enterprise is qualified by our investment in the dignity of our different selves. The conundrum, nonetheless, is more intractable when located in the large categories of conflict-oriented or framework-oriented postcolonial theory than when located in the experiential purchase of literary works, or in the analysis of individual texts, or—dare one say it—in the aesthetic appreciations of a literary turn.

It is widely agreed, for example, that a considerable output of the most exciting contemporary literature emanates from non-metropolitan sources of creativity and concern. Let me permit Salman Rushdie his colourful response to George Steiner's complaint that literary energy is being generated not in the metropolis, but at the edges of the world: "What does it matter...? What is this flat earth on which the good professor lives, with jaded Romans at the centre and frightfully gifted Hottentots at the edges" (Rushdie 1996). We—that is, we in the academy, who have taken the post-challenge seriously— no longer think of Achebe or Gordimer or Coetzee as writing, in reaction, back to the centre. If we are willing to grant Achebe his initial project of re-inserting the African human being in the heart of darkness, then his critical as well as his creative writing—are the two easily separable?—has offered telling adjustments to dominant perspectives on the Western canon, in which the novelist has been always an artist before, as recast by Achebe, a teacher (1988 [1965]). Is Conrad or Bunyan or Shakespeare unifocally a metropolitan writer? Is the Third World writer merely the doppelgänger of the metropolitan counterpart? We may wish to read Toni Morrison as postcolonial, or J.M. Coetzee as both South African and international, or—through his recent work (Coetzee 2005)—as exploratory of the postcolonial as a settler-colony identification: Canberra, or previously Cape Town, placed somewhere 'in-between' London and Lagos.

As I have said, the focus in postcolonial literary studies has remained attached to the elite work in new englishes by the emigré or multicultural metropolitan author (the Salman Rushdie or the Zadie Smith). The oral or indigenous voice, or popular expression on the periphery (African praises, say, or Onitsha market literature), has had limited impact so far on post-debate, where the tendency has been to replace Western canons with Third-World canons (instead of Conrad's *Heart of Darkness*, we have Achebe's *Things Fall Apart*) or where the tendency has been to re-appraise metropolitan 'touchstones' through the telescope of alternative modernities (Shakespeare's *The Tempest* or Bunyan's *The Pilgrim's Progress* in the New World). Such 'elite' constrictions notwithstanding, a literary influence may be fruitfully pursued. It is an influence that can be identified, more recently, even in critics whose interest is principally philosophical, political or ideological.

Although he retains his Marxist predilection for class analysis in his denigration of postmodern sceptics of truth, unity and progress, for example, Terry Eagleton in *After Theory* (2003) suggests a consideration of truth categories—virtue, evil, morality, pleasure, death—which have been in short supply in ideological critique, but which constitute the truth of poetry as opposed to the truth of history (to invoke an Aristotelian distinction). For Robert J.C. Young (2001: 409), to whom I have already referred, literary texts—he names *Passage to India, King Solomon's Mines* and *Kim*—are not an expression of higher or more complex truth, but an aspect of discourse no greater in import than the private letter as evidence in a law court as part of legal discourse: discourse being not the direct or indirect representation or misrepresentation of experience, but a system of statements, or rules, that governs institutional practice. (In Young's attention the practice, of course, is colonialism.) Such a line of argument might seem unpropitious of a literary turn; Young reminds us, nevertheless, that postcolonialism as a spur to thought and activity predates Said, Bhabha and Spivak, the 'holy trinity' of the northern university. Rather, the postcolonial has long had important voices on the peripheries; that, in fact, peripheries may be an inappropriate descriptive term, as perhaps is postcolonial itself, Young preferring tricontinental in

its internationalist ambition. Not only was Gandhi an influential presence—
a kind of embodied creative text, to be interpreted in multiple contexts of
imaginative and ethical challenge—but it is significant that what shaped
those thinkers whose work is synonymous with post- debate—Foucault
and Derrida—was their experience in colonial Tunisia and Algeria,
respectively.[4]

Closer to a literary turn, Bart Moore-Gilbert (1997)—like Ato Quayson
(2000), another critic who has sustained a literary interest[5]—distinguishes
between postcolonial theory and postcolonial practice, and includes as
formative influences not only philosophical and political thinkers, but also
the 'first wave' of Caribbean and African writer-critics of the decolonisation
years. We are reminded that Achebe's landmark essay, "An Image of
Africa: Racism in Conrad's *Heart of Darkness*" (1988 [1975]), was published
three years prior to Said's *Orientalism*; that Ngũgĩ's "decolonising the
mind" (1981)—the phrase had been coined earlier by Es'kia Mphahlele
(1962) in his response to *Negritude*—anticipated the agitation of Spivak,
in particular, for curricular reform; and that both E.K. Brathwaite's theory
of "creolisation" (1971) and Wilson Harris's neologism of "the in-between"
(1967:8) (a means to figure a position between cultures) anticipated
Bhabha's conception of the Third Space. Harris well before Bhabha, in
fact, had defined "the void" as the element which, as in Bhabha, complicates
full translation: the void prevents cultures or cultural forms, which are
being negotiated, from attaining the easy commerce of equivalence or
synthesis, Harris notes, while at the same time the void—the apparent
paradox is key to Bhabha's hybridity—is a place which allows cultures to
mix not by erasing differences, but by "endorsing difference yet creatively
undermining biases" (Harris 1992 [1967]: 20).

I mention the insights of so-called Third World literary figures not to
score 'South' points against the North, but to remind us that what we now
refer to as the postcolonial is, spatially and temporally, an entanglement
of the colony with modernity, in which—as Said (1993) has argued—no
cultures are pure and in which the philosophical home may not be the
nation but the world. Not only in Bhabha or in Harris, but in observations
dating back to Roman and Christian encounters, we may identify—to
return to my earlier point—a post- conundrum: a narrative of causality
suggesting both progress (one stage to the next) and imposition (a
dominating story); or a local story susceptible, also, to its own paradoxes
of difference, as both identity-recognition and ethnicity-identification. It
is a conundrum which, in granting respect for 'my story', may trigger in
'your story' vicious regional competition, as in the Balkan wars of the

1990s: why your story and not my story? Or, whose story has authority? Or, according to post- 'dissensus', is cultural understanding or literary history desirable, or even possible?

Given a rhetoric that is able to paralyse claims of rationality or ethical choice, it is not really surprising to note impulsions to greater nuance and complexity in either/or scenarios. The physical sciences, for example, point out that as in scientific experimentation so in social life, we artificially construct our conjunctures of events. These hypothetical models chart causality according to provisional patterns while subjecting such patterns—which are, after all, constructed patterns—to ever more challenging observation in the pursuit of truer or, at least more invariant, accounts of reality. (See Potter and López 2001) Or, to turn to economics, Immanuel Wallerstein's world systems theory (1974; 1991) in its narration of modernity is not as singular as literary critics of Enlightenment tend to find convenient. While attached to European and now US global expansion, capitalism overlaps differently, at different times and in different spaces, with the intrusions—not simply the passivities—of decolonisation and neocolonialism. (It is not a new observation that South Africa's development invokes the consideration of colonialism of a special kind.)

Such tensions between global universalism—or a mélange of cultural production in US sweatshops at the edges of the world—and the identity politics of regions, even nations, provoke several essays in the collection, *Postcolonial Studies and Beyond* (Loomba et al 2005). The conclusion of the editors, in their Introduction, is that in an era of globalisation debate must move beyond the 'conundrum'—consensus or dissensus—of the past decade, and seek a "new critical language for articulating the linkage between local, lived experience and the broadest structures of global economic and political power" (19). It is not as Said suggests in what for him is an unusual flourish to popular effect that "stone-throwing Palestinian youths or swaying dancing South African groups or wall-traversing East Germans" (1993: 396) by their actions alone collapsed the relevant tyrannies. Rather, it is that metanarratives, as Kelwyn Sole (2005) argues in *Postcolonial Studies and Beyond*, must not be erased, but must be qualified by scrupulous attention to local conditions. Sole illustrates his point in an analysis of the "quotidian experience"—the everyday, as a category—in contemporary South African poetry, which questions the "pseudo freedoms" bred and licensed by neoliberalism in the new South Africa.

At the same time, Sole—alert to the danger of racial division—cannot contemplate a future progressive South Africa simply as an accumulation of discrete observations detached from the trace of a trajectory: a trajectory urging citizens towards a community of awareness. The concept, community of awareness, is Fanon's (1961): his synthesis beyond the antithesis of native resistance. It is quoted approvingly by Said (1993: 262); and it is endorsed by Young in his conclusion as to why, even though he himself prefers the term tricontinental, postcolonialism retains its definitional purpose in globalised times. Postcolonialism marks the fact that, despite setbacks to decolonisation, human beings require a return to what has come to be known as a radical humanitarian tradition. (See Fanon 1961: 315-6, and Young 2001: 67-8)

We touch again on the terrain of the literary, where explorations of the subjective and imaginative life should seek the gradations that are too often erased in the abstractions of postcolonial theory. Sole is unlikely to label himself a postcolonial critic. His caution bears, perhaps, on Said's observation (1993: 264) outside his flourish about stone-throwing youths and toyi-toying (swaying-singing) crowds: the postcolonial paradigm— the West's turning its gaze on its ex-colonies—is least applicable to the topographies, both imaginative and developmental, of countries with particularly complicated relationships to a colonising/anti-colonising dialectic. Said's examples are Algeria, Guinea, sections of the Islamic and Arab worlds, and Palestine and South Africa; and at the conference at Wits University (Johannesburg) in 1996 on "Post-Colonial Shakespeares" Jonathan Dollimore sought both precariously and elegantly to tackle a certain hostility among South African participants to a postcolonial discourse:

> There was, for example, distrust of 'metropolitan' theory, including by myself; a sense that this theory which gestured so much towards difference as a fundamental philosophical premise, disregarded its material realities. But what struck me, as an outsider, as the most hostile divide of all, was that between a materialist tradition of criticism and subsequent developments conveniently (though again reductively) lumped together as "the" postmodern. (1997: 259-60)

How to avoid the either/or dichotomy, or the divide—implicit in northern institutional postcolonialism, despite its best intentions—between a still confident West as the framer of the discourse and the silent, or winking, or rebellious native subjects of the South? As far as academic enquiry is concerned, the response to the travelling theorist cannot be the indigene who, in the blood and the bones, *knows* the local story, and Dollimore's conclusion, even as it feels compelled to retain the European thinker as measure, shifts either/or to both/and:

> I reconsider the place of pessimism within the political project in the spirit of Gramsci's familiar yet never more apposite remark: "Pessimism of the intellect, optimism of the will." (1997: 260)

Optimism of the will reinforces a literary turn, even if such a turn refuses to follow David Punter's own imaginative, sometimes quirky attempt in his study *Postcolonial Imaginings* (2000) to redirect postcolonial theory towards the substance of his subtitle, "Fictions of a New World Order". Instead of postcolonial criticism's "establishing a ground"—what are the forms of colonialism, what is a comprador formation, etc.?—the question, according to Punter, is how to respond to the pressures under which the postcolonial experience is felt, how the narrative, recursive, struggling forward, burdened by setbacks, emerges in image, in speech, in the shocks of its insights, in the complexity of its human interactions. It is an imagination which Punter, in his attempt to turn to the literary, can identify only in "melancholy, ruin, loss" (2000: 186): an imagination (defined by Punter as postcolonial) of violent geographics, displacement, of ghosts in the history house, in which the freight of centuries of colonisation can never be erased.

In the postcolony, however—if South Africa may be designated, tentatively, as a postcolony—the "spectral" (Punter 2002) does not necessarily negate the energies of renewal, even as the in-between space presents an ongoing challenge. How then may the literary intervene? According to Wilson Harris

> the possibility exists for the literary work to involve us in perspectives on renascence which can bring into play a figurative meaning beyond an apparently real world or prison of history.... I believe a philosophy of history may well be buried in the arts of the imagination. (1970: 8)

Or, more recently, according to Hanif Kureishi,

> the only patriotism possible is one that refuses the banality of taking either side, and continues the arduous conversation. That is why we have literature, the theatre, newspapers—a culture... .(2005:19)

* * *

The essays that follow offer independent contributions to postcolonial debate. Insights that have been influential in the definition of the field are neither ignored nor permitted to 'overwrite' the texts of imaginative experience. Matthew Shum's reading of Thomas Pringle, for example, avoids the theoretical formulations that dominate northern institutional postcolonial study. Pringle's settler identity is seen to be less than contained by a landscape poem which, in its local place, requires an adjustment of standard European-Romantic categories of tutored and untutored nature. A close reading is not utilised, in consequence, to entirely deconstructive purposes—to reveal the limits of Pringle's radicalism—as might be the familiar postcolonial manoeuvre. Instead, the close reading returns value to the poem; the complexity of settler identity is captured in Pringle's subjective response to the strange, discomfiting experience.

In Sally-Ann Murray's tilling of the suburban garden, or the garden as text, white South Africans emerge neither as "colonists who will" (Memmi's settlers of conservation or conservatism) nor "colonists who won't" (Memmi's settlers of guilty conscience).[6] If suburban gardening in its importation of hybrid species reveals by analogy jittery identities, gardening reveals also the pleasurable pursuits of settler belonging. If indigeneity has not come naturally to ex-Europeans in Africa, neither will these settlers of over one hundred years vanish in any retreat to a mythical motherland: a motherland now more alien to them than the adopted African soil. There may be potential, therefore, for the forging of new identities beyond nature or nurture. What, after all, is nature, what nurture, in a space that since the Dutch landings in 1652 has experienced translations of Africa and the West?

The anxieties of identity in multiple racial and social contexts are examined, in different ways, by Corinne Sandwith and M.J. Daymond. In a heterogeneous society, class and race identifications raise questions about the authenticity of any discourse: questions that Sandwith pursues in her focus on *The Voice* (1949-52), a little-known black 'township' broadsheet which included the early contributions of writers such as Es'kia Mphahlele. It is the translatability or untranslatability of cultures[7] that Daymond pursues in the interstices of written and oral life stories, English or englishes, or tradition and modernity, or women's voices in patriarchal community. If in Daymond's essay the two subjects of their stories—Mpho Nthunya and Agnes Lottering—occupy Bhabha's Third Space of in-betweenness, then there is no certainty of presencing. When older belief systems encounter Christian teaching in the contact zone, there may be silence, but a silence resonant, paradoxically, of the struggle of incommensurability between contesting worlds. Does academic enquiry probe or respect the othernness?

A scrupulous refusal to inhabit 'otherness' is a mark of J.M. Coetzee's fiction. Monica Popescu asks why Coetzee in 1994, amid momentous change in South Africa, set *The Master of Petersburg* in nineteenth-century Russia. Her enquiry leads to a category shift from 'postcolonial' as vertical-axis consideration of metropolis and colony to "late postcolonialism": a triangulation, or complex interaction, not a turning away from, but an analogous placing of, South Africa's transition in a nuanced, global picture.

Such triangulation also informs the remaining contributions. It is Michael Green's concern that J.M. Coetzee's "Lesson", in *Elizabeth Costello* (2003), on "The Humanities in Africa", glosses stories that in accumulated particularities of time and place may suggest a multifaceted truth of human and spiritual interaction, a reality of Africa and the West. Sweeping generalisations by the two characters in the "Lesson", whether on the nature of African Christianity or Greek classicism, risk evading the needs of actual people. Instead of story yielding the truth of the subject in the landscape, story—as so often in postcolonial discussion—may be manipulated into the service of preferred ideologies. Where does Coetzee, the arch-fictionalist, stand in relation to the characters to whom he gives voice? The question—an intricate question—is posited by Green through a Coetzean device: a lecture which, as in Elizabeth Costello's "Lesson", invites the reader to participate in the making of meaning.

The making of meaning, as Ileana Dimitriu points out in Ato Quayson's study *Postcolonialism* (2000), shifts from consideration of the postcolonial as a set of conditions *out there* to the postcolonial as ongoing process: a coming into being of the new millennium as "a postcolonializing" world (Quayson 2000:8). This suggests increasing migrancy, increasing movements of all kinds across increasingly porous borders, of margins located in centres, and vice versa. As a spectator of a UEFA football match might observe in the composition of the 'multi-ethnic' teams, the ramparts of Fortress Europe have already been breached. Or, more crucially, as a viewer in South Africa of BBC World will see, France in November 2005 experienced the violence of its failure to understand, creatively, its own postcolonialising "presencing". It is the metaphor of postcolonialising that summarises Nadine Gordimer's recent critical and creative writing, and Dimitriu identifies in the diverse landscapes of Gordimer's *The Pick-up* and *Loot* neither metropolitan centres nor African nor Asian nor Latin-American, nor indeed East European peripheries, but multiple margins and centres that are imbued with different degrees of significance. Cheryl Stobie, for her part, turns Barbara Adair's novel of life in a decadent

Tangier to significance in the South Africa of today, in which post-apartheid times have presented the possibilities of challenging new relationships not only across race, but also across gender. Challenges in South Africa, finally, direct Chapman's interview with Robert J.C. Young.

What the contributions have in common is what I have termed a literary turn. Unlike San Juan Jr, the contributors do not regard the imaginative work as an "instance of concrete political practice reflecting the process of national democratic revolution". The new South Africa has not complied in predictable ways with the revolutionary vision: the national democratic movement—if one may still attach the label to the ANC government—has had to adjust its socialist ideals to the complexities of multiple centres and margins within economic and cultural life not only in South Africa, but also in South Africa's relation to Africa and the world. The contributors might be prepared to agree with Derek Attridge (2004: 126-31) that literature defines its "singularity" in its resistance to the all-encompassing frame or idea; that literature although a cultural product is rarely self-contained by the culture; and that whatever its effect or affect on our experience, a literary turn is unlikely either to fast track into power any New Social Movement or to save our souls.

What literature might achieve is its own apprehension of otherness; its capacity to offer surprising articulations of, and insights into, the complexity of human potential and conduct. Despite the utopian pronouncements of many postcolonial projects, the current collection of essays heeds Ania Loomba's more realistic purpose: we academics "should at the very least place our discussions of postcoloniality in the context of our own educational institutions and practices" (1998: 258). The objective is to stimulate our students, and ourselves, to see afresh, and comparatively, across worlds. In this, a literary turn may achieve an ethical dimension.

Notes

1. See Ahmad (1992), San Juan Jr (1998). Also, Fanon (1961), Ali (1993) and Parry (2004).
2. See Chinweizu (1975).
3. See Young (2001), Lazarus (2004), and Loomba et al (2005).
4. See Young (2001), for chapters on "Gandhi's Counter-modernity", "Foucault in Tunisia" and "Subjectivity in History: Derrida in Algeria".
5. For studies that devote greater attention to literary criticism than to theory or political commentary see, also, Ashcroft, Griffiths and Tiffin (1989),

Bassnett and Trivedi (1999), Boehmer (1995), Gilroy (1993), Japtok (2003), King et al (1995), Punter (2000) and Walder (1998).

6. See Memmi (1965).

7. See Budick and Iser (1996).

References

Achebe, Chinua. 1958. *Things Fall Apart*. London: Heinemann Educational.

_____. 1988 [1965]. "The Novelist as Teacher." In: *Hopes and Impediments: Selected Essays 1965-87*. London and Ibadan: Heinemann International: 27-31.

_____. 1988 [1975]. "An Image of Africa: Racism in Conrad's *Heart of Darkness*." In: *Hopes and Impediments: Selected Essays 1965-87*. London and Ibadan: Heinemann International: 1-13.

Ahmad, Aijaz. 1992. *In Theory: Classes, Nations, Literatures*. London: Verso.

Ali, Tariq. 1993. "Literature and Market Realism." *New Left Review* 199: 140-5.

Appiah, Kwame Anthony. 1992. *In My Father's House: Africa in the Philosophy of Culture*. London: Methuen.

Ashcroft, Bill, Gareth Griffiths and Helen Tiffin. 1989. *The Empire Writes Back: Theory and Practice in Post-colonial Literatures*. London and New York: Routledge.

Attridge, Derek. 2004. *The Singularity of Literature*. London and New York: Routledge.

Bassnett, Susan, and Harish Trivedi (eds). 1999. *Post-Colonial Translation: Theory and Practice*. London and New York: Routledge.

Boehmer, Elleke. 1995. *Colonial and Postcolonial Literature*. Oxford: OUP.

Bhabha, Homi K. 1994. *The Location of Culture*. London and New York: Routledge.

Brathwaite, E.K. 1971. *The Development of Creole Society in Jamaica 1770-1820*. Oxford: Clarendon.

Budick, Sanford, and Wolfgang Iser (eds). 1996. *The Translatability of Cultures: Figurations of the Space Between*. Stanford: Stanford University Press.

Bunyan, John. 1987 [1678]. *The Pilgrim's Progress*. Harmondsworth: Penguin.

Chinweizu. 1975. *The West and the Rest of Us: White Predators, Black Slavers and the African Elite*. New York: Vintage.

Coetzee, J.M. 2005. *Slow Man*. London: Secker and Warburg.

Conrad, Joseph. 1994 [1902]. *Heart of Darkness*. Harmondsworth: Penguin.

Derrida, Jacques. 1978. *Writing and Difference*. Translated from the French by Alan Bass. London: Routledge and Kegan Paul.

Dollimore, Jonathan. 1998. "Shakespeare and Theory." In: A. Loomba and M. Orkin (eds). *Post-Colonial Shakespeares*. London and New York: Routledge: 259-76.

Eagleton, Terry. 2003. *After Theory*. London: Allen Lane.

Fanon, Franz. 1961. *The Wretched of the Earth*. Translated from the French by Constance Farrington. Harmondsworth: Penguin.

Foucault, Michel. 1970. *The Order of Things: An Archaeology of the Human Sciences*. Translated from the French by A.M. Sheridan. New York: Pantheon.

Gilroy, Paul. 1993. *The Black Atlantic: Modernity and Double Consciousness*. London: Verso.

Harris, Wilson. 1967. *Tradition, the Writer and Society*. London: New Beacon.

_____. 1970. *History, Fable and Myth in the Caribbean and Guianas*. Georgetown: Ministry of Information and Culture. Reprinted: Harris. 1981. *Explorations: A Selection of Talks and Articles*, edited by H. Maes-Jelinek. Mundelstrup: Dangaroo Press.

_____. 1992. "Judgement and Dream." In: A. Riach and M. Williams (eds). *The Radical Imagination: Lectures and Talks by Wilson Harris*. Liège: Département d'Anglais, Université de Liège.

Japtok, Martin (ed.). 2003. *Postcolonial Perspectives on Women Writers: From Africa, the Caribbean, and the U.S.* Trenton (N.J.) and Asmara: Africa World Press, Inc.

King, Russell et al. 1995. *Writing across Worlds: Literature and Migration*. London and New York: Routledge.

Kureishi, Hanif. 2005. "The Arduous Conversation Will Continue." *The Guardian* (19 July):19.

Lazarus, Neil (ed.). 2004. *The Cambridge Companion to Postcolonial Studies*. Cambridge: CUP.

Loomba, Ania. 1998. *Colonialism/Postcolonialism*. London and New York: Routledge.

Loomba, Ania et al. 2005. *Postcolonial Studies and Beyond*. Durham and London: Duke University Press.

Memmi, Albert. 1965 [1957]. *The Coloniser and the Colonised*. New York: Orion Press.

Moore-Gilbert, Bart. 1997. *Postcolonial Theory: Contexts, Practices, Politics*. London: Verso.

Mphahlele, Ezekiel [Es'kia]. 1962. *The African Image*. London: Faber and Faber: 19-55.

Ngũgĩ wa Thiong'o. 1981. *Decolonising the Mind: The Politics of Language in African Literature*. London: James Currey.

Parry, Benita. 2004. *Postcolonial Studies: A Materialist Critique*. London and New York: Routledge.

Potter, Garry and José López. 2001. "After Postmodernism: The New Millennium." In: J. López and G. Potter (eds). *After Postmodernism: An Introduction to Critical Realism*. London: The Athlone Press: 3-16.

Punter, David. 2000. *Postcolonial Imaginings: Fictions of a New World Order*. Edinburgh: Edinburgh University Press.

_____. 2002. "Spectral Criticism." In: J. Wolfreys (ed.). *Introducing Criticism at the 21st Century*. Edinburgh: Edinburgh University Press: 259-78.

Quayson, Ato. 2000. *Postcolonialism: Theory, Practice or Process?* Cambridge: Polity Press.

Rushdie, Salman. 1996. "The Novel's Not Yet Dead...It's Just Buried." *Mail and Guardian Review of Books* (September).

Said, Edward W. 1978. *Orientalism: Western Representation of the Orient*. London: Routledge and Kegan Paul.

_____. 1993. *Culture and Imperialism*. London: Vintage.

San Juan Jr, E. 1998. *Beyond Postcolonial Theory*. New York and London: St Martin's Press.

Shakespeare, William. 1997 [1623]. *The Tempest*. The Riverside Shakespeare. Boston: Houghton.

Sole, Kelwyn. 2005. "The Deep Thoughts the One in Need Falls Into: Quotidian Experience and the Perspectives of Poetry in Postliberation South Africa." In: A. Loomba et al. (eds). *Postcolonial Studies and Beyond*. Durham and London: Duke University Press: 182-205.

Spivak, Gayatri Chakravorty. 1985. "Can the Subaltern Speak? Speculations on Widow Sacrifice." *Wedge* 7/8: 120-30.

Walder, Dennis. 1998. *Post-colonial Literatures in English: History, Language, Theory*. Oxford: Blackwell.

Wallerstein, Immanuel. 1974. *The Modern World System: Capitalist Agriculture and the Origin of the European World Economy in the Sixteenth Century*. New York: Academic Press.

_____. 1991. *Geopolitics and Geoculture: Essays on the Changing World System*. Cambridge: CUP.

Young, Robert J.C. 2001. *Postcolonialism: An Historical Introduction*. Oxford: Blackwell.

Unsettling Settler Identity

Thomas Pringle's Troubled Landscapes

Matthew Shum

Postcolonial criticism, like its theoretical predecessor colonial discourse analysis, is rarely sympathetic to settler literature, and then only when this literature registers, in some explicit way, opposition to the colonial enterprise. Such an undifferentiated association of colonial writing, especially that of the first phase of settlement, with what Aijaz Ahmad has called "aggressive identity formation" (1992:78), often assumes that the act of enunciation, aesthetic or otherwise, mirrors the processes of material appropriation which establish the colonial state. The assumptions apply particularly, perhaps, to landscape poetry, where the very subject-matter is saturated with implication of the most obvious sort. Even within the metropolitan context, late eighteenth- and nineteenth-century loco-descriptive poetry and painting has been subjected to vigorous critique for its occlusion of the labouring poor, its aestheticisation of political intent, its naturalisation of class interest and so forth. While I do not wish to deny the cogency of these approaches, they have tended to add critical weight to colonial and postcolonial appraisals of landscape depiction as fully implicated in imperial processes. In this paper I take as an example of colonial landscape description Thomas Pringle's "Evening Rambles", a poem first published in London in 1828, but which was in large part composed on the Eastern frontier of the Cape Colony in 1821. In my reading—a close reading, which attempts to respect the dynamics of the text and its complex particularity rather than encode it in a pre-formulated theory—the poem offers a conflicted and uncertain understanding of colonial landscape as a site that both invites and resists the imposition of European schemas. Such a reading goes entirely against the grain of contemporary critical responses to "Evening Rambles", which are united in their disparagement of its derivative intent: the poem is, such readings assert, a transparent attempt to work colonial landscape into imperial paradigms.

The tone is set in J.M. Coetzee's groundbreaking essays on colonial landscape in *White Writing* (1989). While conceding in one essay that the poem's technical achievements (he is discussing the traverses that allow spatial excursus through the landscape) "are accomplished with a fair amount of art" (47), Coetzee returns in another essay to declare the poem no more than an exercise in imperial domestication: "[T]he familiar trot of iambic-tetrameter couplets reassuringly domesticates the foreign content. The underlying argument of the poem, from beginning to end is that, since the African wilderness clearly does not strain the capacities of the English language or even of English verse, it can be contained within the European category of the exotic"(1989: 164). Malvern van Wyk Smith is similarly unforgiving: in his view the poem is a "relaxed domestic contemplation" (2000:28), in which a culpably "selective innocence"(29) enables Pringle to conduct a "controlled and magisterial survey ... confirming ... the operation of the imperial imagination" (29). David Bunn, while locating the poem in a larger argument about colonial landscape, reads in it similarly appropriative intents the fundamental motivation of which is "ideological containment" (1994: 139). Against these assumptions I argue that while Pringle's poem is indeed hinged on certain assumptions about landscape and its representation which are demonstrably British in provenance, and that these assumptions have an inherently imperial character in that they seek to trope colonial landscape into certain regimes of representation, this is by no means the whole story. Far from accomplishing a seamless or untroubled annexure of the African landscape into the generic boundaries of metropolitan representation, the poem, in my reading, problematises this process to the point where such boundaries lose their bearing, and enacts something like the collapse of its informing conventions rather than their imposition. In order to arrive at this reading, however, it is necessary to situate the poem within the numerous descriptions of colonial landscape in the 'frontier' chapters of Pringle's *Narrative of a Residence in South Africa* (1834), descriptions to which the poem does at times allude and descriptions which are indispensable to locating the poem in its proper context.

In those early chapters of the *Narrative* which describe the first years of British settlement on the frontier, we encounter the usual heterogeneous mixture of landscape description, a taxonomy of fauna and flora, observations on animal behaviour, details of progress on the settlement, and a medley of anecdotal accounts of historical and other events. The chapter subheadings, with their telegraphed condensations of content separated by dashes, might offer the appearance of coherence or susceptibility to summary, but the paratactic yoking of discrete particulars ("Valley of the White River—Moravian Settlement of Enon—Anecdotes of the Kaffir Wars") very often indicates something different: the inability to cast the narrative into a containing or generically stable structure. The *Narrative* is not really a narrative at all: it is something more like an eclectic catalogue of events, sights, incidents, observations, anecdotes and polemical interventions strung together along a loose temporal line. This generic eclecticism points towards the difficulty of finding ways to fit the colonial into received templates of representation: a difficulty particularly evident in the descriptions of landscape, where Pringle, as we shall see, often registers reactions that are fraught with ambivalence and, at times, fear. We should bear in mind that for Pringle landscape description is not a matter of mere topographical detail: it is at the deepest level an investment in—or a divestment of—identity itself. Landscape, or the "face of the country" as travel writers of the period called it, as though it were a physiognomy whose decipherment would lead to a revelation of inner character, must be made habitable for the coloniser not only through acts of material transformation or classificatory control, but also through acts of imaginative reclamation whose "shaping perception ... makes the difference between raw matter and landscape" (Schama 1996:10).

The first extended depiction of landscape in the *Narrative* is a ship deck view of the Eastern Cape coast, just beyond the Knysna lagoon—approximately the territory in which the settlers were to be placed:

> This [the ship's tacking off the coast] gave us an excellent opportunity of surveying the coast scenery of Auteniqualand and Zitzikamma, which is of a very striking character. The land rises abruptly from the shore in massive mountain ridges, clothed with forests of large timber, and swelling into the back ground into lofty serrated peaks of naked rock. As we passed headland after headland, the sylvan recesses of the bays and mountains opened successively to our gaze, like a magnificent panorama, continually unfolding new features, or exhibiting new combinations of scenery, in which the soft and the stupendous, the monotonous and the picturesque, were strangely blended. The aspect of the whole was impressive, but somber; beautiful, but somewhat savage. There was the grandeur and the grace of nature, majestic and untamed; and there was likewise that air of *lonesomeness* and dreary *wildness*, which a country unmarked by the traces of human industry or of human residence seldom fails to exhibit to the view of civilized man ...the sublimely stern aspect of the country, so different from the rich tameness of ordinary English scenery, seemed to strike many of the *Southron* [English] with a degree of awe approaching to consternation. The Scotch, on the contrary, as the stirring recollections

of their native land were vividly called up by the rugged peaks and shaggy
declivities of this wild coast, were strongly affected, like all true
mountaineers on such occasions. Some were excited to extravagant spirits;
others silently shed tears. (1966:6-7)

In this first sighting or "surveying" of landscape Pringle employs the two
standard tropes of landscape description, the sublime and the picturesque,
along with their usual connotations. They are, however, "strangely
blended", somehow not the usual sum of their parts:"[I]mpressive, but
somber; beautiful, but somewhat savage". We might gloss the oxymoronic
uneasiness of the above description as sublime but productive of the
sombre rather than an exhilarating sense of the illimitable, and beautiful
or picturesque but lacking ordered containment. Similarly, the "grandeur
and grace of nature" is offset by ("there was likewise") a simultaneous
sense of the strongly scored *lonesomeness*" and "*wildness*". Despite
these complications there is an imperious presumptiveness in the very
syntax of these observations: the landscape offers itself to Pringle's gaze
with a passive allure—"opening", "unfolding" and "exhibiting"—as though
it were a vast and empty "panorama" laid out for survey by "civilized man"
rather than another country with geographical and other features
appropriate to its own social organisation. Though Pringle's gaze over the
colonial landscape will often be directed by the imperious expectation that
it is there to be commanded or mapped onto the co-ordinates of the ways
of seeing he has brought with him, the landscape—as this passage already
demonstrates—will in equal and sometimes greater measure also disturb
these expectations.

In Pringle's subsequent experience as a settler, these initial
apprehensions about the "aspect" of the country he was entering do not
fully abate. In his first venture into the interior—as he rides towards the
London Missionary Society station at Bethelsdorp—he complains of the
emptiness and monotony of a landscape "unenlivened" by human presence,
the blankness of its features "relieved" only by some "lofty and picturesque
mountains" in the distance. The fact that Pringle immediately establishes
such a polarity—let us call it a polarity between the monotonous and the
picturesque—is a clear indication that the latter category possesses for
him an associational significance that goes beyond mere 'pleasure'. It is
as though Pringle were eagerly scanning the surrounding country for
sights—and sites—that will offer the legible differentiations of the
picturesque rather than the unreadable blankness of landscape that is
merely "monotonous". As Pringle's party journeys towards the land

allocated to them, he continues to read landscape in terms which emphasise privation –"a country so waste and lonesome that it seemed almost totally devoid of inhabitants"(1966:27)—occasionally punctuated by more picturesque detail. In the following short passage we see the often abrupt transition between the two types of landscape: "The features of the country changed alternately from dark jungle to rich park-like scenery, embellished with graceful clumps of evergreens; and from that again to the desolate sterility of savage mountains, or of parched and desert plains ..." (26). Pringle's use of the term "picturesque" is not definitionally specific; in general application it exists mainly as an antonym to the predominantly "waste" or "sterile" or "savage" character of the landscape. Its substantive applications are varied, as the following passage illustrates:

> The scenery of the upper part of the dell is very picturesque. Accompanying the course of a stream, as it meanders through the meadows, you have, on the right, lofty hills covered with woods of evergreens, and broken by *kloofs* or subsidiary dells, filled with large forest timber. On the left the hills are lower, but also covered with copsewood, and in many places diversified by rocks and cliffs of deep red and other lively colours. ... At every turn the outline of the hills varies, presenting new points of picturesque scenery; while, scattered through the meadows, or bending over the river margin, appear little clumps of evergreens, willows, and acacias; and sometimes groves of lofty forest-trees ... enrich the vale with a stately beauty not always met with in South African landscape. This combination of the wild, the grand and the beautiful, is heightened in its effect by the exotic appearance of the vegetation. The meadows, too, or savannahs along the river banks, are richly embellished ... with large purple flowers. ... (1966:84-5)

There is a painterly attention to detail in this passage most evident in verbs which serve a compositional purpose by evoking variation in perspective ("At every turn the outlines of the hills *varies, presenting* new points ...") or verbs ("diversified by", "enrich", "heightened", "embellished") which emphasise textural nuance. Pringle responds to this scene, which he acknowledges as atypical, with a lyricism of particularity rare in his descriptions of South African landscape. In contrastive terms, this is a veritable sanctuary of the picturesque, rich in the "variety, ornamentation, and detail" (Bermingham 1994:87) typical of picturesque taste. Even here, however, in what is the most extended picturesque description in the *Narrative*, this is not a made-to-order metropolitan picturesque but a colonial hybrid, a "combination of the wild, the grand, and the beautiful" even further "heightened" by the "exotic". The very fact that Pringle 'composes' this passage with such detail is an indication that such a landscape has a significance that goes beyond its topographical features: it is a landscape whose differentiated detail, despite its excess, can be read as responsive to European aesthetic categories. The colonial landscape becomes picturesque when it resembles, however imperfectly, those metropolitan landscapes which the picturesque is typically thought to describe.

In March 1821, barely a year after his arrival, Pringle left the settlement at Glen Lynden to accompany Robert Hart, the superintendent of a government farm in Somerset East, "on a journey which he had occasion to make through a part of the country very seldom traversed even by the colonists" (1966:77). This journey was to take Pringle into mountainous and wooded territory that was both visually spectacular and, a decade earlier, the scene of violent conflict between the Xhosa and colonial forces. The first leg of the journey was to a Moravian mission at Enon and required an ascent of the successive ridges of the Zureberg (Suurberg) mountains. The initial stages are described by Pringle in terms already familiar to us: the landscape is "monotonous" and "enlivened only now and then" by the presence of indigenous fauna. As the ascent continues, Pringle finds distraction in the scattered novelty of bird, plant and animal life even though, typically, he recognises that the terrain has no productive capacity and is "unprofitable for the occupation of civilised man". Then, as if to counter this recognition, or at least to soften its implications, he invokes the religious language of providential design, the "beneficent arrangements of a creation where nothing—not even the sterile desert or naked rock—is placed without design, or left utterly unproductive" (80). Pringle then goes on to liken what he calls the "climate and productions" of the region to "ancient Palestine" and quotes from the psalms to corroborate this comparison. As it happens, exactly the same sentiments were expressed by Pringle shortly after the arrival at Glen Lynden where he observes that : "On this and other occasions the scenery and productions of the country reminded us in the most forcible manner of the imagery of the Hebrew Scriptures" (38) before quoting again from the psalms. In both these descriptions it is as though Pringle, denied the productive associations of the picturesque, must go back to an older biblical template to map or make sense of the barrenness of the country. It is all the more curious, then, that immediately after Pringle appeals to providential design as evidence that the Zureberg is not simply a useless excrescence of nature, he should encounter a scene that entirely baffles his imagination. The occasion is a forced ascent to the top of a mountain ridge:

Here my companion had told me that an extraordinary prospect awaited
us: but all my previous conceptions fell infinitely short of the reality. On
the left, a billowy chaos of naked mountains, rocks, precipices, and
yawning abysses, that looked as if hurled together by some prodigious
convulsion of nature, appalled and bewildered the imagination. It seemed
as if this congeries of gigantic crags, or rather the eternal hills themselves,
had been tumultuously uptorn and heaved together, in some pre-adamite
conflict of angelic hosts, with all the veins and strata of their deep
foundations disrupted, bent, and twisted in the struggle into a thousand
fantastic shapes; while, over the lower declivities and deep-sunk dells, a
dark impenetrable forest spread its shaggy skirts, and added to the whole
a character of still more wild and savage sublimity. (1966:81)

This extraordinary passage, which splices back in time to the elemental or
pre-human, traumatically disrupts the referential schemas into which
Pringle has hitherto transcribed his experience of landscape. The usual
perceptual or phenomenological distance between viewer and viewed
evident in Pringle's other landscape descriptions undergoes a bewildering
reversal: here the colossal, demonic landscape overwhelms the viewer,
forcing him to confront it on terms which are entirely its own. The
"imagination" which in the picturesque mode is transformative, working
on the landscape, is "appalled and bewildered", stunned into passivity;
and though Pringle does not allude to this, the appeal to providential
"design" in the preceding paragraph is made to appear wishful. When
Pringle eventually gropes for a suitable descriptive epithet for this
convulsive disturbance of the earth itself, he does so by using a sexualised
metaphor that renders the scene before him even more disturbing: "while
over the lower declivities and deep-sunk dells, a dark and impenetrable
forest spread its shaggy skirts, and added to the whole a character of still
more wild and savage sublimity". This autochthonous or indigenous
sublime both threatens and abases the imagination; it is unnerving,
infernal; its intensities carry the threat of self-dissolution. Why, we must
ask, does the sublime, so productive an aesthetic category in its European
context, become utterly unbearable when evoked by the experience of a
South African landscape, where it becomes a sublime of terror in which
nature itself seems unnatural? I shall work through other aspects of
Pringle's response to a local sublime before returning to this question.

Finally, there are those occasions when landscape is viewed not solely
as the terrain of nature and its "scenes and productions" but as bearing
the imprint of the historical; these configurations or superimpositions of
landscape and history are unfailingly disturbing. In a passage in the same

chapter in which the Zureberg experience is evoked, for example, Pringle writes: "In the midst of this mountainous scenery we arrived at a spot where the elder Stockenström, landdrost of Graaff-Reinet, had been treacherously slain by the Caffers in 1811"(96). Pringle then goes on to describe, in some detail, the events which resulted in the death of Stockenström and fourteen of his men. He concludes this account as follows:

> From this spot I looked down the scenery which I have attempted to describe; and I could well fancy the effect of the savage shout of exultation (described to me with sensations of horror by some of those who were present) pealed forth by two or three thousand barbarians, as they stood over their fallen enemies .... The sonorous power of the Caffer voice, the stern and stupendous features of the country around, and the dismal spectacle of the field of slain, must have given to the scene at that moment a character indescribably terrific and appalling. (101)

Here the visual scene is infused with historical memory and the violence of the colonial past, with its "sensations of horror", impinges on the present in a manner that, like the savage sublime itself, threatens the limits of expressivity: a scene "terrific and appalling" lines up on the same level of threat and fracturing incomprehension as one that is "appal[ling] and bewilder[ing]".

There is a crucial difference between these two experiences, however, in that Pringle's evocation of the events of 1811 are not the product of an intense immediacy; they depend upon the mediations of "fancy" to bring together landscape and historical event. Such imaginative moments might be rare in Pringle, but they signal the emergence of something like a historicised poetics of landscape borne out of the colonial encounter itself. Another such moment occurs when Pringle is again on an "excursion", this time into the 'ceded' or 'neutral' territory from which the Xhosa had been driven in order to create a buffer zone between them and the impending British settlement. Pringle was well aware of these circumstances: "During my residence at Eildon," he writes, "I made various exploratory excursions into the waste country lying between our valley and the New Caffer Frontier, which had remained totally unoccupied since the native inhabitants were driven out of it in 1819" (115). The reference to "waste country" acknowledges depopulation as an act of colonial intervention rather than an inherent attribute; neither is Pringle insensitive to the effects such interventions have on the landscape itself:

> The scenery both of this and of the other chief branches of the Koonap
> river was of a very impressive character. The aspect of the country, though
> wild, was rich and beautiful. It was watered by numerous rivulets, and
> finely diversified with lofty mountains and winding vales, with picturesque
> rocks and shaggy jungles, open upland pastures, and fertile meadows along
> the river margins, sprinkled as usual with willows and acacias, and
> occasionally with groves of stately geelhout. ... But the remains of Caffer
> hamlets, scattered through every grassy nook and dell, and now fast
> crumbling to decay, excited reflections of a very melancholy character, and
> occasionally increased, even to the most painful degree, the feeling of
> dreary *lonesomeness* which the wild grandeur of the scenery tended to
> excite. (1966:117)

In a manner reminiscent of Pringle's earlier description of coastal scenery,
this passage again underscores the contrariety of the local landscape: it
has a "wild grandeur" that hints at the sublime, while being at the same time
"rich and beautiful" in the picturesque mode. But it is the final sentence
of the passage, which focuses our attention on the eviction of the land's
original inhabitants, that even further complicates these already
contradictory schemas. The "dreary *lonesomeness*" which afflicts Pringle
is first of all attributed to the "wild grandeur of the scenery", whereas
earlier (on the shipboard viewing) a similarly italicised "lonesomeness"
was held to result from the fact that the land was "unmarked" by signs of
industry or habitation. In this passage "lonesomeness", the condition of
feeling alone or, we might say, of having no sense of an integral or
identificatory relationship with one's surroundings, is a consequence of
a colonial landscape which suggests sublimity, but which does not invite
any sense of participatory belonging or expansion of being. Adding to this
original estrangement and exacerbating it even to the "most painful
degree" are the "melancholy" thoughts or "reflections" occasioned by the
sight of the abandoned Xhosa villages which, unlike European ruins, do
not bear the imprint of temporal erosion and are simply disappearing into
the landscape. Pringle does not elaborate on the nature of his "reflections",
but we may reasonably assume that their "melancholy" cast is not
unrelated to this evidence of the aftermath of colonial conquest and
eviction.

   In considering Pringle's traumatised renderings of scenes or imagined
events that in a more accustomed context would be occasions for the
expansion of being normally associated with the sublime, we need to ask
why this should be so. Though never definitively explicit, Pringle's use
of the word "sublime" appears to be loosely derived from its theorisation

in Edmund Burke's influential *A Philosophical Inquiry into the Origin of our Ideas of the Sublime and the Beautiful* (1757). Burke's work marked a shift from the rhetorical sublime derived from Longinus to a sublime associated with a variety of natural phenomena. The natural sublime was in turn displaced by the Romantic sublime which regarded sublimity as subjective force arising from within, a more Kantian emphasis on the powers of the mind as opposed to the objects perceived. That Pringle's use of the word "sublime" is conditioned by Burkean conceptions is evident in the fact that he always uses it in connection with an overwhelming impression derived from external sources, and we have already examined the occasions of this use. In a well-known passage on the sublime in nature, Burke begins by asserting that "The passions caused by the great and sublime in *nature,* when those causes operate most powerfully, is astonishment; and astonishment is that state of the soul in which all its motions are suspended in some degree of horror. In this case the mind is so entirely filled with its object, that it cannot entertain any other, nor by consequence reason on that object which employs it" (1969:49). These lines describe, in an approximate way, Pringle's "appalled and bewildered" reaction to the scene at the summit of the Zureberg . But Pringle moves away from these prescriptions when this experience does not subsequently yield the positive payoffs of the Burkean sublime: "the ... effects [of] admiration, reverence, and respect" (1966:49). One might speculate here that in the metropolitan context the experience of the sublime in nature is likely to be occasional, something only encountered out of one's daily round; the sublime has the force of novelty, but does not intrude into the conduct of everyday life. But in a colonial context where the social fabric is fragile or even non-existent, sublime experiences are more threatening because they are in no way counter-balanced by the elaborate feminine sociality of the beautiful, whose relation to the sublime is also formulated by Burke in terms of the duality "Society and Solitude".

If one were to take the first of these terms and water it down almost to non-existence, it would change the homeostatic balance between the two categories. This might, in part, explain Pringle's clear reluctance to embrace the sublime in conditions where "society" scarcely exists. We must also consider that for Burke the sublime, a notoriously unstable category anyway, is by no means always experienced as "delightful" and can, in the wrong circumstances, produce a terror unmediated by aesthetic distance: "When danger and pain press too nearly," he writes, "they are incapable of giving any delight, and are simply terrible; but at certain distances, and with certain modifications, they may be, and they are, delightful, as we everyday experience" (1969:36). As far as what I have called the "historical sublime" is concerned, Pringle's apprehension of these moments as painful and threatening bears witness to the violence on which settlement is founded and an awareness, perhaps, that land, or in an expanded sense, "territory", is an ongoing locus of conflict and dispossession that no forms of representation will abate. Sarah Suleri has noted Burke's alertness to the "potential historicity of the sublime" and in particular his tendency to deploy the sublime in colonial contexts (she has India in mind) where the European imagination must negotiate "the psychic proximity of aesthetic discourse with the concomitant intimacy of cultural terror" (1992:36). In a similar manner, Luke Gibbons observes the "volatile intersection between aesthetics and politics" (2003:5) evident in Burke's evocation of an Irish "colonial sublime", where the abuse of imperial power calls up an illimitable sense of suffering and reprisal. In both these instances, the sublime—albeit a sublime conceived from a metropolitan vantage—presents itself as an apposite category for the excruciating and conflicted experience of colonialism. The fact that Pringle admits the sublime in only the most fleeting manner, and never develops it in the body of his work suggests, at the very least, that his experiences on the Eastern Cape frontier were calamitous to his understanding and that the shock of the sublime called not for representation but for repression.

If we look back over this assemblage of landscape description in the *Narrative,* it becomes all too clear that Pringle's engagement with the terrain of his new country was by no means a secure and confident reading of it into European registers. He seems, rather, to be more conscious of the resistance of the landscape to his gaze, its often abrasively novel character, and its almost involuntary excitement of unexpected emotions. While there are also occasions when the landscape offers the reassurance of the familiar, these occasions are never sufficiently continuous to accumulate into something settled and durable. One must stress again that for a frontier settler like Pringle, landscape is the predominant element in the physical world; how landscape is read, interpreted or acted upon, in both literal and figurative senses, is the first and indispensable step into the future: it is freighted with a significance that it would not necessarily have in its metropolitan context. Before going on to examine Pringle's set-piece landscape poem, "Evening Rambles", however, we need very briefly to detour into the conventions informing the picturesque, the generic mode to which the poem is most obviously indebted.

John Barrell has observed that both the etymological and the cultural roots of the word "landscape" mean that we cannot use it without denoting "notions of value and form which relate not just to seeing the land, but to seeing it in a certain way—pictorially"(1972:1) and the various conventions of the picturesque, in its multifarious forms, are the direct product of an eighteenth-century register of landscape viewing as a socially and culturally distinctive practice. "To display a correct taste in Landscape," writes Barrell, "was a valuable social accomplishment" (5). I can only gesture towards the complexities of critical understandings of the picturesque, but it is perhaps worth remarking on the broad consensus that the picturesque was so pervasively determined by its social context as to be, in Alan Liu's words, "in every sense a form of social control ... the frames of vision it created should be seen to participate in the basic institutions of control ... that supervised the British state" (1991:5). If such readings insist (see also Pfau 1994:17-140) on the indissolubility of the social and the aesthetic, and emphasise moreover that the aesthetic acts as a form of dissimulation, covering its investment in forms of 'social control', then we must immediately ask if such doubling of inscription is possible in a colonial context like the Eastern Cape frontier where, among other considerations, there was no social aggregate of sufficient density to constitute a class, middle or otherwise. In seeking to understand how metropolitan forms might acquire an altogether different valency when deployed in contexts remote from their site of origin, the work of Paul Carter on the Australian colonial picturesque is an indispensable resource. For Carter, the colonial picturesque is an entirely mutated form which has "nothing to do" with "canons of taste formulated in Regency England"(1987: 259), but must instead be understood as a tentative attempt to elicit a "feeling of being at home in the world" (243). In the unsettling spaces of a new landscape, the settler puts familiar forms to new uses, and the picturesque functions not so much as a reproduction of what is already known but as one means of "civilizing the landscape, bringing it into orderly being"(58). Carter also recognises—and here the application to Pringle is obvious—that this projective use of the picturesque means that its empirical or referential sense is cancelled by its contradictory usage and that it often depended on "contrast ... with the preceding country rather than its own intrinsic qualities" (349). My abbreviation of Carter's arguments about colonial landscape has been severe, but let it at least serve to underscore the point that the colonial picturesque cannot be understood as a mere recycling of metropolitan conventions.

* * *

"Evening Rambles", the poem of Pringle's that offers the most sustained engagement with local landscape, was first published in 1828 in *Ephemerides*, the first London edition of Pringle's poetry. Its date of composition is given as 1822 but, as we shall see, there are reasons to believe that two of its six stanzas are the result of later interpolation. The very title of the poem—the allusion to Wordsworth's *An Evening's Walk* (1793) is surely not accidental—indicates its allegiance to a locodescriptive/picturesque genre of some lineage, but even so it begins with what we might construe as an oblique denial of its informing conventions. In the first stanza the relieving of "sultry" African heat by the "low and languid" breezes of the early evening releases the scent of mimosas, a "fragrance faint" that is immediately transposed ("it seems to tell") onto soothing memories of a "Scottish dell" where "primrose-tufts ... peep[...] forth in tender spring/When the blithe lark begins to sing". The second stanza decisively interrupts this reverie:

> But soon, amidst our Lybian vale,
> Such soothing recollections fail;
> Soon we raise the eye to range
> O'er prospects wild, grotesque and strange;
> Sterile mountains, rough and steep,
> That bound abrupt the valley deep,
> Heaving to the clear blue sky
> Their ribs of granite, bare and dry
> And ridges, by the torrents worn,
> Thinly streaked with scraggy thorn,
> Which fringes nature's savage dress,
> But scarce relieves her nakedness. (1989:ll,11-22)

The repetition of "soon" emphasises how the Eastern Cape landscape ("Lybian" is here used as an accepted shorthand for "African") very rapidly overwhelms any attempt to fit it into those descriptive formats which accommodate "tender spring", "the blithe lark", and so forth. One could be forgiven for imagining that Pringle would either end the poem after this stanza or look beyond metropolitan protocols to write another sort of poem altogether. That he does neither but elects instead to find ways of contriving a frontier picturesque might be understood as an evasion: the more telling point, perhaps, is that the poem signals an awareness of the contradictions with which it must deal. The "prospects wild, grotesque and strange" which enclose the valley of the settlement emphatically refuse the desiderata of the picturesque; Pringle explicitly acknowledges that such a landscape cannot be absorbed into the "soothing recollections" of a Scottish prototype and is therefore resistant to those paradigms of the picturesque to which he is accustomed. He then sets out to work this unpromising material into recognisable poetic form by elevating his angle of vision so as to screen out the "amphitheatre of steep and sterile mountains": "But where the Vale winds deep below", begins the third stanza, "The landscape hath a warmer glow". With these lines what had earlier been a "Lybian vale", defined primarily through the stark and unrevealing differentials of rock and sky and lacking any intimate compositional detail, now receives a dab of painterly colour: a "warmer glow". If the stage is now set for Pringle to rehearse familiar locodescriptive techniques, we are at least in a position to register the detours he has had to take to arrive at this point.

In direct contrast to "prospects wild, grotesque and strange" or the muted memories of Scottish dells, a natural environment vivid with plant and animal life animates the next two stanzas. Local flora—the spekboom, the aloe, the bean tree—provide an exotic profusion of colour in the third stanza, with the light from the descending sun "blending" this potentially unruly display into the softer and more familiarly European matrix of "the deep green verdure". In the fourth stanza Pringle manoeuvres himself to ground level—"Let me through the mazes rove"—where he encounters, or is immersed in, an animal world of untroubled sociability signalled through the sounds of mating birds and humming bees. Here human presence is barely felt as an intrusion: even the nervous Duiker only skitters away at the sound of the poet's approaching footfall. These two stanzas reclaim colonial space by transforming it into a poetic habitat where the designs of artifice coincide with the life of nature itself. This colonial Arcadia, in which flora perform a veritable dance of display ("spreads ... rears ... shakes") for the observing eye and fauna all but invite the poet into their domestic intimacy, is invested with an incriminating degree of fantasy. It is as though Pringle feels the need to reverse the impact of the "sterile mountains" which has so precipitately cancelled "soothing reflections" with the counterweight of this natural idyll. Paradoxically, however, the abruptness of this inversion unsettles our reading: what kind of poem is this that can only vacillate between extremes?

The fifth stanza, the poem's centrepiece, may be read as an attempt to mediate these extremes, or at least to bring them within a single frame. The stanza begins with Pringle installing himself in the panoptic centre of a fully selfconscious "prospect" poem:

My wonted seat receives me now –
This cliff with myrtle-tufted brow,
Towering high o'er grove and stream,
As if to greet the parting gleam.
With shattered rocks besprinkled o'er,
Behind ascends the mountain hoar,
Whose crest o'erhangs the Bushman's Cave,
(His fortress once and now his grave,)
Where the grim satyr-faced baboon
Sits gibbering to the rising moon,
Or chides with hoarse and angry cry
The herdsman as he wanders by. (ll,49-60)

It is immediately apparent that Pringle is unable to sustain the idyll of the earlier stanzas. Though he begins conventionally enough with an unimpeded vision over the generic "grove and stream", he has still to negotiate—or feels the need to negotiate—what he *cannot* see from his prospective vantage: a Bushman's cave above him, now occupied by a menacing baboon. David Bunn has argued that in this stanza Pringle is attempting to write the (in fact coeval and competitive) Bushman out of the landscape by displacing him to an earlier era and that "the poet performs another act of containment by placing the Bushman outside symbolic systems through his contiguous association with the 'grim satyr-faced baboon' that now occupies the site" (1995: 157). This may be so—Pringle does something similar with the Bushman in "The Emigrant's Cabin"—but the treatment of the Bushman's cave in "Evening Rambles" is, I think, far more hesitant than Bunn is willing to allow. It is complicated, for one, by the contiguity of Pringle himself and his "wonted seat" to the cave and its cluster of associations. I would argue that this contiguity does in fact disturb the sovereignty of Pringle's gaze by deflecting his focus upwards and away from the scene "spread out below", which has to wait for the next stanza. The site of the cave introduces a brief but troubled interruption into the conventional unfolding of a prospect poem with its reminder that the commanding height of vision is not untroubled by adjacent presences. Furthermore, the lines "Whose crest o'erhangs the Bushman's Cave/ (His fortress once and now his grave,)" call up an intertext in *The Autumnal Excursion*, Pringle's first extended venture into the picturesque, published in Scotland in 1819. This is the full context of the relevant lines:

"How lovely seems the simple vale

Where lives our sires heroic tale!
Where the wild pass and the mountain flood,
Hallow'd by dying patriots blood, –
The rocky cavern, once his tent,
And now his deathless monument, –
Rehearse to memory's kindling thought,
What Faith inspired and Valour wrought"! –
(1819:13)

These lines celebrate the memory of the resistance of Scottish Covenanters
to English persecution in the seventeenth century. In this poem Pringle
is able to recall the impress of history on the landscape in ways that
corroborate the present by lending texture to "memory's kindling thought",
something he cannot do in a colonial context which demands, not
necessarily successfully, that precolonial history submit to its own
erasure. The relevant intertext with "Evening Rambles" is obviously the
couplet "The rocky cavern, once his tent,/ And now his deathless
monument" and, on the face of it, would seem to suggest some analogy
between slaughtered Bushmen and heroic Scottish resistance to English
rule. I would not pursue the analogy this far (if only because the full range
of Pringle's writing would not support such a claim) but what this intertext
does suggest, at the very least, is that the Bushman's abandoned cave has
disquieting resonances that Pringle cannot quite banish.

   Having completed yet another detour, Pringle is finally in a position to
invoke the full compositional detail of the extended view. In taking up this
prospect over the colonial landscape, he is repeating a gesture endemic
to locodescriptive poetry since the seventeenth century: "the troping of
a moral vantage point by means of an elaborate description of 'literal'
spatial elevation"(Pfau 1997:38). The implied linkage between visual
command, with its descriptive plotting of the landscape into complex
ordered forms and what Pfau later calls "a coalescence of authorial and
readerly sensibilities in an all-encompassing subjectivity of sound moral
and aesthetic judgement" (43) is a similarly recurrent feature of such
poetry. We need to ask if "Evening Rambles" is able to exert such authority
over the very different topographical details of the colonial landscape and
bring these details into the orbit of its controlled vision. The answer, I
would suggest, is certainly not a straightforward yes. Pringle begins
conventionally enough: the vista of the valley is "Spread out below" and
"full displayed" to his gaze, with the accustomed dispersion of light and
shade. Once again invoking generic "nooks", "bowers", "meadows" that
are adjectivally secured by the familiar "sheltered" and "sylvan", Pringle

looks set to create a landscape on an accustomed pattern. From this point, however, rather than ranging through different planes and details of vision as prospect poetry normally does, with "the order of description ... from foreground to horizon" (Barrell 1972:44), the stanza instead focuses rather obsessively on the "tortuous bed" of the river course running through the valley. In describing this river as being "like a dragon spread" Pringle alludes faintly to the imagery of the Zureberg where the Sunday's River is described as being "like the path of some mythological dragon"(28); but it is his description of the "ravage" left by the flooding of this river that we may more fully detect, in displaced form, the aftershocks of the Zureberg experience:

> Lo there the Chaldee-willow weeps
> Drooping o'er the headlong steeps,
> Where the torrent in his wrath
> Hath rifted him a rugged path,
> Like fissure cleft by earthquake's shock,
> Through mead and jungle, mound and rock.
> But the swoln water's wasteful sway,
> Like Tyrant's rage, hath passed away,
> And left the ravage of its course
> Memorial of its frantic force. (ll,69-76)

The description of the river's "tortuous bed", the very sinuosity of which suggests force and resistance, dominates this first section of the stanza, just as its aftermath dominates the second. It is worth pointing out here that in the *Narrative* Pringle expressed exasperation over the definitional attributes of the word "river" in the South African context: an example of how even the most simple designations could be confounded in the colonial context. "In speaking of *rivers*," says Pringle, "I may here remark, once and for all, that this appellation is applied by the African colonist to every brook that merely exhibits a rill of running water ... so that the term often appears, to a European apprehension, very unappropriately employed" (1966:104). To this he adds:

> The rivers of South Africa, with but few exceptions, are little else than periodical torrents, usually flowing with a diminutive streamlet, at the bottom of a huge chasm or glen, the banks of which rise on either side ... these tremendous yawning gulfs, when filled by the sudden and excessive rains to which this climate is occasionally, though not frequently subject, are swollen ... with a mighty and furious torrent, which defies all control and obstructs all passage. (1966:104)

A river, then, is both a definitionally or semantically unstable term and a natural phenomenon subject to abrupt and destructive changes which "def[y] all control". From William Plomer's "The Scorpion" to Ruth Miller's "The Floating Island", riverine floods have functioned in South African poetry as a metaphor for an intrinsic natural violence, "Anarchy ... leapt beyond mischance", as Miller puts it. It is perhaps fitting that the first extended nature poem written in English in South Africa should have at its centre a landscape formed predominantly by the "frantic force" of a flooded river. And while such a poem might be prospectively appropriate in its South African setting it is, perhaps for this reason, anomalous in its informing context of British landscape poetry which takes its cue from a very different set of material specifics (where rivers, for example, are notable for their calm and amplitude: "Broad rivers bold and bright", as Pringle put it in "The Autumnal Excursion").

If we return to that section of the stanza quoted above, we notice first the pattern of disrupted expectations which has already begun to characterise the poem, here evident in the sudden transition from the generic picturesque of nooks, bowers and meadows to the "headlong steeps" carved out of rock by the sheer force of the "torrent in his wrath". Pringle's gaze, far from being an excursus or unimpeded roaming through an extended prospect, is here fixated downward into the geological strata of the earth itself which he imagines as having been convulsed by elemental forces: "like fissure cleft by earthquake's shock". This is the same imagery of geological upheaval used in the Zureberg passage where "gigantic crags" and the "hills themselves" seemed to have been "tumultuously uptorn and heaved together". The "headlong steeps" through which the floodwater has "rifted ... a rugged path" also operate as a horizontal recrudescence of the "rough and steep" mountains, suggesting that the division between these two features of the landscape is not as absolute as it at first appeared.

Although the poem might render the Zureberg sublime in a controlled and muted form, the very fact of its "recollection" points to a sense of a landscape disturbed in its very formation and Pringle's next move is an attempted cancellation of this disturbance by immobilising the river bed as a "Memorial", something secure in the safety of the past. The simile of geological rupture gives way to one of temporal succession: the inconceivable power of water blasting through the elements has "passed away"; it is a moment of excess, aberration, and waste, a "tyrant's rage" now safely subdued. By associating the geological with a disturbed and

tyrannical historical moment and dispatching it to the temporal distance
of a "memorial", Pringle is able to suggest that, like that other site of
evacuated agency, the "Bushman's grave", the violent force of water and
its aftermath may safely be consigned to a past whose convulsions have
been buried in the rocky strata of the earth itself. A space is also cleared
for the stanza to return to the present tense:

> – Now o'er its shrunk and slimy bed
> Rank weeds and withered wrack are spread,
> With the faint rill just oozing through,
> And vanishing again from view;
> Save where the guana's glassy pool,
> Holds to some cliff its mirror cool ... (ll,77- 82)

A more conventional picturesque allows Pringle to follow the receding
"faint rill" of a water course until it gathers into the reflective surface of
a "glassy pool". Such mirroring effects, usually achieved by the calm
surfaces of lakes, are a common picturesque motif and suggest a 'natural'
aesthetic, free of any mediation. But we must also remark that much of the
imagery used in this stanza, from "fissure cleft" to the engorged and
swollen water and its aftermath in the "oozing" of a "shrunk and slimy
bed", is unmistakably if unconsciously sexualised. While it is something
of a critical commonplace that the picturesque deploys erotic effects,
these are generally ascribed to the nature of the picturesque gaze which
looks intently but cannot possess and hence invests "heavily in the
erotics of denied desire" (Modiano 1994:197) whose characteristic locus
is in the seductive glimpse and concealment associated with "intricacy",
which Alan Liu calls "the great fetishistic zone of the picturesque"
(1989:63). Pringle's sexual figuration is a lot blunter than the mannered
"deshabille" (to quote Liu again) of the metropolitan picturesque and
brings back into circulation the sexualised sublime of the "deep sunk
dells" and "impenetrable forests" of the Zureberg passage. Earlier
characterised as a "memorial" the river bed is in fact a swamp of oozy
fecundity whose origin is that "fissure cleft by earthquake's shock" in the
earlier line. The geological ur-act of the sublime is not so easily banished
and this colonial picturesque cannot surmount its uncomfortable proximity
to a primordial past.

Pringle's eye then moves upward to the enclosure of the "palmite's
leafy screen" and an adjacent rock-ash from which are suspended the
nests of weaver birds. The stanza ends with the following lines:

> In cradle-nests, with porch below,
> Secure from winged or creeping foe –
> Weasel or hawk or writhing snake;
> Light swinging, as the breezes wake,
> Like the ripe fruit we love to see
> Upon the rich pomegranate-tree. (ll,87-92)

What interests me here is the way in which these protective nests function both as an image of a secure animal domesticity *and* a threatened one. Furthermore, the associative transfer of the pendant nests to the plenitude of "ripe fruit" implicitly carries that threat to the "rich" harvest of the pomegranate tree. David Bunn offers the intriguing hypothesis that the embowered nests, like the paired, conjugal animals in stanza three, prepare the way for colonial settlement by "anticipating the white settler household adapted to South African conditions" (1994:145). While not wanting to dismiss this speculation, I would still argue that such anticipations are fraught: turtle doves and honey bees are not emblematically South African animals and in the case of the weaver nests one encounters the paradox that an aesthetic effect—"these beautiful nests" as Pringle calls them in a note—is achieved in consequence of an evolutionary survival technique: "to secure their offspring from the assaults of their numerous enemies, particularly the serpent race"(1989:93). In this new landscape, even the effects of 'picturicity' are liable to reveal themselves as embedded in adaptive behaviours that respond to a dangerous natural environment.

One cannot be absolutely certain, but I would argue that the next two stanzas, which deal with colonial labour, are the product of an interpolation prior to the poem's 1828 publication. There are a number of reasons to suspect this: in the period of Pringle's residence on the frontier he employed neither slaves nor migrant Bechuana labour. Neither is there any evidence that at this time he took any interest in the abolitionism with which his name is so often associated because of his later tenure as Secretary of the British Anti-Slavery Society. These stanzas are pointedly homiletic in tone and do not use the presence of the labourers to any kind of picturesque effect; even on an expressive level, the verse is formulaic, and sacrifices the compositional detail of other sections of the poem to a tendentious denunciation of slavery. In all these respects, the two stanzas fall out of the customary range of locodescriptive or picturesque poetry altogether, and their placement here is anomalous. The first of the stanzas begins with a (much belated) recognition of the furthest point of perspective ("But lo the sun's descending car/Sinks o'er Mount Dunion's peaks afar")

and immediately resorts to description by privation: the "brown herder"
is not a shepherd from a "Scottish dell", possesses a gun and not a crook,
has no "flute", "book", "rustic song" and so forth. It seems odd, especially
since these privative details are of little interest in themselves and
approach mere enumeration, that Pringle should re-introduce a technique
that he had earlier explicitly discarded as inappropriate to his setting. The
intention of these lines might be to designate the herder as "the White
Man's thrall" and to bring his legal destitution to the attention of the
British reading public: the description, nonetheless, carries the implication
that indigenous people are destitute of their own resources. The Hottentot's
rhetorical construction in terms of a lack accentuated even further by
circumstance suggests that his privation is immanent, and that his future—
as the negative comparisons imply—lies in the 'improving' model of a
Scottish peasantry. The "poor Heathen Bechuan" fares only marginally
better: though he "Bears on his brow the port of man" because not
"debased by slavery" he remains a "poor heathen" humming a "tuneless
song". Whether enslaved or not, indigenous labour is cast as a failed
peasantry in desperate need, one assumes, of humanitarian intervention.
Just as he did in "The Emigrant's Cabin", though on a mercifully smaller
scale, Pringle has taken the original version of the poem, added to it,
perhaps revised some lines in the original, but in his additions has
attempted to appropriate the original into the explicitly reformist agendas
then preoccupying him.

When Pringle returns to landscape prospectus in stanza nine, the verse
is drained of referential specificity: ten of sixteen lines have no distinctive
locality and these lines typically employ a contrived figural generality
("Now, wizard-like, slow Twilight sails/ With soundless wing adown the
vales") that seems to act as a delaying or suspending device to postpone
direct descriptive engagement. Even when a local "villain Lynx" and
"thievish porcupine" make their personified appearance, their presence is
revealed by the "lamp" of an "enamoured fire-fly"—"Link-boy he of
woodland green/ To light fair Avon's Elfin-Queen"—straight out of the
pastoral fantasia of *A Midsummer Night's Dream*. What Pringle is delaying
or blocking here is clearly the threatening advent of night itself:

> But lo! The night bird's boding scream
> Breaks abrupt my twilight dream;
> And warns me it is time to haste
> My homeward walk across the waste,
> Lest my rash tread provoke the wrath

Of adder coiled upon the path,
Or tempt the lion from the wood,
That soon will prowl athirst for blood.
—Thus, murmuring my thoughtful strain,
I seek our wattled cot again. (ll,139-48)

Though ending the poem the stanza also returns to its beginning: just as
the recollections of a Scottish dell failed to screen the enclosing
"nakedness" of its colonial counterpart, so here too is an admission that
the pastoral reverie in the preceding lines was a "twilight dream" attempting
to block out the actual scene by transposing onto it another set of
associations. The shattering of this narcoleptic reverie by a night-bird's
ominously "boding scream" acts a chthonic warning to the poet immediately
to abandon his "wonted seat" (and with it his fantasy of transposition) in
order to escape the threat of impending nightfall and the dangers that it
brings. In this context, lingering too long on landscape can be the death
of you. The poem ends rather incongruously with a meditative "murmuring"
of the poet's "thoughtful strain" where the previous lines suggest that the
"haste" of his "homeward walk across the waste" will not allow such
tranquil recollection.

In Pringle, whose consciousness has contracted into protective reverie,
the "wakeful bird" is a harbinger of danger: the landscape is closing in
around him, threatening him; "murmuring my thoughtful strain" suggests
the repetition of a protective spell rather than reposed contemplation, and
the improvised "wattled cot"—significantly the only mention of settler
habitation—seems hardly able to offer the protection he seeks. Far from
having achieved any reciprocation with landscape, the consciousness of
the poet retreats into monadic isolation: what we have at the end of the
poem is not closure, but flight. Here the very title of the poem is misleading
in its suggestion of leisurely meandering: while Pringle may contrive some
visual traverses, for most of the poem he is immobilised in a prospect
position which he has eventually to abandon under some duress.

* * *

I have argued that from its beginning, where Pringle acknowledges, quite
explicitly, that the settler landscape will not lend itself to an unproblematic
emulation of European models, the poem is disconcerted by antitheses
which it cannot resolve. While there are times when Pringle proceeds as
if this were not the case, such as the richly ornamented depictions of
natural life in stanzas two and three, these moments of apparently normative

evocation never lend themselves to ongoing development. What we have instead is something very much like dialectical movement within the poem between landscapes which invite or prefigure human occupation and landscapes which refuse it. That the poem is unable to resolve these tensions or antitheses indicates, I think, an unspoken recognition that colonial experience requires another set of representations altogether. These are not supplied, of course, but the very failure of the poem to accomplish this speaks strongly to a sense of uncertainty, of a spatial bewilderment in which memories of home and the landscape of the colony blur into an indeterminate place: the settler experience is laid open to the dangers of its own futurity while at the same time losing its grip on the hand-holds of inherited convention. As such, the poem seems to me to deserve a foundational place in "white writing" precisely because it is anti-foundational: it admits to its own contingency and clears the space for a set of representations that are not axiomatically tied to derivative models.

"Evening Rambles"—if we excerpt the interpolated sections—attests to a very much more embattled and insecure coloniality than that which finds expression in those later poems of Pringle's in which he adopts an indigenous persona and a position of humanitarian advocacy. Paradoxically, many of the poems of Pringle's which are associated with his status as a 'good' humanitarian and reformist colonial were written or extensively revised when he lived in London and did not have to contend with the abrasions of colonial life (from which he had fled). In this poetry Pringle assumes a subject position which is assured in its ventriloquising of an indigenous voice and secure in its moral authority. Is it not time, perhaps, to regard these poems as belonging in a very much more imperial lexicon than a poem like "Evening Rambles", with its fraught sense of settler consciousness and its manifest failure to complete the generic and tropological objectives which might first have motivated it? And might we not also consider that in formulating approaches to colonial South African literature, we need to be attentive to the complexities of the texts themselves and their specific location rather than forcing them into the prescriptive theoretical formulations which have tended to dominate postcolonial studies? Such 'close reading' will not make us new critics; instead, it might enable us to produce new, situated forms of postcolonial understanding.

References

Ahmad, Aijaz. 1992. *In Theory: Classes, Nations, Literatures*. London: Verso.

Barrell, John. 1972. *The Idea of Landscape and the Sense of Place, 1730-1840: An Approach to the Poetry of John Clare*. Cambridge: Cambridge University Press.

Bermingham, Ann. 1994. "The Picturesque and Ready-To-Wear Femininity." In: S. Copley and P. Garside (eds). *The Politics of the Picturesque: Literature, Landscape and Aesthetics since 1770*. Cambridge: Cambridge University Press.

Bunn, David. 1994. "'Our Wattled Cot': Mercantile and Domestic Space in Thomas Pringle's African Landscapes." In: W.J.T. Mitchell (ed.). *Landscape and Power*. Chicago: Chicago University Press.

Burke, Edmund. 1969 [1757]. *A Philosophical Enquiry into the Origin of our Ideas of the Sublime and the Beautiful*. New York: P.F. Collier & Son Corporation.

Carter, Paul. 1987. *The Road to Botany Bay*. London & Boston: Faber & Faber.

Coetzee, J.M. 1988. *White Writing: On the Culture of Letters in South Africa*. Sandton: Radix.

Copley, S. and P. Garside (eds). *The Politics of the Picturesque*. Cambridge: Cambridge University Press.

Gibbons, Luke. 2003. *Edmund Burke and Ireland: Aesthetics, Politics and the Colonial Sublime*. Cambridge: Cambridge University Press.

Liu, Alan. 1989. *Wordsworth: The Sense of History*. Stanford: Stanford University Press.

Modiano, Raimonda. 1994. "The Legacy of the Picturesque: Landscape, Property and the Ruin." In: S. Copley and P. Garside (eds). *The Politics of the Picturesque*. Cambridge: Cambridge University Press.

Pfau, Thomas. 1997. *Wordsworth's Profession: Form, Class, & the Logic of Early Romantic Cultural Production*. Stanford: Stanford University Press.

Pringle, Thomas. 1819. *The Autumnal Excursion, or, Sketches in Teviotdale; with Other Poems*. Edinburgh: A. Constable.

————. 1966 [1834]. *Narrative of a Residence in South Africa*. Cape Town: Struik.

————. 1989. *African Poems of Thomas Pringle*. Edited by Ernest Pereira and Michael Chapman. Pietermaritzburg: University of Natal Press.

Schama, Simon. 1996. *Landscape and Memory*. London: Fontana Press.

Suleri, Sara. 1992. *The Rhetoric of English India*. Chicago: Chicago University Press.

Van Wyk Smith, Malvern. 2000. "Origins Revisited: Dissent and Dialectic in Early South African Writing." In: E. Lehmann, E. Reckwitz and L. Vennarini (eds). *Constructing South African Literary History*. Essen: Die Blaue Eule.

Indigenous Gardening, Belonging, and Bewilderment

On Becoming South African

Sally-Ann Murray

While 'flora' have provided South African stamp designers with a portmanteau iconography of place able to represent both the national and an ostensibly apolitical 'natural history', gardening, indigenous or otherwise, is not a prominent subject in South African literary-cultural analysis. Nor is it especially visible in South African imaginative writing, although those offshoots of indigeneity considered to be of greater national-cultural consequence—identity, language, heritage—have enjoyed comparative attention. Gardening's close cousins, 'conservation', 'the/environment', 'the land', 'the farm', do feature, possibly because these intersect at the levels of materiality and metaphor, with the South African historical dramas of colonialism, apartheid and the postcolonial,[1] the last being an in-between space where new intellectual growth areas and growing numbers of researchers over-run the manicured lawns of the G8 club and even threaten to unsettle the more open field of English Studies.

In this essay I position 'indigenous' gardening within the ambit of postcolonialism as among the erratically 'sub' (-versive, -terranean, -cultural…) practices of colonialism which Ashcroft, Griffiths and Tiffin (1989) identify as influential precursors—from *within* settler culture—of what is more usually envisaged as *post*colonialism. The Ashcroft et al position has been criticised as politically disingenuous in its bid to discover "strategies of resistance and articulations of post-coloniality" in the literary traditions of *colonial* settler culture; it is viewed as mere balm to the conscience of those burdened by the colonial inheritance in the present day (Childs and Williams 1997:85). Yet does it not remain possible that something like a "network of disidentificatory traditions" (Slemon 1991:3) may feature as an elusive and a fugitive form of identity available to *the coloniser*, as well as the colonised? I intend to suggest this in relation to the emergence of indigenous gardening in South Africa.

In tussling with the meanings of gardening, let me take a literary turn, although this will not bring me to ground more stable than a real South African garden. Think back to 1984, and Nadine Gordimer's review of J.M. Coetzee's novel *Life & Times of Michael K*, where she emphasises that even the "The *Idea* of Gardening" (my italics) has been rendered dubious by the political pressures which have shaped the South African imagination. Gordimer takes no issue with that part of Coetzee's narrative in which the author establishes Michael K's beginnings in De Waal Park as a municipal gardener who develops a preference for black, rich, loamy soil. Gordimer can also grant the symbolic value of having K bury his mother and affirm an earthy, a nurturing attachment to the soil which holds her. However, she rejects Coetzee's decision to have his simple character turn from politics by gestating, through his careful tending of a pumpkin seed, a tentative belief in himself as a gardener. Raising her eyebrows in sceptical interrogation, Gordimer asserts: "It's better to live on your knees, planting something?" (1984:6).

Yet given the philosophical sophistication of both Coetzee and his apparently simple-minded protagonist, is Gordimer not wrong to imagine that Coetzee was naively constraining the field of social action by depicting K as a gardener? Does her conditioned belief in gardening in South Africa as an avoidance of politics—even the subsistence gardening to which Michael K is driven by a desperate will to survive—not lead her to miss a crucial aspect of Coetzee's fictional project? For in relation to a range of ongoing, familiar, even mundane human activities through which life in the putative South Africa of his novel is sustained and imagined in circumstances both ordinary and extreme—building, walking, eating, fighting, sleeping, talking, naming, dreaming, imprisoning, lying, fellating—Coetzee depicts Michael K as "an out-of-work-gardener in Africa in the late twentieth century" (1992:198) in order to situate gardening, or at least the idea of gardening, as a social *problematic*, with all the attendant hopes, self-interestedness and limitations that this might involve. (This is suggested by Michael K's joyful, solitary savouring of the one pumpkin he has grown, as Gordimer would have it, "hidden from the just and unjust of marauding history" [1984:6]. It is also suggested in Michael's observation: "the truth is that I have been a gardener, first for the Council, later for myself, and gardeners spend their time with their noses to the ground" [1985:181].)

The tension between Gordimer's reservations about tending the garden and Coetzee's persuasive representation of the possibilities and dead ends of 'gardening' as practice prickle in me a number of responses. To what extent is 'gardening' a humanly essential (and environmentally crucial) commitment to earth action that rightly takes precedence over blunt politics? Does 'gardening' inevitably mean attending to—and over-diligently *tending*—an abstracted 'Nature' while ignoring historical-political consequence? Does 'gardening', as an allegory for action in the world, necessarily lead writers and readers into realms of pleasurable indulgence remote from material forms of praxis? Further, when it comes to indigenous gardening, what are the implications of trying to effect, without obvious *affectation,* an 'indigenous' or vernacular garden style? And how might a better understanding of particular local histories of gardening—and the histories of 'the idea of gardening' as philosophy—help me to think of South African identities as historically and geographically contingent?

Indigenous gardening in South Africa has been part of erratically emergent 'postcolonial' cultures of settler belonging in a context in which 'the indigenous' while variously exotic and/or frightening, was widely entrenched as an inferior category. If tensions between 'strange' wilderness and 'familiar' domesticity have informed understandings of South African space for gardeners and tourists alike, the wild has been often, well, 'the wild', 'Africa', definitely *not the garden.* As Holmes observes of a middle-class white Australian settler garden, "refined nature" was the mark "of *difference* from the land around her" (2003:183), the "garden was her monument to a different world. It mediated the harshness of the surrounding landscape, providing a retreat from the unnaturalness of that barren land" (181). Similarly, the garden, for those who became white South Africans, was a symbolic place in which were nurtured the seeds of 'proper' garden plants, generally herbaceous border and bedding species traditional to Anglo-European cultivation, plants whose beauty was celebrated beyond the garden in the related aesthetic genres of poetry, painting, and prose. Or, by post-settler generations during the 1960s, the garden was treated as a canvas for painterly experiments in the flowerings of horticultural modernism exemplified by Roberto Burle Marx. (More of this later.) Whatever grew in 'the veld' and 'the bush' may have been lovely, or curious, or intimidating, or useful, or attractive as borrowed landscape, but it was not initially imagined to be suitable, in terms of either tasteful propriety or of successful propagation, for transplanting to the cultivated environs of the domestic garden.

Still, these boundaries were not fixed, as is indicated in the letters of Ellen McLeod of the Byrne Valley, written to her sister in England between 1850 and 1888, and subsequently collected by Ruth Gordon as *Dear Louisa: History of a Pioneer Family in Natal* (1970). McLeod's correspondence illustrates how, for an early white settler woman in South Africa, the clearing of land for a garden—and the clearing of imaginative space for new forms of habitation in a strange place—involved a complex exchange of seeds, slips, memories and present experiences of unfamiliar indigenous plants. The process contributed to the formation of a life sufficient to sustain physical being and it strained after the mental-emotional sustenance of much-loved places, people, and plants, left behind. McLeod's letters also imply that if gardening and 'the garden' helped to domesticate the vast unknown into habituated place, this entailed challenging, often unpredictable shifts between containment and extension, volition and happenstance.[2]

There is also a fascinating Roberto Burle Marx 'Durban story' which suggests the difficulty, for the settler and coloniser, of coming to value indigeneity over romanticised exoticism. Burle Marx was a Brazilian landscape architect (and painter, singer, designer of jewellery, fabric, stage sets…), who is widely considered to be the creator of the modern garden. As Sima Eliovson's 1991 monograph shows, there is much in his work that might lead us to categorise him as modernist: painterly sweeps and blocks of plant colour, combined with equally dramatic, sinuous abstract effects in paving, mosaic and hard landscaping, plus an inspirational assimilation into his planting designs of bold decoration that borrows from a Portuguese heritage as well as from the styles of traditional body art practised by the Amazon Indians. Even more evidently in that tradition of monumentalism favoured by high modernism is Brasilia, which Burle Marx co-designed as a replacement capital for Rio. The sometimes cold principles of modernism aside, however, a major part of Burle Marx's reputation derives from what might well be envisaged as a horticultural subset of organic modernism: his unusual emphasis, for his time, on the development of an indigenous botanical aesthetic, advocating the use of native plants in gardens for purposeful stylistic effect. When "Marx started designing, Brazilians wanted European gardens with imported lilacs, boxwood and roses, which of course struggled and died in their climate. Through his designs, Marx showed the beauty and utility of their own native flora" (Easton 2001:n.p.).

In Brazil, Burle Marx actively campaigned for the use of indigenous plant species in landscaping and collected numerous native plants still at the time undescribed by science. However, as the Durban gardeners' grapevine has it, when he came to Durban for a series of talks in the early 1960s, inspired gardening enthusiasts and council horticulturalists misinterpreted his point about the use of appropriate native species in garden design. Anecdotal memory suggests that for many Durbanites— whether tending private domestic gardens or involved in municipal parks and gardens landscaping—Burle Marx signified 'modernity'. They were hungry for horticultural innovation: eager to shrug off provinciality and outdated, traditional English botanical repertoires, and perhaps hankering after the aura of borrowed 'cosmopolitan' glamour. The city's gardeners went on a Brazilian botanical binge involving heliconia, calathea, bromeliads, crotons, any vaguely 'tropical exotic', among them plants which Burle Marx had struggled to make remarkable for the Brazilian gardening imagination, bringing them from the obscurity of jungle vegetation to a place of distinction in the aesthetic vocabulary of South American horticulture.

Pointedly enough, Burle Marx had himself come to appreciate the value of taken-for-granted rainforest species from his home country when, as an art student in Germany in 1928-9, he saw them presented as precious, spectacular floral specimens by German botanists in the Brazilian plant greenhouses of the Dahlem Botanical Gardens in Berlin. Only when directed by vectors of 'the other' was 'indigeneity' available for rehabilitation as a pertinent category from the perspective of the person sharing nativity with the plants. In their immediately 'post-Marx' period, instead of celebrating plants native to South Africa or to specific South African biomes, Durban gardeners were possessed by an unprecedented passion for plants from Latin America, their hot colours and striking forms sultry as the samba, seductive as the girl from Ipanema. Perhaps Brazilian plants declared a vibrant, sophisticated counter to the generic sameness of white South African sub-urbanity that would later be characterised by Stephen Watson: inescapable "drab declensions of suburbs" where, at "the end of a thousand lawns, dying in the heat or burnt beige by cold", nature "sprawl[s], as if it...had been pulled through a bush backwards" (1990:187). Perhaps, in a horticultural unconscious, 'Latin America' was for white South African gardeners a relief from the heaviness of historical and geographical identity, an inspirational style which promised the breath-easy joy of pure 'buenos aires' against the 'mal aria' of South Africa's sociopolitical unease. And what if Brazil had favelas, the analogue of the human refuse dumps that apartheid was institutionalising for black South Africans? These grew beyond the immediate garden context, and favela does not mean flower in any language.

Through such dense clumps of desire and difference do the meanings attached to 'the indigenous' and 'the exotic' struggle to emerge, often leaving little trace. The mango, that familiar Asian exotic, all the more enjoyable, now, for being at least non-invasive if not indigenous, is as characteristically 'Durban' as the insistent yellow pungency of marigolds. In 2005 the relative lushness of the Durban sub/urban cityscape cannot declare its own provenance, cannot attest, for the city's black, white, Indian and mixed-race inhabitants, to its makings as a modern garden under colonial town planning even as different plantings were happening in other peri-urban pockets. The South American plant craze that once swayed so many of the city's gardeners has been naturalised, both ideologically and through vegetal incorporation, into a verdant sub-tropicalism, a green coastal city whose bushy, treed, gardened slopes, understorey and canopy shot through with bright, saturated colour, seem to wrap 'Durban' in a variously gracious, languid, floridly brash distinction that mark the city's difference from Johannesburg, Pretoria, Cape Town. And which continue to demarcate the leafy, established, early-settler suburbs of Berea, the Ridge, and Glenwood from the comparative 'wildernesses' of Cato Manor shackland and the manicured corporate enclave that is Umhlanga Ridge.

Barely distinguishable from the coastal bush, for most people, regardless of the categorical classifications of the Conservation of Agricultural Resources Act (CARA) or the efforts of Working for Water, is another type of 'other' vegetation, which flourishes upon 10.1 million hectares of South African land, and threatens biodiversity and water security despite repeated attack by herbicide, panga, chainsaw, and biological control agent. Bugweed, Lantana, Sesbania, Spanish reed: they seed almost anywhere a bird may fly, and a person walk, threatening the carefully holistic indigenous garden; going under cover among the clipped shrubberies of the townhouse complex; flourishing rampant on freeway traffic islands; masquerading as shade trees between patches of mealies and cabbages dusty with the exposure of informal settlement. Whatever the place, whoever the gardener, the Othered vegetation manages to take root. Of course something must be done, and CARA, in theory if not always in practice, provides the national policy ('policing') framework necessary for the eradication of invasive aliens and the concomitant sustenance of indigenous biodiversity.

But indigeneity is disputatious when it comes to those invasive plants that have acquired personal or cultural consequence. Consider the outcry among some residents of the Outer West region of Durban—Hillcrest, Gillitts, Kloof—at the felling of non-indigenous trees, among them traditional, symbolic 'pioneer' settler species such as poplars, gums, wattles and pines. Such vegetation, in its longevity and extra-human scale, seemed a fundamental feature of the rural, green belt topography of these suburbs, and many feared that with the trees would fall a 'way of life', partly because the felling coincided with the changing human landscape of democracy, where residents of previously white suburbs perceived the threatened intrusion of 'other' races. In this emotive public space, the bio-legal rationalisations of CARA against invasive alien species held little sway, and 'the exotic' was imaginatively habituated not as other but as self, not as *invasive* or *alien,* but as a self-justifying, even natural bulwark against the increasingly vociferous claims, in the new South Africa, of economically dispossessed indigenous people. To adapt the Comaroffs: the anxiety over the felling of 'foreign flora' "gestured towards a submerged landscape of civic terror and moral alarm" (2001:630).

Or let me turn to a more minor, personal passion like *Psidium guajava.* The guava, Category II alien invader according to CARA, is a species to be regulated with permit. Permit me, though, to mention how delicious they taste, so rich a food source that even the earth digests them quickly when they fall to the ground. And how deceptively smooth the bark, despite its dramatic visual variegation. Such responses: not permissible; illegitimate? I must discipline the senses into the necessity of an environmental responsibility which proscribes certain parts of my identity. Not easy. Neither is it easier if I allow that this proscription occurs not in the name of abstract nationally-decreed dictat, but for the sustainability of life— including human life—on earth. Delete 'c' from delectable, designate the dangerous species undesirable, 'deletable'. How difficult it is to dictate the bounds of what plant life is proper, and what bears the stigma of impropriety. As the Comaroffs remark, "controversies over indigenous plants and alien-nature" permit "a vocalisation of anxieties and conundrums not easily addressed by politics-as-usual": what are the limits of belonging, what is the 'nature' of the nation, what are the associated rights of the human subject? (2001:651). For me as a South African, a South African gardener, the process of indigenous gardening entails many forms of self-denial, as well as inconsistent refusals and recognitions of the moral complicity between discourses of environmental control and vestigial racism. Both restrict movement across borders, and indeed the right to settlement, of supposedly undesirable, migrant populations who, it is feared, would quickly take root, take over, if but given the chance. The ecological necessity of managing plants by 'permit', controlling plants which are environmentally permissive, may also, beyond awkward discursive overlap with subtle new forms of racism, infringe upon human need. The truth is that non-native and even categorically invasive plant species have become important to the cultural, religious, economic and dietary sustenance of the various groups of people who have come to call South Africa, home. For instance, with a slight change of perspective, alien plant species become "people's plants" which provide valuable fuel supplies; the supposed Other of botanical indigeneity may be simultaneously "one person's livelihood and another's apocalypse" (Comaroff 2001:650).

It is also pertinent that a South African interest in indigenous plants is not an expressly home-grown phenomenon, notwithstanding a vast, still only partially-recorded wealth of knowledge about the medicinal-cultural use of indigenous species among black South Africans. South African interest in indigenous gardening is a local version of a knowledge type that is emerging around the world, although 'indigenous gardening' in this country will take particular shape from the characteristics of the national-geographical space designated "South Africa". Some of these particularities arise from topography, climate and soil, and others from the peculiarities of sociopolitical environments inherited from apartheid, which made 'home and garden' the entitlement of white South Africans while re-producing generations of black people in a relation to the land premised on labour migrancy and domestic/garden work. That said, the debates around indigenous gardening are not restricted to South Africa, and they spill beyond the containment of 'the garden' into unsettled areas of national identity, polity and heritage. They appear in Germany, where idealistically progressive Greens are suspected of fascist-reactionary plant policing in order to achieve an environmental purity which would also weed out undesirable non-native human immigrants. They emerge in Australia, where national Weedbuster Week against invasive aliens (among them South African arum lilies, acacia species and various senecios) became the model for the South African government's Department of Water Affairs and Forestry's Working for Water "AlienBusters" campaign. (This has since been re-launched as "Weedbuster Week" on account of the xenophobic overtones of the initial branding.) In England, too, botanical indigeneity is evident in ecologically motivated but contentious plans to rehabilitate a rural landscape that has become visually and experientially familiar as "the English countryside". This would mean replanting land that now comprises meadow grasses, flowers, and hedgerows (land potent in the public imagination as already under threat from highways and residential-commercial development), with the far less picturesque, but more authentically original vegetation of the bosky thicket. A return to the native planting is widely considered unappealing, even threatening, not least of all to the popular, economically productive and emotionally reassuring view of English heritage as a green and pleasant land.

Clearly, knowledge of botanical indigeneity in South Africa is increased through the comparative and international dissemination of scientific-environmental research, environmental policy programmes and ecological advocacy groups. All are forms of agency which prompt South Africans towards consciousness of the habitats and species diversity of their own immediate environments. In the not-necessarily ecological space of South African gardening, however, other models have exerted their influence upon indigeneity, primarily the design and planting by contemporary practitioners of naturalistic, wild, and grassland gardens, a repertoire given visual reference in coffee-table books, television programmes, garden shows and décor magazines. Here, we might name Piet Oudolf of Holland, founder of the New Wave 'naturalistic-artistic' planting movement, and the English plantswoman and 'gravel gardener' Beth Chatto. Both Oudolf and Chatto favour water-wise species, textural contrasts, harmonious plantings and a natural aesthetic which have proven adaptable to plant varieties and conditions in South Africa's temperate, highveld and mediterranean regions. Their convictions and ideas can also be made to intersect with those of local landscapers and plant specialists who are 'indigenous' to various degrees: Geoff Nichols, for instance, presently the horticultural consultant for the elite and contentious Hawaan Forest Estate development on the KwaZulu-Natal North Coast, has a considerable history of indigenous botanical involvement. At the Silverglen municipal nursery he worked to develop stock (and knowledge) of indigenous plants for traditional herbal-medical use, and in doing so also helped to grow the idea of suburban and council indigenous gardening in KwaZulu-Natal. Or think of Phil and Lynn Page, who in the same province have popularised the possibilities of indigenous landscaping across domestic, civic, and corporate settings. And we might even stretch our ideas of 'the indigenous' to include the landscaping of Patrick Watson, designer of the extensive 'botanical gardens' of the sumptious Lost City African-themed casino resort, who well before the present culture of television makeover represented horticultural indigeneity as an idea able to be 'made over', demonstrating how plant species, both indigenous and exotic, may be used to stage African 'indigeneity' as a commercial-national identity.

It is equally important to recognise that an interest in indigenous plants in South Africa cannot be separated from the rise, prompted by international interest, of 'the indigenous' as a broad theme *across* the disciplines of horticulture, architecture, décor, cuisine and fashion. This has seen attention given to the development of style vocabularies, materials, and construction methods derived from and appropriate to ethnic cultural contexts. As we know, in 2005, South Africans' own appreciation of the cultural capital associated with 'national identity' (as opposed to the isolationism of Afrikaner Nationalism) is being emphasised by this country's global post-apartheid cachet as a convenient, 'modern African' long-haul tourist destination. Overseas tourists wanted to experience 'Africa', and designers across various specialisations obliged the foreign visitors by updating the colonial look of upmarket boutique hotels and game lodges into an idiom closer to the stylish neo-modernism of "ZenZulu", or the earthy sophistication of "EcoEthnic", with landscaping in indigenous species to complement, mimic or refine the expected 'wilderness' or 'bush'. Such quasi indigeneity gradually shifted into the residential market, acquiring the persuasive, shape-shifting influence of an opinion leader for those white South Africans who hankered after an 'African' identity able to be simulated through design. Such design-led innovation gave the issue of indigenous form and content an unprecedented popularity among white South Africans, transforming the more overt, even threatening discourses of indigeneity as they appear in the arena of political democracy—demands for racial representivity in the workplace, for indigenous language mastery and tuition in the university—into a 'reasonable' and desirable style repertoire that is 'easy to live with' and easy to achieve using either relatively poor or extremely costly, 'indigenous' materials.

Indigeneity, we understand, has not come naturally to 'ex-European', non-native white South African gardeners. They have had to *learn* how to become indigenous; how to acquire practical horticultural knowledge about local plant species; and how to conceptualise these species in relation to established gardening aesthetics. At the time of my writing, the popularity of South African indigenous plants for the local domestic garden is enjoying a wave of interest that began in the late 1980s, a phenomenon both aided by and attested to in the number of generalist and specialist plant nurseries that propagate and supply indigenous stock. In addition, the specifically indigenous interest has resulted in gardening initiatives that tweak the established garden club practices of open garden days and gardening competitions, in order to focus on indigenous South African plants. In KwaZulu-Natal, for example, visitors come in their thousands to three established annual events on the local horticultural calendar: the Kloof Conservancy's Indigenous Open Gardens; "Wild Gardens" hosted by WESSA (Wildlife and Environmental Society of South Africa), and the plant sale of the KwaZulu-Natal branch of the Botanical Society, a market branded through the apt moniker, "Go Wild".

Such events may specifically attract the dedicated, already-knowledgeable aficionado; but they also reach the merely interested or curious, and in doing so contribute to a climate of awareness which informally educates several publics into new ways of seeing and thinking about the possibilities of indigenous planting, garden design, and environmental issues. The same is true of books such as Charles and Julia Botha's popular volume *Bring Nature Back to Your Garden* (1995), designed with specific South African regions in mind. The English edition has sold over 10 000 copies, and an isiZulu edition has also been published. The book has succeeded in attracting a wide readership precisely because it communicates crucial scientific information and persuasive opinion in a non-scholarly register based on sound practical advice about gardening in environmentally 'friendly' ways; it uses a 'down-to-earth' rather than proselytising, serious tone, and a cartoon-inspired homiletic of illustrative sketches. Even the relatively specialist genre of the field guide to trees and flowers has valuable educative potential, as is evident from the success of Elsa Pooley's guides to trees and wildflowers. These combine scrupulous Linnaean scientific description (crucial for accurate plant identification) with detailed forms of regional local knowledge, giving common names in isiZulu, isiXhosa, Afrikaans and English, as well as information which places advice concerning garden cultivation in relation to traditional medicinal, cultural, spiritual and culinary use.

Yet indigenous gardening in South Africa is not quite a 'phenomenon', or a zeitgeist; it remains very unevenly in evidence. Consider, for example, a locally-conceived and produced gardening and décor magazine like *South African Garden & Home,* which has only in the last few years begun regularly to publish features and inserts on indigenous and water-wise gardening as a mode of being 'responsibly South African'. And this represents more dedicated page-space than in the analogous, though more exclusive, expensive title from the international *Conde Nast* stable, *House & Garden,* which tends not to highlight 'indigenous gardening' per se as a practice to be widely encouraged and enjoyed, but rather, exemplary, noteworthy gardens, and/or influential garden designers or landscape architects, often as adjuncts to the 'house beautiful' in aesthetic embodiment of the integrated indoor/outdoor lifestyle. While a Proudly South African design ethos *is* sometimes encouraged, more often the pressure to localise, in this title, is construed as an obsessive, illiberal provincialism, and stories praise local design for an originality which yet retains connection with the international trends that reconcile local idiosyncrasy to the interests of the market. The indigenous, here, is configured not as an affordable, commercialised popular or as ecological necessity, but as exclusive top-end design style intended to distinguish the buyer's *taste* from more parochial, common-place expressions of 'South Africanness'.

In South African garden and home magazines—notwithstanding the slim, recently-established titles dedicated to gardening as special niche— the scant page space and the interrupted focus given to indigenous gardening are partly a function of the consumer magazine as a genre: a piecemeal, fragmented text-format which relies on an incidental, erratic phenomenology of composition and reading held only loosely together by periodic formulae such as the conventionalised departments of 'décor', 'food', 'outdoors', etc. In part, though, the irregular visibility of indigenous gardening in South African lifestyle magazines may be ascribed to the realities of a consumer-driven South Africa: socio-cultural identities remain so volatile, so unevenly influenced by the contingencies of world historical trend, regional ethnicity, community interest group and the like, that the claim of the indigenous is obliged to survive amid a mêlée of discourses. 'Indigenous gardening' is not yet a firm conceptual category and therefore cannot carry through into coherent practice. It appears in the magazine pages amid a clamour of competing voices which represent plant developers, import nurseries, environmentalists, government, advertisers, garden designers, competition organisers.... Whatever the reasons for the fragile, fragmented representation of indigenous gardening in local periodicals, however, the potential of the popular magazine as an educative forum should not be dismissed. We may recall that to a Victorian reading public popular periodicals were far more influential than books in familiarising and explaining new discoveries in science, technology, medicine and understandings of human culture (Cantor et al 2004).

If democracy has pushed white South Africans into previously unimagined conceptual relations with 'indigeneity' (gardening being but one), it is feasible that the political and economic opportunities associated with democracy have brought new imaginative-experiential possibilities for black South Africans, especially those who have the capital and leisure to afford a middle-class lifestyle. For such black South Africans, home ownership and gardening might represent appealing ways of being 'South African', and of claiming entitlement to this South African place. What may I safely assume, here? More than likely, very little. Perhaps for black South Africans now resident in the previously white 'garden suburbs', being at home may entail the need to become familiar with domestic plant and design knowledges that were once the privilege of the oppressor. Such garden knowledge was permitted to black people only through the menial labour of 'the garden boy'. Now, for contemporary middle-class black South Africans, arrival in the suburbs might best be entertained neither through personal mastery nor the 'garden boy', but through outsourcing to professional garden services. Furthermore, in such domestic gardens, indigenous plant species may be as foreign to the black South African as to the white, any coherent body of supposedly traditional knowledge or an inherited ethnobotanical patrimony having long been cut across by vectors of apartheid modernity.

If I cannot but accept that indigenous gardening is a practice which has as much to do with culture as with nature, I might still, as a gardening academic (never merely an academic gardener), dig over the ideas of Homi Bhabha (1993), who doubles and splits Fanon's notion that the fantasy of the native is to occupy the master's place. Developing Bhabha's suggestions about "masking" for the colonised being not a neat division but a "dissembling image of being in at least two places at once" (1993:44), I could propose that one of the erstwhile master's fantasies, after decolonisation and with all the irregularities of 'the postcolonial', might be to occupy something of the *native's* place. There *are* many deceptions involved here, for the coloniser *already has* occupied this place through strategies of force which, especially in an age of democracy, render the occupation evidently illegitimate, and the shift in consciousness provoked by a realignment of sociopolitical power makes uncomfortably undeniable the long-suppressed acknowledgment that this was never 'the master's' place in the first place. And with this comes the need to imagine new identities beyond those of native and alien.

These moves towards identification with place and people have a complicated historical circuitry, and much depends on the degree of cynicism or sympathy we are willing to extend. In the rightly influential *White Writing* (1988) J.M. Coetzee, for example, draws attention to settler identifications with indigeneity almost as dispassionate statement of fact rather than critical position, figuring the process somewhat mechanistically in doing so: the settlers attempted a "projection of consciousness into the alien: into the African himself, into the African fauna or landscape" (74). The lines of identification, here, are possibly too unmediated, implying (oddly, for Coetzee) a conception of colonialism as a successfully dominating big idea, a 'projection' which visibly, assertively, broadcasts the colonisers' cultural authority even as they seek to connect with the local. Nothing breaks down, or intervenes; all is 'projection'? There are none of the gaps, inconsistencies, failures and clumsy splices of situation, action and belief that scholars have come to acknowledge as the unexpressed underside of colonialism's history. David Bunn, for his part, looks beyond history as 'projection', suggesting that a traveller such as Le Vaillant tried imaginatively to invent "his authority for being in Africa by imitating indigenous forms", in this case, campsite shelters modelled after the indigenous Khoikhoi hut. These imitative designs, Bunn writes, then became "a sign of Le Vaillant's authorship, his ability to respond creatively, benevolently, and unobtrusively to the foreign environment" (1994:133), but he goes on to admit that this is, of course, "a conceit" not a truth, one which is "present throughout colonial landscape painting and poetry" (133) and, I am suggesting in this paper, South African indigenous gardening.

With even less ideological reserve Stephen Watson develops this line of thought in an essay on the limits of literary romanticism in South African poetry, contending that in white South African writers' "various efforts to establish a subjective intensity and wholeness, to attain that internal paradise in which the distinction between internal and external, subject and object, mind and world is momentarily elided, may be read…the efforts of aliens to *overcome* [my italics] the other that rendered them alien" (1990:60-1). In the context of my own argument about the ambiguous nature of indigenous gardening as a form of contemporary identity for white South Africans, the expression "to overcome" is wonderfully layered. It implies the familiar narrative of historical conquest in which the colonists attempt to 'overcome' the other by force, but it also hints at the alien conquerors' reluctantly growing sense that what needed to be 'overcome' was that part of the very colonial self which resisted incorporation. Indeed, this is made clear in Watson's subsequent move in the essay from which the above quotation is taken: he admits the massive psychic-experiential ruptures and inconsistencies which arise in the settler's struggle to become African while being simultaneously recalcitrant about relinquishing cultural authority. For the "colonisers found themselves in a place where they did not belong, where continuities became discontinuities, certainties anxieties, the familiar eccentric, their own selves strangely other" (1990:61). And it is traces of this which even now shape the practice of indigenous gardening popular among increasing numbers of white South Africans.

In this way, it is possible to see analogies with the colonial poetic practice in which the white poet "finds it necessary to construct a *transitional object*...that enables transactions between metropolitan conventions and colonial conditions", and in many cases this was "a landscape" (Bunn 1994:138). In this respect, indigenous gardening may be a problematic mode of representation, open to the same criticisms levelled against white South African poetry: poets tend "to retreat into a stone or shell, into that moment of fusion with the symbolic piece of Africa, the pebble in his hand" (Watson 1990:74). As Watson explains, "the poet's tendency to invest all his or her attention and love in something very far from the human image, identifying in an object, a plant, an animal, ...[the] sense of reality, morality or of the self" is an "act of sympathetic identification" which might not "provide anything like an adequate metaphor for life in society, in history" (74).

The growing tendency in South African indigenous gardening has been to *efface* the hands of culture and politics, and to rehabilitate the domesticated garden through both indigenous plant content and planting style, as a simulation of the unauthored, pre-nation state of 'natural wilderness'. For the white South African gardener, the desire to shape, plant and grow an indigenous garden embodies a paradox, for at least one aspect of the motivating desire is to erase the tracks of a residually European self, hence the culture in which most white South Africans, at least until now, have been nurtured, however insidiously. So in one sense, the turn to indigenous plants in the historically 'exotic' suburban garden "marks the settlers' burgeoning reconciliation with place and increasing national identification with the land" (Roberts 1999:128). Even beyond the national boundary, the indigenously-styled garden gestures towards a shamanistic faith, a powerful sympathetic magic through which white South Africans hope to "call up a memory of a nature beyond the confines of cultivation", an "interior wilderness" of human being (Madsen 1999:37,36) that is symbolic of a better self. Yet in another sense, as a South African indigenous garden movement gathers strength, white South Africa's generational hold on the land is being challenged by state-driven mass housing projects; the recommendations of the Land Claims Commission; and CARA legislation which makes landowners ethically and financially responsible for the management of invasive alien species on their properties. Indigenous gardening, therefore, is not only a pleasurable or recreational leisure pursuit; it is a jittery informing context in which the idea of indigenous gardening comprises an awkward white South African rapprochement with place and space, even as it carries with it the uneasy subjectivity of various selves in history. It would take an Ivan Vladislavić to tell this tale, a suitably preposterous, not improbable, provocative, inventive, politically-incorrect addendum to his collection of short fiction, *Propaganda by Monuments* (1996). Let me write this:

Jan van Riebeeck, Dutch commander at the Cape, organises a tree planting ceremony to which is invited the standard South African mélange of guests. We are there (very unsure of who we are supposed to represent), struggling to make ourselves heard above the strains of "All Things Bright and Beautiful" being played by members of a combined band from the Working for Water/Woolworths Trust EduPlant schools' permaculture gardening project. The scholars, all identified as indigent, play on ingenious indigenous instruments fashioned from gourds, seed pods, and twigs, with shakers that look suspiciously as if they were once Coke cans. Uncanny how even these cans can be recycled. We glance around the crowd. There is H.B. Rycroft, one-time director of the National Botanic Gardens at Kirstenbosch, reading—against the wind and other rackets—a eulogy to Van Riebeeck as the first ecologist in Africa, since "on October 26th, 1657, Van Riebeeck instructed his forester...to manage and, therefore, conserve the forest above Kirstenbosch and not to harm it by reckless felling" (Eliovson 1979:19).

As he finishes, Rycroft strides purposefully (how else?) through the crowd distributing free mini samples of Bounce Back compost stapled to publicity brochures for The Botanical Society of South Africa. The brochure invites us to support South Africa's floral heritage by donating money (in the form of estate bequests, trusts, or charitable donations) to the society, explaining that such financial support "is the most enduring and far-reaching way of ensuring that your interest in, and concern for, our natural heritage lives on into the future" and automatically makes you a member of the "Heritage Circle" of the Botanical Society of South Africa. We read on, gratified to learn that this is an "exclusive group of people who feel, as you do, that our efforts to preserve our rich diversity of flora—much of it unique to southern Africa—must continue beyond our own lifetime. As a member of this select group, you will receive invitations to exclusive functions, where you will meet specialists in the field and mix with those who share your vision. You will also be presented with a beautiful photograph album of hand-made paper. This could be your memorial: a living, green space that will endure way beyond your lifetime as a testimonial to your vision and hope for the future".

Despite our digital sophistication, we quite fancy the idea of the crafted photo album (beautiful images, cherished memories, history standing the test of time...), but we watch as one man peers at the pamphlet and then discards it, along with the Bounce Back. We might think him uncivilised except that we know him from news features on television: an elderly Bushman whom authorities are planning to move from the Richterstveld, his home since birth and before, to make way for a national park. He turns to leave the junket, but is cornered by a pathbreaking environmental historian doing field work for an academic enquiry into Cape farming practices: "'Conservationists,' the Bushman spits, *'Hulle sorg vir die halfmens, maar gee niks om vir die hele mens nie* '". He goes, without a trace, although there are masses of other indigenous people milling, ready, waiting to take his place. Many of them have come to barter sheep and the medicinal herb 'kanna' for commodities from Van Riebeeck's men. *!ke e:/xarra //ke* they seem to be saying to us. We have seen this motto emblazoned on the coat of arms, but it and they are still incomprehensible, so we nod, politely, uncomprehending. (They are also nearly naked, which is something else to see. And rather distracting.) The Swedish botanist Thunberg succumbs, wilts, but perhaps he is overcome by the heat, or merely with the linguistic effort of trying to get his tongue accurately around the sound of a plant name in the vernacular. Khanna, kannie, canny, can he, cunny; he eventually resorts to the so much simpler 'Sceletium', a lonely half in the Linnaean binomial taxonomic system.

Thunberg turns to the person on his left for help; it is Zoë Wicomb, the coloured South African writer, home from intellectual exile for a visit, savouring the smell of *'hotnotkooigoed'* crushed between her fingers: hmmmmhhhh. Unforgettable. You *can't* get lost in Cape Town. Her hair is wild, like the bush, her face planed with traces of a vanished but longed-for past. He would like to crush her to his breast, then release himself into her aromatic fynbos. She seems, to Thunberg, so wonderfully familiar, just the Other he knew he would encounter by travelling to Africa. She looks more truly African than the President, he thinks, when cross-categorising against the prominent posters displaying an urbanely dark gentleman in an expensive suit. Thunberg's tired retinas for one moment play a Tretchikoff on him, superimposing the after-image of Wicomb's hair on the man's manicured head. (Pulling the wool from his eyes, Thunberg wonders about the old adage: indeed, maybe two birds in a bush *are* better than one in the hand? It's so difficult to tell, isn't it?)

Mbeki, we see, is not with us (not, of course, that he is against us), and we assume he was invited, but presume he is travelling out of the country, as is so often the case with the indigenous plants and people who have been burdened with carrying the South African flag. Still: it seems that Mbeki wants guests to understand the difficulty of reconciling indigeneity with divergent identities, even though the hybrid *Iaman African* he planted years ago has struggled to take root: as his official stand-in at today's event he has chosen Martinus van Schalkwyk, the new Minister of Tourism and Environmental Affairs. All the better to mingle with the mense, Van Schalkwyk has disguised himself as a schoolboy, and little boys bollock around, all of them in short pants, joshful of hope that their teacher will soon release them into the natural wonders of the games arcade at The Heritage Mall that has recently been built on the slopes of Table Mountain. We remember that this development was stop/start for years, until the Environmental Impact Assessment people and the city council gave the green light. The buildings twinkle at us from their lofty heights, a neon sign in the shape of a massive 'King Protea' phasing through a rainbow of colours which flashes *'The Heritage', 'the Heritage', 'The Heritage'....* Thunberg tears himself away from Wicomb and wonders whether he will be able to buy one of those Madiba shirts.

All the while, the Administrator of what will one day become the Transvaal works the crowd present at this public gathering to test the speech he plans to read on the occasion of the Republic Festival of 1966. He wants, in particular, to praise the publication of the specially-commissioned book *Sixty-six Transvaal Trees* (De Winter et al, 1966) as "an occasion of thanksgiving for the mighty blessings we have received.... It can assuredly not be regarded as inappropriate if on such a joyous occasion we happen also to think of the great gift from nature, our wealth of indigenous trees, which Providence gave us before we even asked for it" (De Winter et al 1966:6). The crowd's response is mixed: roars of approval, shouts of dissent, perplexed inclinations of the head.... Some hooligan chucks a *snotappel* fruit, two lovely girls give Sir a mixed bouquet of carnations, glads and arums, all held together in a flurry of babies' breath. There is a sangoma burning bunches of *imphepho,* and an imbongi looking for the president to praise. *Aikhona.*

Fixed with the satisfied look of the successful captain of industry, there is Mehring, stepped out from *The Conservationist.* He is a guest of honour, and he stands ready with spade in one hand to plant, yes, but also to deal with the body of the black man that will certainly be displaced by meddling with the earth through mining and farming. This much his maker has taught him; and as we know she has her own ideas about gardening. In his other hand is Mehring's "companion volume to the wild-flower book, a book on indigenous tree species" (Gordimer 1974: 212), for he has been invited specifically to advise Van Riebeeck on tree type, and position. His author does not approve; she knows him for a character both complacently complicit and insistently ignorant, despite opportunities to be otherwise. Anyway, here it is; you can't keep a good man down. Mehring's preference is for "superimposing two large chestnuts in flower (pink or white?—he forgot to ask the nurseryman, but perhaps one doesn't know until the first blooming?) at various points in his landscape" (Gordimer 1974:213). But now he's conflicted and lacks the authority to make a stand: "The first hole is ready and they move on to make the next. It was difficult to decide where to plant the trees. They ought to be near the farmhouse, really—a farmhouse as one thinks of one. Two great round chestnuts dark over the stoep.... It would be something extraordinary. But on the other hand"—the one in which he holds his spade, remember—"indigenous trees would be better in such a definitive position, Yellowwood, Eugenia or something—as a general rule one should plant indigenous trees wherever possible, not even ordinary exotics like eucalyptus and poplar.... He stands with his hands on his hips, for balance, looking down into the hole". He thinks—oh my God, has he, in this day and age, said it aloud?—"Whatever else they may or may not be able to do, they know how to dig" (1974:212). 'Strue. We have made sure of that.

Burrowed somewhere in all of this is Michael K, waiting for his season. Will we, do we, recognise him and what he is doing? Does he plan to sell organically-grown pumpkins in an exclusive Woolworths range developed from his one remaining seed? Or has he gone indigenous, with public-private funding for a small business in medicinal plants? Or is he, still, patiently and persistently, drawing liquid from a well with a bent teaspoon so that he, if no-one else, can water the supposedly water-wise saplings that the committee has just planted and will nonchalantly neglect when the PR jamboree concludes? But wait... wait. He does not move, still as a root, knotted in the clasp of the earth. Is he dead, his body returned in spirit to the inevitable, inhospitable seed-bed that the guests cannot see, and upon whose decay they plant a hedge against their bets?

Is this the end?

(Disclaimer: the author—I—would like to declare that the texts, persons, and situations referred to are factual or based on fact. While grafts and slips have been made for the purposes of propagation, no names have been changed in order to protect identities. I am happy to share more detailed information with you in exchange for seeds or similar. Financial assistance towards this project from the National Research Foundation is gratefully acknowledged. However, even more so than usual, the opinions are solely those of the author—me, mine—and should not be attributed to the NRF or any of its affiliates, or indeed, in the case of the concluding story, to Ivan Vladislavić.)

Notes

1. Especially relevant work here is that by Jean and John Comaroff (2001), as well as William Beinart and Peter Coates (1995). In addition, research by

William Cronon (1983) and Henry Hobhouse (1992) suggests that natural ecosystems and all forms of plant life comprise largely unrecognised factors in the historical process.

2. It was Julia Martin's *Writing Home* (2002) which moved me to look at the Mcleod letters. Martin's book is a collection of poetic stories in which plants, people, and place are linked to memory and identity.

References

Ashcroft, Bill, Gareth Griffiths and Helen Tiffin. 1989. *The Empire Writes Back: Theory and Practice in Post-Colonial Literatures.* London and New York: Routledge.

Adam, Ian and Helen Tiffin (eds). 1991. *Past the Last Post: Theorising Post-Colonialism and Postmodernism.* Hemel Hempstead: Harvester Wheatsheaf.

Bhaba, Homi K. 1993. "Interrogating Identity: Frantz Fanon and the Postcolonial Prerogative." In: *The Location of Culture.* London and New York: Routledge.

Beinart, William and Peter Coates. 1995. *Environment and History: The Taming of Nature in the USA and South Africa.* London and New York: Routledge.

Botha, Charles and Julia Botha. 1995. *Bring Nature Back to Your Garden.* Durban: WESSA.

Bunn, David. "'Our Wattled Cot': Mercantile and Domestic Space in Thomas Pringle's African Landscapes." In: W.J.T. Mitchell (ed.). *Landscape and Power.* Chicago: Chicago University Press: 127-73.

Cantor, Geoffrey, Gowan Dawson, Graeme Gooday, Richard Noakes, Sally Shuttleworth and Jonathan R. Topham (eds). 2004. *Science in the Nineteenth-Century Periodical: Reading the Magazine of Nature.* Cambridge: Cambridge University Press.

Childs, Peter and R.J. Patrick Williams. 1997. *An Introduction to Postcolonial Theory.* New York: Prentice-Hall.

Coetzee, J.M. 1985 [1983]. *Life & Times of Michael K.* London: Penguin Books.

_____. 1988. *White Writing: On the Culture of Letters in South Africa.* Sandton: Radix.

Comaroff, Jean and John L. 2001. "Naturing the Nation: Aliens, Apocalypse and the Postcolonial State." *Journal of Southern African Studies* 27(3):627-51.

Cronon, William. 1983. *Changes in the Land: Indians, Colonists, and the Ecology of New England.* New York: Hill and Wang.

De Winter, B., Mayda de Winter and D.J.B. Killick. 1966. *Sixty-six Transvaal*

Trees. Pretoria: The Botanical Research Institute and the Department of Forestry.

Easton, Valerie. 2001. "First, Make Good Dirt." *The Seattle Times*. <http://seattletimes.nwsource.com/pacificnw/2001/1028/plant.html>

Eliovson, Sima. 1979. *Garden Beauty of South Africa*. Johannesburg: MacMillan South Africa.

_____. 1991. *The Gardens of Roberto Burle Marx*. Portland, Oregon: Timber Press.

Gordimer, Nadine. 1974. *The Conservationist*. London: Jonathan Cape.

_____. 1984. "The Idea of Gardening: The *Life and Times of Michael K*." *New York Review of Books* 3(6):1-6.

Gordon, Ruth (ed.). 1970. *Dear Louisa: History of a Pioneer Family in Natal, 1850-1888*. Cape Town: A.A. Balkema.

Hobhouse, Henry. 1992 [1985]. *Seeds of Change: Five Plants that Changed the World*. New York: Harper & Row.

Holmes, Katie. 2003. "'In Spite of It All, The Garden Still Stands': Gardens, Landscape and Cultural History." In: H. Teo and R.Whites (eds). *Cultural History in Australia*. Sydney: University of New South Wales Press:172-85.

Madsen, Virgina. 1999. "The Call of the Wild." In: M. Thomas (ed.). *Uncertain Ground: Essays Between Art + Nature*. Sydney: Art Gallery of New South Wales: 29-43.

Martin, Julia. 2002. *Writing Home*. Cape Town: Carapace.

Pooley, Elsa. 1993. *Trees of Natal, Zululand & Transkei*. Durban: Natal Flora Publications Trust.

_____. 1998. *A Field Guide to Wildflowers of KwaZulu-Natal and the Eastern Region*. Durban: Natal Flora Publications Trust.

Sherry, J.S. 1971. *The Black Wattle*. Pietermaritzburg: University of Natal Press.

Slemon, Stephen. 1991. "Modernism's Last Post." In: I. Adam and H. Tiffin (eds). *Past the Last Post: Theorising Post-Colonialism and Post-Modernism*. Hemel Hempstead: Harvester Wheatsheaf.

Teo, Hsu-Ming and Richard Whites (eds). 2003. *Cultural History in Australia*. Sydney: University of New South Wales Press.

Thomas, Martin (ed.). 1999. *Uncertain Ground: Essays Between Art + Nature*. Sydney: Art Gallery of New South Wales.

Vladislavić, Ivan. 1996. *Propaganda by Monuments and Other Stories*. Cape Town: David Philip.

REVOLUTIONARIES OR SELL-OUTS?

AFRICAN INTELLECTUALS AND *THE VOICE OF AFRICA*, 1949-1952

CORINNE SANDWITH

A contribution of postcolonial studies has been the recognition of the various forms resistance or complicity may take in the colonial situation. In Homi Bhabha, for example, we move from Fanon's psychology of violence and its attendant material effects to the psychology of display: the native mimicking the master. The danger of such a shift—what is called the cultural turn in postcolonial studies—is that a focus on the expressive manifestation (or 'text') may divert attention from the shaping pressures of historical context. One such pressure that has been relatively neglected by the cultural turn is that of class. Yet to erase considerations of class is to erase a significant category of explanation even when the cultural manifestation suggests race or identity as the predominant factor. I wish to consider the character of response—resistance or complicity—in a little-known but in its day influential community newspaper, *The Voice*, published in English between 1949 and 1952 by a group of African intellectuals living in Orlando township, near Johannesburg. My purpose is to utilise *The Voice*, therefore, as paradigmatic of a discourse of colonialism, one that continues to characterise the 'postcolony' today, especially as global capitalism impinges upon even the most local of endeavours. *The Voice* is an intriguing subject for this discussion: while its politics are those of an outspoken African nationalism, it simultaneously evinces a regard for Western 'High Culture'—expressed both at the level of style and content—and an ambivalent attitude towards indigenous cultural forms, which could well be interpreted as the unmistakable sign of political 'complicity'.

I begin my exploration of *The Voice* with an equally paradigmatic example: on 8 June 1940, Walter M.B. Nhlapo, journalist for the government-compliant newspaper, *Bantu World*, wrote an article condemning the

deteriorating standards of the Johannesburg Bantu Men's Social Centre
(BMSC). The Centre, it seems, had begun to attract a "motley crew of
patrons" whose behaviour was not in keeping with the elevated traditions
of this once respectable establishment. Alcohol, single women, people
dressed in "sportswear" and "ordinary clothes", as well as a tendency for
patrons to keep their hats on while dancing were just some of the signs
that "the veneer of civilisation [was] falling in this place". These people,
he wrote, have "lowered the value of [the Centre's] erstwhile educative
and social atmosphere". A common enough feature of "'tsaba-tsaba' and
marabi gatherings", this kind of behaviour was out of place in a centre that
had been established for the intellectual and cultural edification of a
respectable African elite. "A place for such a person," Nhlapo continues,
"is not the Centre, but a bench in the park" (*Bantu World*, 8 June 1940:5).
A month later, another article by Nhlapo, this time on the behaviour of
patrons at orchestral concerts (again at the BMSC), suggested that a more
"orderly" state of affairs could be ensured if "simple courtesies" like
"silence", "applause", "no fidgeting" and "no leaving while music is on"
could be encouraged by means of signs held up at appropriate intervals
during the concert (*Bantu World*, 13 July 1940:12).

Nhlapo's views on 'civilised' behaviour had their counterpart in
arguments on 'civilised' art. Disturbed by the ever-growing popularity of
jazz music on the Rand, which, he complained, was lowering artistic
standards and drawing people away from 'High Culture', Nhlapo advocated
what he described as the less ephemeral pleasures of Marlowe, Shakespeare,
Boswell, Beethoven, Schubert, and Handel. A "low type of noise full of
cheap sentiment", jazz "has deafened and blinded our appreciation for art.
Art's visage is too high to hit our senses, and our expressions are but a
clumsy revelation of ignorance" (*Bantu World*, 24 February 1940:14).

Nhlapo's defensive early 1940s diatribes against an emerging urban
working-class culture are an amusing example of a well-documented
African elitism in contexts of colonial rule (see Couzens 1985; Kavanagh
1985; Orkin 1991). Elsewhere, invoking dubious narratives of African
evolutionary progress, and deeply uncomfortable with a growing mass
militancy in African politics, Nhlapo appears to reiterate the familiar stance
of someone who has bought into the cultural and social hierarchies of
Western capitalist societies. What is also interesting about these comments
is that the kind of cultural capital which Nhlapo implicitly invokes as the
outward sign of social respectability includes not only the familiar cultural
icons of Shakespeare or Schubert, but also such things as behaviour,
accent, style of dress, manners and general demeanour, or what Pierre

Bourdieu (1986) has described as a cultural capital which has in a sense become "embodied". This kind of deference to the fine social distinctions of the dominant culture is common. One need only look at newspapers such as *Bantu World*, *Umteteli wa Bantu*, and the Cape Town-based *Sun*. It is against this background that I consider the cultural politics of *The Voice*.

The Voice of Africa was edited by Es'kia Mphahlele, Isaac Matlare and Khabi Mngoma, and ran from September 1949 to February 1952.[1] Produced on a shoestring budget in rough, cyclostyled form, this idiosyncratic community newspaper has been neglected by historians and literary critics alike. Completely absent from Mphahlele's autobiography, *Down Second Avenue*, it appears briefly in Peter Walshe's history of the African National Congress, but is erroneously linked with a number of pan-Africanist broadsheets produced by members of the ANC Youth League in Orlando.[2] Originally the inspiration of a small community discussion group, the Orlando Study Circle (whose members included Mphahlele, Mngoma, Matlare, Barney Ngakane and the afore-mentioned Walter Nhlapo), *The Voice of Africa* is a remarkable document of a particular place, a distinctive community and a peculiar historical moment. With virtually no support from advertisers, bar a few local Orlando businesses, the costs of producing *The Voice* were borne almost completely by the editors themselves who were able to make use of printing and roneoing facilities provided by the South African Institute of Race Relations (Manganyi 1983:70). In a landscape dominated by white-owned African newspapers which, at this time, were unashamedly engaged in the promotion of a conservative politics while cynically marketing first-world commodities to a fast-growing urban African population, *The Voice* was a rare example of an independent, black-owned newspaper. Rejecting those papers that "serve the interests of the capitalist, cold-blooded moneyman", *The Voice* committed itself, instead, to a policy which was "guided by the needs of the masses" (September 1949:4). In stark contrast also to "that archangel of political cowardice" *Bantu World* (January 1950:8), *The Voice of Africa* offered both a militant response to an increasingly repressive apartheid state and a scathing attack on the compromised politics of conservative African leaders.

Primarily an organ of political commentary, analysis and critique, *The Voice* also acted as a township chronicle. It provided news of local community events (particularly the numerous cultural and social activities of the popular Donaldson Community Centre) and addressed local community issues such as housing shortages, the high cost of transport, and the ever-present menace of the South African police. In this sense, as Mphahlele's biographer puts it, it was "very Orlando in flavour" (Manganyi 1983:101), balancing a concern for a wider political scene with the more intimate address of a community news-sheet. With a substantial literary focus which included book, theatre and music reviews as well as short stories and poetry by Mphahlele, Mngoma and Nhlapo, *The Voice* anticipated the by now well-known literary renaissance which a few years later was to emerge in *Drum* magazine.[3]

Anxious to intervene in the impasse of South African resistance politics in the wake of the shock victory of the Afrikaner National Party in 1948, *Voice* writers asserted a strong 'African Nationalist' project in the interests of radical political change. The paper was tolerant of a wide range of political solutions within this more militant nationalist position, and made a point of avoiding what it termed the unnecessary "political pea-shooting" (July 1950:2) of internecine political squabbles amongst the oppressed. In fact, the discussion group (the Orlando Study Group) from which the newspaper emerged seems to have been deliberately created in order to allow for the expression of the widest possible range of political views (Manganyi 1983:70). One of its regular contributors, Isaac Matlare, for instance, was a member of the Progressive Forum, a Johannesburg-based group which fell under the wing of the All African Convention and the Non-European Unity Movement (Mphahlele 1959:212), both of which (by this time, at least) were antagonistic towards the ANC.[4] Zeph Mothopeng, a teacher at Orlando High, was a member of the Africanist wing of the ANC Youth League (Lodge 1983:80). Mphahlele and Mngoma, also teachers at Orlando High, were amongst a group of younger teachers who were engaged in a struggle against the more conservative old-guard in the Transvaal African Teachers' Association. Walter Nhlapo—another regular contributor to *The Voice*—is something of an anomaly in this group. Erudite and articulate, and still holding onto something of his earlier cultural elitism, Nhlapo stands out from his co-contributors on *The Voice* in his obvious sympathies with the more gradualist and reformist political approach of a familiar South African liberalism.

Clearly, the strong desire to avoid unnecessary "political pea-shooting" was an important factor in the success of the newspaper. A collaborative effort in which contributors were given a free hand, *The Voice of Africa* reflected the diversity of African opinion on the Rand. Thus in October 1949, while Nhlapo argues that "white and black can live together" if whites would only "do away with prejudice" (October 1949:7), another editorial reacting to the upcoming celebrations of the newly-erected

Voortrekker Monument angrily denounces this "Klu Klux Klan orgy", where "beards [are exchanged] for hoods". "In these circumstances," the piece continues,

> it does nobody any earthly good...to court their co-operation or appeal to their finer feelings, or even hope for a change of heart. They do not want our co-operation, but our labour, on their own terms.... If the whites ever possessed any finer feelings, they lost them over 200 years ago. We can do nothing else but give back hate for hate, bitterness for bitterness, insult for insult. (November 1949:1)

Contradictions of this kind make it very difficult to speak of any unitary 'voice'. And, since the names of editors and many contributors remained a closely guarded secret in order to protect them from the scrutiny of the South African government (and from the pique of insulted community leaders), it is also virtually impossible to identify any of the original authors. There were a few exceptions: Mphahlele's articles were usually written under the by-lines "Naledi" and "Edi Mento", while Mngoma tended to use the initials K.B.M.V. or K.M.V. Most of the other pieces were published under pseudonyms like "Orpheus", "Scorpion", "Pedagogue" and "Politicus Africanus".

Never reducible to a single position, it was the job of its two main editors, Mphahlele and Mngoma, to bring coherence to the publication (Manganyi 1983:69), and while neither Mphahlele nor Mngoma was a member of the African National Congress or its more militant Youth League wing, there is evidence that both were sympathetic to the more radical, left-inclined position of certain elements within the League.[5] Their experience as teachers in a racist education system acted as a strong politicising agent and a spur to their efforts in the public domain. Both products of missionary education and recipients of university degrees, they had nothing but contempt for government plans to introduce an inferior form of "Bantu Education" (Mphahlele 1980:168).

Interest in the bulletin appears to have been immediate and widespread. Manganyi puts circulation figures at around 500 copies. The paper was sold by a team of volunteers in Orlando for a penny and, according to Manganyi, it was "keenly sought after", it was "really hot stuff" and the "people lapped it up" (1983:70). An apology published in the second issue of the newspaper regretted that it could only meet a small proportion of its demands, and immediate calls from readers for a letters page appear to confirm this claim. As early as the second issue, *The Voice* was confident about its role and value in the community:

> 'The Voice' has come to the people of Orlando as a blessing. They feel
> that at last there is an organ which can voice their opinion freely and
> clearly, because it is a paper, free from the control of vested interests.
> Unlike many of the so-called African papers which most of the time echo
> the opinion of the capitalist daily papers, even when that opinion is
> inimical to African aspirations, the 'Voice' will seek to serve the healthy
> interests of the Black Man. (October 1949:5)

Ranging in tone from angry denunciation to wry satire, the newspaper
retained an irrepressible equanimity and optimism, even in the face of an
increasingly repressive and intolerant political regime. Idiosyncratic,
playful and ironic, *The Voice* was as critical of the conspicuous failures
of the liberation movement as it was of the apartheid state. Reacting to
widespread apathy and self-doubt amongst the oppressed, and fiercely
opposed to what it saw as a deferential, self-serving and complacent
African intellectual class, its principal concern was to educate, politicise
and mobilise its readers in the interests of meaningful change. The first
editorial begins:

> There is a general political inertness among us. Nothing...ever awakens
> our political consciousness. For most of the time, we are apathetic and
> contemptuous, even destructively suspicious of any person or group of
> persons who try to revive our spirits. Then we sigh and feign boredom or
> cry down such attempts by nauseating criticism. Why do we wait until
> a few Whites have initiated any struggle on our behalf before we snap out
> of this hangover? Something MUST BE DONE...we are thwarted
> everywhere we go, thwarted by weak and undisciplined leadership; by our
> own indifference and corrosive habits.... No. Self-pity never solved
> personal or national problems: it is a maladjustive reaction.... Suffice it
> to say we know what we want. No nation ever attained its liberation by
> accident or by the visitation of some fairy godfather. (September 1949:1)

In this regard, *Voice* journalists tended to dismiss a liberal emphasis
on the quiet politics of negotiation and compromise as ineffectual "gas-
talk" (July 1950:1) and, like the ANC Youth League, reiterated the urgent
need for a change in political tactics as a response to a renewed state
onslaught on black South Africans in the post-war period and in relation
to an increasingly visible "master-race cult" (November 1949:1). One of the
incidents that invited strong condemnation from *Voice* journalists was the
state response to the 1950 May Day protests against the Suppression of
Communism Act. Clashes between crowds and a 2000-strong police force
in Alexandra, Sophiatown, Benoni and Orlando resulted in the deaths of

eighteen people, three of whom were school children (Lodge 1983:34).
According to *The Voice*, this was "government by a police-state where the
masses of Non-Europeans are fodder for the sjamboks, batons and guns
of savage policemen" (May 1950:1).

Afrikaner Nationalism, not surprisingly, came in for a great deal of
criticism. In his regular column "Rabelais at Large", Mphahlele took
delight in satirising a stereotypical Afrikaans racism through the figure of
Baas Pieter, inhabitant of the fictional world of Rooikop. For the most part,
Mphahlele's satire in these columns is directed at a myopic Afrikaner
Nationalism which could see no value in other cultures. This satire is also
concerned with exposing the moral bankruptcy at the heart of its supposedly
Christian morality. In conversation with a friend, for example, Baas Pieter
on one occasion declares,

> There is nothing Wordsworth or any other English poet ever wrote which
> can ever surpass DIE VLAKTE by Cilliers. There is also too much fuss
> about 'daardie kêrel' Shakespeare. The only good thing about that bloke
> was that he was a Nationalist. Instead of a learned man translating
> MACBETH into Afrikaans, he should have written a tragedy on Paul
> Kruger. (April 1950:4)

Admittedly, the joke depends on one's acceptance of an unfavourable
comparison between Afrikaans culture and that of the supposedly superior
English variety. Here, it is interesting to consider to what extent it is an
exclusively Afrikaans culture that comes under attack, and to what degree
British or European culture is subjected to a similar kind of scrutiny. (I shall
return to this question in a moment.) In the meantime, it is important to
recognise that as far as the general politics of *The Voice* are concerned,
English liberals were also subjected to harsh criticism. In this regard, while
"Rabelais"/Mphahlele rudely exposes the ignorance and racism of someone
like Baas Pieter, he also takes an occasional stab at the pecuniary
underpinnings of the British Christian 'civilising' mission. An editorial
published in October 1951, for example, comments obliquely on the
question of the notorious "civilisation test", and also accuses white
liberals of "[sowing] confusion among the very people who they claim to
protect":

> [The Liberal's] vision Splendid is that which envisages in a distant future
> a change in attitude on the part of his government towards the poor black
> slave; he believes in gaining an inch in 10 or 20 years towards his ideal;
> he believes in protests through the medium of the telegram, or memorandum,

or deputations to the government to ease off the pangs that are imposed on us day after day; he has a hazy idea of equality among races, but gets mixed up in his qualifications of such quality e.g. the education or civilization qualifications – only those black people who can exercise the vote "intelligently" should have it.... He is primarily a white man and secondarily an apostle of freedom for all: hence his satisfaction in merely keeping within the Constitution;...hence his resentment of any revolutionary step we want to take because he would be involved. He is ready to wage any "fight" constitutionally, to avoid arrest, and then he tells himself that if he acted against the law, he would be depriving us of the help of other would-be white sympathisers.... (October 1951:1)

While sympathetic towards the ANC Youth League, *The Voice* preferred to retain its own independence. Mphahlele and Mngoma in particular were wary of a more exclusive 'Africa for Africans' stance propounded by an influential faction within the League. Instead, they saw a more politically effective strategy in co-operation with others amongst the oppressed (August 1950:2). This strand in a broader South African national project, which embraced both so-called Coloured and Indian groups, was a position which, from the late 1950s onwards, was to become the cornerstone of ANC policy. Once again in opposition to ANC leaders, *The Voice*—in a position close to that of the Non-European Unity Movement—advocated an uncompromising principle of non-collaboration "with all councils of state which are segregatory", and condemned "those who serve on such councils and boards, and any other people or organisations which seek to perpetuate these councils" (January 1950:11).

The more militant brand of African nationalism in *The Voice* reflected a new mood in African politics. Post-war disillusionment with empty wartime promises had fed into a growing radicalism which was first seen in the emergence of popular, grass-roots resistance movements, and only later adopted by more aggressive elements in the ANC. In 1949, a document produced by the African National Congress Youth League was finally accepted at the annual ANC conference held in Bloemfontein. The ANC "Programme of Action" rejected the 'cap-in-hand' moderation of the Congress old-guard, and committed the organisation to the strike, boycott, civil disobedience and non-collaboration tactics of a more militant mass movement. In the words of ANC Youth League secretary, Joe Matthews, this was a transition from "urban gentleman with clean hands to a militant people's movement" (*Spark* 1952:1). A more assertive nationalist philosophy, inspired in part by the success of anti-colonial struggles abroad, it accommodated a range of positions from the Garveyite 'Africa for the Africans' stance to a more left-inclined, class-based analysis (see Gerhart 1978; Lodge 1983; Simons and Simons 1983; Walshe 1987). Whether they propounded an unapologetic ethnic nationalism or a more inclusive form of anti-colonial resistance, members of the ANC Youth League were united in their dissatisfaction with existing ANC leaders.

While those in the ANC Youth League tended to temper their criticism in the hopes of initiating reform from within the ANC, *Voice* journalists took little notice of such political niceties. Instead, they argued that in its insistence on following only constitutional methods of resistance—at the same time adopting an extremely patronising attitude towards the 'backward' poor majority—the "lethargic and slow-moving ANC" (November 1949:3) had become isolated from its people. Accordingly, the ANC was in danger of degenerating into "an exclusive fashionable club where the educated elite wallow in intellectual theory juggling", imagining its domain as a kind of "Mount Olympus where intellectual demi-gods delight in chatting about the fates that harass the mortal masses" while sitting around "waiting for the masses to raise burnt offerings to them". These intellectuals "have never shared the miseries, poverty and the helplessness which are the lot of ordinary man". Content to "bask in the warmth of applause from their own clique, and to eat of the crumbs from the white liberal table", they ignore the "yawning gap between intellectual armchair theorists and the people" (March 1951:9).

The ANC was not the only target of this critique. African professional classes are dismissed on countless occasions as "crumb-beggars" (July 1950:2), "belly crawlers" (March 1950:3), "black boot-lickers" (December 1950:4) and "yes men" (September 1950:4). In many ways, the early success and growing notoriety of *The Voice* was directly linked to its ongoing preoccupation with the conservative and obsequious politics of local community leaders. In an editorial entitled "Yes-Men must GO", the writer rails against the class of "Good Natives" who "have failed the people by putting [their] personal interests first". "Doormats of liberals", and "oppressor's puppets", "their jobs have deadened their consciences" and they are "no longer able to tell the difference between selling out and playing straight" (March 1950:1). Instead, African leaders are urged to "come down to mother earth", to "forget [their] intellectual snobbishness", and to "stop wandering in the Utopia of [their] political ideals!" (November 1949:7). The high levels of aggression and hostility in these attacks bear testimony to the enormous significance of these issues for those concerned.

Particularly galling in this regard was the treacherous role played by teachers in fostering servility and deference to authority amongst the poor: instead of preparing the youth for their role in shaping a more just social order, teachers were "actively assisting the ruling class in keeping the non-white in a state of ignorance and servitude" (October 1949:3). Fort Hare University, for example, is described as "tower[ing] conspicuously above [other institutions] as the brightest beacon light of suppression and repression". The products of such universities are "learned fools with haloes", "harmless, angelic, subservient, insensible dullards" who are "shamefully indifferent to the cries, miseries and struggles of their people" (June 1950:1). Closer to home, in response to its willingness to go along with the new syllabuses of Bantu education, Orlando High School was dubbed "Orlando Tribal High". Rural chiefs are treated no more politely. Described as the "hypnotised snakes" of government officials, who "[dance] to the jarring music of white domination" (October 1949:9), they are accused of being complicit in the oppression of their own people.

The hostility of these attacks had much to do with the particular character of Orlando itself. Described "as a glorified Marabastad" by Mphahlele (1980:203), Orlando was in fact held up as a model African township, set up by the Johannesburg municipality as part of its efforts to establish alternative accommodation to the more centrally-located (and, therefore, more threatening) freehold African settlements like Sophiatown and Alexandra. Situated much further away from Johannesburg, Orlando attracted a slightly more affluent petit-bourgeois class, which had gained the reputation of being politically passive and unconcerned with the struggles of ordinary people (Lodge 1983:15,89). *The Voice* was unequivocal on this point, frequently berating Orlando residents for their "yellow-livered cowardice" (May 1950:1). Distinguishing between "two streams" in the Orlando community—the "majority group" of "loving and lovable good folk [who bear] their own burdens and miseries with a kind of stoical bitterness and tragic humour" and the group of "untouchables" who "live in houses you dare not breathe when you pass, lest the windows break"—*The Voice* made no secret of its primary allegiance to ordinary black South Africans (January-February 1952:17). Like the radical intellectuals of the Western Cape-based Non-European Unity Movement, *Voice* journalists repudiated any connection—despite their own relatively more privileged position—with an elite African class, claiming instead the role of people's champion: *The Voice* was "the journal of the people, by the people for the people" (January-February 1952:17).

In the same spirit, *The Voice* was also careful to distance itself from the conservative politics of 'good native' African publications like the *Bantu World*. Described on one occasion as a paper which "aims at keeping the

African under the perpetual tutelage of the white man", its argument that "'both races can live in this country peacefully, not as masters and servants, but as partners, the white race playing the role of senior partner'" leaves "the whole concept of white supremacy intact". "Small wonder," the article continues, "that even a liberal author dubbed the BANTU WORLD 'the voice of Caliban'—a deformed sub-human slave of Prospero's in the TEMPEST. This Frankenstein monster of white supremacy must go, whatever its shape or form" (June 1950:6).

Interestingly, in contrast to the generally Rabelaisian and anti-elitist ethos of the paper, articles addressed specifically to women readers had a decidedly more moralising and admonishing tone, even to the extent of reiterating the conservative social and cultural prescriptions of the dominant culture. So while in one article women are chided for their snobbish and status-conscious behaviour—for using their women's clubs to show "how many tea-sets they have" and "how expensive their wardrobes are" (April 1951:7)—they are also exhorted to refrain from unacceptable conduct like gossiping, flirting and laughing out loud. In the manner of a more conservative cultural tradition, women's clubs are described as places of moral and cultural upliftment: "You will as a member of a club with high ideals, learn that life is not a thing to be idled and frittered away; it is a sacred trust that implies true and laudable service to God and man. It is a school where one's boldness is restrained and where the vulgar outburst of coarse high spirits is repressed" (December 1950:13). When it comes to the subject of women, it seems, the cultural prescriptions of the dominant culture are anxiously applied rather than satirically dismissed.

Not surprisingly, *Voice* journalists made themselves profoundly unpopular with the leaders of the day, both black and white. Coming under the scrutiny of the Johannesburg Special Branch in the early 1950s—the school principal of Orlando High School, Godfrey Nakene, had secretly submitted copies of *The Voice* to the Transvaal Education Department— the paper was banned from Orlando High on account of its recklessly anti-government stance. According to Mphahlele's biographer, Nakene felt himself personally attacked in its columns, and wasted no effort in getting Mphahlele and some of his co-conspirators expelled. In spite of the fact that more than half the school came out in protest, Mphahlele and Zeph Mothopeng were dismissed towards the middle of 1952 (Manganyi 1983:71; Mphahlele 1980:169).[6]

* * *

Writing on the emergence of nationalist movements against forms of colonial oppression, Frantz Fanon points to a stage in the development of national consciousness when, feeling "like a stranger in [their] own land" (1990:176), assimilated African intellectuals throw off their allegiance to the culture of the colonised and attempt to "renew contact with the oldest, most pre-colonial springs of life of their people" (169). Although Fanon is critical of its tendency towards 'exoticism' and sceptical of its real political effects, he describes this rejection of Western culture in positive terms as "a phase of consciousness which is in the process of being liberated" (177). After a period of "unqualified assimilation", the native "decides to remember who he is". According to Fanon, while the attempt to revive the ancient customs of a culture under colonial rule is an important stage in the development of national consciousness, what tends to emerge as the liberation struggle slowly gathers strength is a "fighting culture" (179). Eventually abandoning their quest for an increasingly chimerical pre-colonial past, African intellectuals begin to identify with the revolutionary struggles of the masses.

The Voice of Africa presents an interesting problem for this influential model of anti-colonial resistance. While consistently promoting a militant African nationalist project—actively contributing to its progress in the practical realm of local community politics—*Voice* journalists were so steeped in the literature and culture of the West that it not only forms part of a deeply-felt literary sensibility and overarching world view, but also provides the terms of reference in which an anti-colonial resistance is expressed. The left-inflected African nationalism of *Voice* politics, in other words, is articulated in an idiom drawn almost completely from the world of European literature: Podsnap, Don Quixote, Micawber, the Ancient Mariner, and the Scarlet Pimpernel are just some of the literary figures who find themselves in the pages of *The Voice* as it negotiates, puzzles over, and rails against an increasingly oppressive regime. Similarly, Dickens, Austen, Shakespeare, Swift, Shaw, George Eliot, and the Romantic poets are all freely appropriated, cited, echoed and 'rewritten' in the interpretation and critique of the contemporary political scene.

The narrator of Jane Austen's *Pride and Prejudice*, for example, finds herself in unfamiliar company as she is unceremoniously enlisted in a materialist argument concerning the operations of ruling-class power: "It is a truth universally acknowledged," the article begins, "that the intellectuals of any nation hardly ever constitute a class of their own, but are as a rule the representatives of some class or other" (January 1950:8). Similarly, a short piece on a recent Voortrekker celebration in the Northern

Transvaal town of Lydenburg concludes, "We know enough of Voortrekker 'Christian plundering' and rule by rifle [and] Bible...to be able to say like Banquo: 'Thou hast it now...and, I fear thou play'dst most foully for it'" (October-November 1950:6). In the most explicit re-writing of Western literature, Milton's "Paradise Lost" and Byron's "Vision of Judgement" are subjected to extensive and ironic re-fashioning in the service of an anti-colonial politics. Both these re-writings—prefaced with tongue-in-cheek apologies to the writers concerned—are significant examples of the confident and playful appropriation of Western 'High Culture' for radical political ends.[7]

In addition to such reliance on the resources of an imported culture, *Voice* journalists insisted on their right to unrestricted access to forms of European 'High Culture' (classical music, in particular): a participation which was being withdrawn under the specious apartheid logic of the need to protect a traditional 'Bantu' way of life. Instead of "spurning those acquisitions which make him a stranger in his own land" (Fanon 1990:177), the African intellectuals of *The Voice* conspicuously embraced such acquisitions as part of an Africanist project. While there was anger at the European distortions of pre-colonial history and culture and pride in the achievements of the past, *Voice* journalists were wary of the tribalising connotations of government calls for the "Bantu" to return to pre-colonial traditions and culture.

What brought many of these issues to a head was a proposed series of concerts by world-famous violinist, Yehudi Menuhin; concerts which were confined to white audiences. Reacting angrily to comments in the press by the Minister of the Interior that Africans were unable to appreciate music in the "high idiom", Khabi Mngoma in his regular music column rejected the conclusions of these so-called "European experts on Native affairs":

> [Government officials] believe that instead of concert halls where Africans can listen to symphony, arenas should be built for them where half-naked and dressed in their traditional costumes, they would sing and dance to their own music. Africans are wary of such statements because they reek of apartheid with all its nefarious motives, i.a. oppression. People may have their folk music, but it is absurd to confine a people's appreciation, composition and performance of music to their indigenous music. When people come into contact with Western culture, they die out, unless they adapt themselves to it. We are suspicious of "experts" who want to isolate us and probably annihilate us, as has been the fate of the American Red Indian, Australian Black Fellow, the Bushman and Hottentot, who are fast

dying out. It is stupid to expect an African born and bred in town to take
as active a part in indigenous music as the rustic. The former has the
Western influence, and he comes into contact with music that is
predominantly Western. To the urban African, indigenous African music
can be as new and strange as it can be to the average European. (November
1949:9)

That Mngoma's position on 'indigenous' music did not include a rejection
of the emerging working-class musical idiom of marabi is clear from an
earlier article in which he defends marabi by emphasising its continuities
with more established modern swing bands such as the Harlem Swingsters
and the Merry Blackbirds (October 1949:10).

Interestingly, *The Voice* also directed its views on the dangers of 're-
tribalisation' and 'indigeneity' at Africans themselves. Reacting to
arguments by the ANC Youth League that Africans should "resign from
anything European", the anonymous editor responds:

Perhaps they would rather see us play the isiba rather than the oboe, jungle
drums rather than the piano; dressed in beshu instead of suits; live in huts
instead of villas, and so on. When nationalism takes this trend, the attitude
is strikingly uncongenial to a progressive temperament: it is a poisonous
and disastrous transition of thought that must narrow and stereotype
men's outlook on things, forcing them to see no glory in Debussy,
Baudelaire, Maurois and others who are unAfrican. (December 1950:
inside cover)

The tendency to conflate nationalist projects with the repudiation of
Western culture is, to an extent, understandable. Cultural assimilation or
Western acculturation—viewed with suspicion by many historians and
literary critics—may be regarded as a litmus test of 'oppositionality': a
clear sign that an individual has internalised the Manichaean cultural and
social divisions propagated by the West. Conversely, and despite Fanon's
warnings, the corresponding return to the cultural resources of a pre-
colonial state of grace may be regarded with more sympathy. Are these
journalists, then, examples of Fanon's "race of angels": assimilated
African intellectuals—target for radicals and African nationalists alike—
who have "thrown themselves greedily upon Western culture" (1990:176);
who regard their traditions with horror; and who have lost touch with their
people and their history? Do we dismiss such African intellectuals as
political sell-outs, members of a relatively more privileged elite, who value
their financial security more than their freedom, and who preach moderation
and argue along with colonial governments for the qualified franchise?

The Voice's overt nationalism and its antipathy towards conservative African leaders make any easy assumptions about either colonial deference or reactionary politics equally difficult to defend. In order to unravel the conundrum of the assimilated colonial subject who simultaneously resists, it is necessary to consider both the range of arguments put forward, as well as their historical location. In a context in which pseudo-scientific racial theories still held sway, this position was both a reaction to cultural exclusion and a claim to equal participation in South African cultural and political life. A strong assertion of a shared humanity, it also drew on and echoed the powerful arguments of the early nineteenth-century African-American intellectual, W.E.B. du Bois (1905), whose arguments were quoted with much enthusiasm in *The Voice*:

> I sit with Shakespeare and he winces not. Across the color line I move arm in arm with Balzac and Dumas, where smiling men and women glide in gilded halls. From out the caves of evening that swing between the strong-limbed earth and the tracery of the stars, I summon Aristotle and Aurelius and what soul I will, and they all come graciously with no scorn or condescension. (October 1949:8)

Mphahlele's response to the Yehudi Menuhin concert, mentioned above, provides a particularly illuminating example of the way in which Africans resisted the ever-intensifying cultural exclusions of the apartheid era. Eventually allowed to attend a special concert for Africans only, Mphahlele registers his anger at this kind of cultural apartheid in the following ironic conflation of the European Romantic tradition:

> It is all over now – the Menuhin concert. I'm not a music critic and all that: I listened with my native ear, surrendered myself to the effect of that music. I don't know anything about E Minor or E Major. They mean nothing to my simple untutored mind.... But Bach's concerto in E Major and Mendelssohn's in E minor brought that night "sensations sweet, felt in the blood, and felt along the heart" and "feelings too of unremembered pleasure," as Wordsworth says.... So, if on hearing that music I may have seen some maiden "amid the alien corn" "faery lands forlorn," "the crystal streams," a river flowing "through caverns measureless to man down to a sunless sea," or "meandering in a mazy motion," or "alone upon a branch that's bare, a trembling leaf left behind," or may have heard the wailing of "a God in pain," it is because the height of poetic truth reached by the composer...struck on the lyrical strings of my being. (April 1950:10)[8]

The repudiation of an ideology of racial backwardness and inferiority implied in this response was also accompanied by an interrogation of the meaning of a 'national' culture, which was partly indebted to British educationist, Victor Murray (1929), also quoted in *The Voice*. In a defamiliarising strategy very like the opening pages of Conrad's *Heart of Darkness*, Murray reminds his European audience of their debt to cultures other than their own:

> For [the African] as for us the treasures of the world's past have been heaped up. We receive the treasures of the East, Rome and Judea, and have added to them. And if for us Barbarians and Gentiles, Plato thought, and Virgil sang and Jeremiah agonised, and Christ died, these things happen for the African too. For him also in later days Beethoven played, Leonardo painted, Shakespeare wrote, Pascal disputed, and James Watt invented. (October 1949:8)

Interestingly, this position—in which culture is understood not as the fixed preserve of particular nations but as the unstable and ever-shifting combination of many cultural streams—was also the position adopted in 1944 by the African National Congress Youth League, and reiterated in their "Basic Policy" of 1948:

> Culture and civilisation have been handed down from nation to nation and from people to people, down to historic ages. One people or nation after another made its own contribution to the sum-total of human culture and civilisation. Africa has her own contribution to make. The Congress Youth League stands for a policy of assimilating the best elements in European and other civilisations and cultures, on the firm basis of what is good and durable in the African's own culture and civilisation. In this way, the African will be able to make her own special contribution to human progress and happiness. (In Karis and Carter, 1987:326)[9]

If *Voice* journalists claimed an authoritative space for Africans in the broader field of cultural endeavour, thereby rejecting the 'backward' cultural designations of the apartheid state, it is equally true that they held no illusions about Western pretensions to moral and cultural superiority. While the hegemonic Western narrative of benevolent colonial emancipation and economic development is contradicted with stories of plunder and oppression, *Voice* journalists also take every opportunity to point to the "immorality" of government policy in the present. An article by Mphahlele which attacks the "stupidities of white civilisation", for example, offers an embryonic sense of an alternative (African) value system to counter the dominant Western model. Commenting on white "laziness", "greed", hypocrisy and an endlessly competitive spirit,

Mphahlele—in the often impolite and satirical guise of his alter-ego "Rabelais at Large"—takes pleasure in reflecting on the peculiarities of white South African culture: "These white demi-gods…are afraid of laughing out loud; they get rich and starve and beat their labourers in the process, and when they are 80 and feel the tug of the grave, give out their money to charities so as to die peacefully…." His conclusion is deliberately flippant: "Civilisation??!! No-no-no-no, I refuse to go!" (August 1951:3). On a more serious note, his five-part series (beginning in January 1951), entitled "What it means to be a Black Man", provides another important counterpoint to the moral pretensions of white civilisation by offering a detailed exposition of the role of the South African legal system in keeping non-Europeans in continued subjection.[10] Expressing the same mixture of moral outrage, hostility, anger and cynicism, which characterised similar arguments in the Non-European Unity Movement, *Voice* journalists repeatedly attack the moral superiority of the West. This hostile stance, however, is also marked by the defensive, even pessimistic, tone of those who are painfully and acutely aware of their own subordinate social position: if Western civilisation is, as one commentator described it, "fickle", "foppish", "bragging", "cowardly", even "stark raving mad" (June 1950:4), it has nevertheless effected a seemingly impenetrable hegemony.

Western moral superiority is also frequently contested on the grounds of culture itself. Regular literary reviews—on a range of literary-cultural texts including Oliver Walker's *Proud Zulu* (April 1950:7), Adamastor's *White Man Boss* (December-January 1950:11), the film *Jim Comes to Jo'burg* and popular magazines such as *Drum* and *Zonk*—become vehicles for a forthright interrogation of colonial rule. Adopting an overtly politicised approach, *Voice* reviewers test the claim of Western moral superiority against examples of racist distortion and stereotype in contemporary South African culture. A few illustrations will suffice. Rejecting the derogatory representations and "cheap roles" in "Jim Crow" films like *Jim Comes to Jo'burg*, one writer argues:

> We have had enough of being called 'Jim' and 'boy' by Europeans without films like these adding to the humiliation. By all decent means let us have African film actors, but let the dignity of the African also be maintained. We should accept roles that show the African in better light than as incorrigible servant, the frightened animal, the blundering idiot, the criminal or dunce. We also have noble feelings and ambitions in life…. Films like "Jim Comes to Joburg" and "Zonk" [magazine] are just one more grain of dust in the African's eye! (July 1950:10)

Turning to Afrikaans fiction, another writer looks at the frequent recourse
to racist descriptions like "kaffir", "outa", "ayah", and "meid", as well as
the use of terms like "vreet" and "trop", which assume a connection
between Africans and animals. Nothing more than an "immoral linguistic
display", this fiction remains "outside of the realm of noble and dignified
literature" (April 1950:2). The anonymous reviewer of John Buchan's
Prester John also takes up the issue of the representation of Africans in
fiction. John Buchan, the reviewer suggests,

> [belongs] to the political school known as the Milner Kindergarten.... A
> Word of Caution! The unwary reader must realize that John Buchan's
> mind, as revealed in this book, is typical of the mind of most whites which
> fabricate 'risings that must fail' in the hope of discouraging for all time any
> attempt on the part of the African to shake off the fetters of oppression.
> The author has lamentably failed to show that the rising would have been
> an undoubted success if it had had as its basis an effective organisational
> machinery. The writer should have created not a mere neurotic self-
> seeking visionary out of Laputa, but a more substantial personality with
> clearly defined political principles and a dynamic far-reaching programme:
> but then his Lordship was part of the ruling class! (April 1950:7)

By contrast, white South African writers who oppose the distortions of
colonialist histories are treated more sympathetically. In this regard,
Oliver Walker's *Proud Zulu* and Adamastor's *White Man Boss* are both
singled out for their more progressive reading of South African history.
According to one reviewer, Walker is to be commended not only because
he depicts "the dishonesty, the chicanery, and the complete lack of moral
scruples" which characterised the Boers in their dealings with Africans,
but also because he understands the equally duplicitous role played by
"the representatives of Her Majesty the Queen" (April 1950:7).

As the above illustrations suggest, a simple equation between Western
acculturation and political 'complicity' would have failed to offer an
adequate account of the cultural and political preoccupations of *The
Voice*. In the first place, *Voice* journalists understood that any attempt to
renew contact with pre-colonial culture as part of a developing African
nationalist project was more likely to hinder than advance their political
cause. Cynically manipulated by the state as a reason for excluding
Africans from full participation in the economic and political life of the
country, indigenous culture—linked in apartheid social engineering to
're-tribalisation'—was regarded as a disingenuous justification for
apartheid segregation. For an African to embrace 'indigeneity' in such a

context, therefore, was to provide support for existing government policies: a move which almost certainly guaranteed one's political and economic isolation. Simultaneously, any recourse to notions of an "African mind or African psychology" (August 1951:2) would endorse the ideology of the apartheid government. Interestingly, in their outright rejection of race classifications in favour of a more "universal" understanding of human psychology (April 1951:1), *Voice* writers advocated a position significantly at odds with the influential Negritude movement.[11]

In the context of South Africa in the 1950s, then, the conspicuous display of Western cultural 'proficiency' becomes a conscious strategy of political resistance. In this sense, and despite its deep affinities with Western culture, *The Voice* articulates a position that is in fact close to Fanon's "fighting phase" (1990:179). Recognising the value of the past, *Voice* journalists are clear that it is the present that demands the greater attention. Eager to embrace the reality of an industrialising and urbanising society, increasingly reified indigenous cultural practices are "like the setting sun, 'lingering like an unloved guest'" (August 1950:8). Although Mahmood Mamdani (1996) cautions against explanations of South African society which treat South Africa as a special case, it seems to me that the response of African intellectuals, outlined above, cannot be understood without an acceptance of the specificities of South African society in the early 1950s. I do not wish to exaggerate the distinctions between the segrationist initiatives of the Smuts government and the elaborate apartheid engineering which followed. The newly-elected National Party government, however, was determined to reverse a worrying trend which had accelerated during the Second World War, namely the massive increase in the numbers of Africans settling in urban areas in response to crippled rural economies and deepening poverty levels. In this sense, the nationalists embarked on what Mamdani describes as a process of "de-urbanisation": an attempt to reinstate 'tribal' authority in a more systematic way than the previous advocates of trusteeship had dreamed possible. For the likes of Mphahlele and his colleagues, the most glaring indication of this policy change was the establishment of differential systems of education for Whites and "Non-Europeans", and an increasing reliance in official discourse on the notion of "Bantu culture". Accordingly, this 'moment' in the history of resistance in South Africa is an ambiguous one: Africans who had benefited from the sectional privileges bestowed on a small elite now faced the inevitable prospect—together with the poor and uneducated—of being forced into the ghetto of a 'race' identity.

The complexities of historical context notwithstanding, there are other reasons why it is more appropriate to understand *The Voice* as an example not of complicity but of anti-colonial resistance. In the first place, *The Voice of Africa* articulates a version of African nationalism quite distinct from the gentlemanly and self-serving politics of an older generation of ANC leaders. This is evident in its emphasis on the political and economic emancipation of all South Africans, its strong identification with the struggles of the poor majority, and its deeply-felt unease with all forms of social hierarchy and privilege. In this sense, *The Voice* articulates an African nationalist project which recognises in the poor majority not just a tool of resistance—a powerful 'muscle' of revolution to be abandoned as soon as power had changed hands—but an ally in the creation of a just social order: one in which the working classes are not excluded while a new black elite prospers. Of all the issues which emerge in the pages of this newspaper, the problem of the petit-bourgeois sell-out is considered by far the most urgent. Whilst the intensity of this attack on collaborationist leaders is partly a result of sensitivity about the journalists' own relatively more privileged position, it is also a powerful attack on the social and cultural distinctions which sustain the entrenched inequalities of Western capitalist societies. In their repudiation of notions of cultural 'respectability', in their rejection of 'civilisation tests', and in their explicit attacks on the snobbery of conservative petit-bourgeois leaders, *Voice* journalists articulate a forthright opposition to the routine social exclusions of the dominant white culture. What *The Voice* represents, in other words, is not the conservative politics of a socially aspirant petit-bourgeois elite. Neither is it the kind of elitist defence of Western values against a 'debased' African working-class culture represented in Walter Nhlapo's attack on a new generation of patrons at the BMSC.

Strongly repudiating existing class and race divisions amongst the oppressed, *The Voice* gave an unapologetic Rabelaisian 'up yours' to the dominant culture. What was rejected was not Western culture per se, but the set of social relations of domination and subordination in which the acquisition of Western cultural capital figures as both powerful signifier and determinant of social dominance. A strong affinity with Western culture does not necessarily entail an acceptance of the fine social distinctions upon which this culture is premised. For this reason, I suggest that in order to assess the 'complicity' or 'resistance' of particular examples of African colonial response, it is necessary to qualify questions of cultural identity and allegiance with those of class. Anti-colonial 'resistance' or 'oppositionality' is best defined not in terms of cultural identity, but as the articulation of a particular political stance, one which is based on an overt contestation of the race *and class* exclusions of the dominant social order.

Notes

All quotations from *The Voice* are reproduced in exactly the same form as they appeared in the original text, including all typographical and grammatical variations and idiosyncrasies.

1. The newspaper appeared once a month between September 1949 and August 1950. From September 1950, it was only issued every two months. It was at this time that its name was changed to *The Voice of Africa* (Switzer and Switzer 1979:64). I use the two titles interchangeably.

2. It is also given brief mention in Couzens (1985:317). Switzer and Switzer give a fuller description (1979:64).

3. It must be emphasised that, aside from the shared aim of publishing new writing by black South Africans, there was very little similarity between the two papers. *The Voice*'s strong anti-government stance and its characteristically earnest style are in marked contrast to the market-driven ethos of its more famous competitor.

4. The Non-European Unity Movement was established in 1943. A formidable oppositional political movement, which operated mainly in the Western Cape, it remained bitterly opposed to the ANC (Alexander 1986; Lewis 1987; Drew 2000).

5. Mphahlele joined the ANC in 1955, but retained some sympathy with the position of the leftist elements in the All African Convention. (See Mphahlele 1980:188-91.)

6. Mphahlele, Mothopeng and Matlare were arrested on charges of public violence and inciting the school boycott. They were imprisoned for four days. They were acquitted on the evidence of some of the pupils at the school who testified that they had been forced to sign affidavits incriminating the three teachers on pain of being sent to a reformatory (Mphahlele 1959:169).

7. For similar examples of cultural refashioning and appropriation, see Stephanie Newell's *Reading Cultures in Colonial Ghana* (2002).

8. "sensations sweet, felt in the blood, and felt along the heart" and "feelings too of unremembered pleasure" are taken from Wordsworth's "Tintern Abbey"; "Faery lands forlorn" and "amid the alien corn" are from Keats's "Ode to a Nightingale"; "the crystal streams" is found in Robert Burns's "Young Peggy"; "through caverns measureless to man down to a sunless sea," and "meandering in a mazy motion" are from Coleridge's "Kubla Khan" and "a god in pain" is a line from Keats's "The Eve of St. Agnes".

9   Incidentally, the use of the pronoun "her" in this document to describe the
    generic African subject is an interesting (and unusual) departure from
    conventional gender norms.

10 Much of this discussion was prompted by a letter expressing the "views of
    a European reader" which rehearsed the traditional argument that non-
    Europeans were not quite ready for European civilisation, and argued that
    instead of "cursing [the white man], Africans should be grateful for the
    benefits they had already received, not least of which was Shakespeare,
    Beethoven and 'medical science'" (August 1951:8). For another caustic
    response, see October 1951:inside cover page.

11 Mphahlele's encounters with Negritude while in exile in Nigeria are recorded
    in a fascinating series of articles which were published in the Communist Party
    journal, *Fighting Talk*, in the early 1960s.

References

Alexander, Neville. 1986. "Aspects of Non-Collaboration in the Western Cape,
    1943-1963." *Social Dynamics* 12.1:1-14.

Bhabha, Homi K. 1994. *The Location of Culture*. London: Routledge.

Bourdieu, Pierre. 1986. *Distinction: A Social Critique of the Judgement of Taste*.
    London: Routledge.

Couzens, Tim. 1985. *The New African: A Study of the Life and Work of H.I.E.
    Dhlomo*. Johannesburg: Ravan Press.

Drew, Allison. 2000. *Discordant Comrades: Identities and Loyalties on the South
    African Left*. Pretoria: Unisa Press.

Du Bois, W.E.B. 1905. *The Souls of Black Folk*. London: Constable.

Fanon, Frantz. 1990 [1961]. *The Wretched of the Earth*. London: Penguin.

Gerhart, Gail. 1978. *Black Power in South Africa: The Evolution of an Ideology*.
    Berkeley: University of California Press.

Karis, Thomas and Gwendolyn M. Carter (eds). 1987. *From Protest to Challenge:
    A Documentary History of African Politics in South Africa*. Stanford, California:
    Hoover Institution Press.

Kavanagh, Robert Mshengu. 1985. *Theatre and Cultural Struggle in South Africa*.
    London: Zed Books.

Lewis, Gavin. 1987. *Between the Wire and the Wall: A History of South African
    Coloured Politics*. Cape Town: David Philip.

Lodge, Tom. 1983. *Black Politics in South Africa since 1945*. Johannesburg: Ravan
    Press.

Mamdani, Mahmood. 1996. *Citizen and Subject: Contemporary Africa and the
    Legacy of Late Colonialism*. Cape Town: David Philip.

Manganyi, N. Chabani. 1983. *Exiles and Homecomings: A Biography of Es'kia Mphahlele*. Johannesburg: Ravan Press.

Mphahlele, Ezekiel. 1974 [1962]. *The African Image*. London: Faber and Faber.

_____. 1980 [1959]. *Down Second Avenue*. London: Faber and Faber.

Murray, A. Victor. 1929. *School in the Bush: A Critical Study of the Theory and Practice of Native Education in Africa*. London: Longman's Green.

Newall, Stephanie. 2002. *Reading Cultures in Colonial Ghana*. Manchester: Manchester University Press.

Orkin, Martin. 1991. *Drama and the South African State*. Johannesburg: Witwatersrand University Press.

Peterson, Bhekizizwe. 2000. *Monarchs, Missionaries and African Intellectuals: African Theatre and the Unmaking of Colonial Marginality*. Johannesburg: Witwatersrand University Press.

Simons, Jack and Ray Simons. 1983. *Class and Colour in South Africa: 1850-1950*. London: International Defence and Aid Fund.

Switzer, Les (ed.). 1997. *South Africa's Alternative Press: Voices of Protest and Resistance, 1880s-1960*. Cambridge: Cambridge University Press.

Switzer, Les and Donna Switzer. 1979. *The Black Press in South Africa and Lesotho: A Descriptive Bibliographic Guide to African, Coloured and Indian Newspapers, Newsletters and Magazines, 1836-1976*. Boston: Hall.

Walshe, Peter. 1987. *The Rise of African Nationalism in South Africa: The African National Congress, 1912-1952*. Johannesburg: Ad Donker.

Self-Translation, Untranslatability

The Autobiographies of Mpho Nthunya and Agnes Lottering

M.J. Daymond

For people in South Africa, autobiographical storytelling and writing has long been an important mode of counter-asserting the existence and value of the cultures and individual lives that state apartheid (as a special form of colonialism) attempted to occlude and even to obliterate. From the early examples, such as the autobiographical strand in a pamphlet written in 1915 by the herbalist, Louisa Mvemve (2003),[1] to the fully-fledged autobiographical writing of the 1950s—for example, Peter Abrahams (1954), Ezekiel Mphahlele (1959), and in 1963 Bloke Modisane (1986)—the will to counter the official denigration and suppression of selfhood of black people is evident. Women made their mark a little later in this nation-wide project of cultural resistance and reconstruction when, influenced by Black Consciousness (see Driver 1990; Daymond et al 2003:45-51), writers such as Ellen Kuzwayo (1985) and Emma Mashinini (1989) presented their lives in order to speak metonymically with their people, especially with the women of their communities, and to construct a united identity in their struggle.

Autobiographical writing has continued unabated into the period of South Africa's first democratic elections in 1994. Introducing their account of "the flourishing of the autobiographical voice" in these years, Sarah Nuttall and Cheryl-Ann Michael suggest that while this voice works alongside the Truth and Reconciliation Commission in testifying to the suffering of the past, it is now also a "symptom of the decompression, relaxation, and cacophony of the post-apartheid moment in general" (2000:298). While the stories appearing in the post-apartheid moment are still, despite the prefix, shaped in relation to the racism of the past, they now present a greater variety of selfhoods and personal histories, and some recent autobiographical writing is beginning to indicate that there is no longer a crucial encounter between hegemonic-colonial and subordinated-indigenous cultures. This archetype of the colonial encounter was, in fact, always too reductive for South Africa where the colonial past gave power to both English and Afrikaans (the latter an indigenously developed language), and since the 1990s language roles have been yet more fluid, with each language a differently performing factor in the ever more complex intercultural engagements of a further, usually localised rather than national, stage in the development of living-in-community.

If the autobiographies of the 1950s and sixties that I note above fit the familiar definition of postcolonial cultural production as a "writing back" to the imperial centre, in the landmark phrase taken up by Ashcroft, Griffiths and Tiffin (1989), those that I discuss here support a recent critical interest in forms of intercultural translation. They are, as I shall show, examples of a movement away, or aside, from asymmetrical power relations and towards new kinds of border crossing. Furthermore, attention to the difficulties such autobiographies pose for cross-cultural utterance and interpretation challenges a current postcolonial critical aspiration, which Stephen Slemon has articulated in order to problematise: "the practice of comparative critical analysis in pursuit of cross-cultural mutuality" (2003:11). He argues that the politics of popular reporting of cross-cultural negotiations are such that their intertwining of resistance with reconciliation is seldom acknowledged. The contention in the latter part of my essay is closely related: just as the othering of the indigenous voice under colonialism was most severely felt in the disempowerment inflicted by separatism (apartheid), so an insistence on mutuality at the expense of difference, on translation in the face of untranslatability, may today result in another kind of occlusion: this time originating in the opposite desire (local as well as global) for similarity, or even in the more accommodating search for mutuality. The two autobiographies to which I shall turn recall lives that did not enact the anti-apartheid imperatives of the autobiographies of the 1950s and sixties. The paradoxical consequence of what was once the relative marginality of the lives that they represent is, however, that readers today may recuperate these narratives as a foretaste of the "decompression" of the post-apartheid moment: as a glimpse of what living-in-community in postcolonial circumstances in South Africa might entail.

Agnes Lottering's *Winnefred and Agnes* (2002) is set in KwaZulu-Natal while Mpho Nthunya's *Singing Away the Hunger* (1996) is set mostly in Lesotho. They have in common, nonetheless, two apparently incommensurate features. On the one hand is the fact that since the 1950s the South African government's apartheid-driven economic policies have shaped the lives of people in the whole region; on the other is the perhaps surprising fact that in their accounts of their daily participation in several of the cultures of southern Africa, neither writer indicates that the then dominant languages (English or Afrikaans) played a key role in her cross-cultural encounters. Taking up the use of 'english' (Ashcroft et al 1989:7-8) to indicate a break away from the past hegemony of standard English throughout the British Empire and the development in the colonies of varieties of 'english', it would be more accurate to say that english is for these autobiographers the means of reaching the widest possible audience rather than the sign of a will to resist the colonising power in an act of abrogation and appropriation. The absence of linguistic anxiety from their texts may have come about because neither Lottering nor Nthunya positions herself as an intellectual and neither claims a capacity to stand back from daily cultural engagements in order to conceptualise what is happening in a wider world. Whether or not this is a significant factor in the writing, the absence of linguistic anxiety in daily life does allow each autobiographer to approach intercultural engagements with attitudes that are new, or at least inadequately accounted for in the established critical models used in anti- or postcolonialism. In fact Lottering's explicit point in writing is that hers is a history (lived partly in english) that has been overlooked in the nation-wide identity-gathering of the last two decades. What she particularly wants to bring forward is her family's pride in its racially-mixed lineage (which I outline later) and their long having lived in community, and at times in intimate contact, with their Zulu neighbours.

Negotiating across cultures and languages was usually an outcome of the crowded lives of city townships, as Mphahlele and Magona (1990; 1992) indicate in their autobiographies, and as Nthunya's brief account of her schooling confirms:

> ... I was in Benoni Location, many years in school, and we used to speak Xhosa, Zulu, Sesotho, Afrikaans, Tswana, and Pedi. We would talk English in the classroom, and also at times Afrikaans and Sesotho, or even Xhosa. You never knew from day to day what language you would speak that day. Sometimes when you arrive in the morning the teacher will tell you, "I don't want any more Xhosa. We will talk only Sesotho today." Other days he will say, "we are going to talk Afrikaans the whole day." (1996:122)

Nthunya attended school before the days of 'grand apartheid' when linguistically marked divisions had not yet been driven into the educational system. At that time schooling seems to have responded to a comparatively non-hierarchised array of languages in township life; in some ways it was dealing with a set of educational issues similar to those which follow from the present, post-apartheid policy of eleven official languages. Nthunya's account also suggests that the country's hegemonic languages (chiefly English, but increasingly Afrikaans too) were treated as relatively benign co-presences with one of the indigenous languages ("Afrikaans and Sesotho"), and that township dwellers willingly acquired a capacity for code-switching. What is most remarkable in Nthunya's description is the sheer quantity of languages that she had to negotiate each day.

In its rural setting, Lottering's autobiography depicts a less dense, and an even less stratified co-presence of indigenous and colonial languages. The intercultural negotiations which happened in the remote Ngome forest of northern KwaZulu-Natal where her family farmed were less *ad hoc* than those of the townships and they had a history that probably went back to the early nineteenth century. Continuity of practice was possible because the little world of Ngome had, until the 1960s, escaped the full impact of apartheid; as she writes Lottering looks nostalgically at her own childhood as relatively untouched by the orchestrated quest for 'racial purity' of colonial and early apartheid rule. For this reason, her choice of english as her written language has about it a lack of self-consciousness that indicates her confidence in her right to that language and culture.

Lottering's relative security in several cultures would have been bolstered by her immediate family's economic independence: they rented their farm from the State and their comfortable circumstances continued until the 1960s when all the families living in the area were moved because it had been declared a State Forest Reserve (2002:226). She is able to strengthen this note of confidently shared cultures in a comparatively tranquil world by telling her mother's story (a generation even less exposed to state racism) in the first half of her narrative. Nthunya's material circumstances in adult life and her writing position are, on the other hand, shaped by a different set of rural conditions. After marriage, she and her husband moved to live with his family in Lesotho's Maluti Mountains because the region offered them refuge from the tensions of township life. Once there, she and Alexis became prosperous farmers and, when times were hard he worked on the roads being built for the Katse Dam (1996:99). When Alexis died, however, Nthunya had to sell off her remaining cattle and abandon her homestead to move nearer to Roma, where her mother lived, in order to find work. Since 1968 she has "clean[ed] houses" (106) at the University of Lesotho; as she depicts this stage of her life, class issues arise and she finds that her linguistic skills work largely against her. One African employer, hearing her speak English on the phone, asks "'How can this *lekhooa* (white person) talk with you? I thought you said you don't speak English. I thought you could only speak Sesotho, but one day I heard you talking Xhosa, and my children tell me you understand Zulu and speak many languages. I think you are a liar'" (121). Nthunya's narrative shows the extent to which migrant labour in South Africa undermined Sotho family structures, but, although she is disturbed by the resultant symptoms of deprivation (such as jealousy of others who enjoy even the smallest of advantages), her identity as a Sotho woman is a matter about which she, like Lottering in her way, is quietly confident.

Drawing on the history of assimilation, syncretism and mutual translation in the three hundred years of colonial and apartheid rule that is represented in South African autobiography, J.U. Jacobs has argued that Said's postcolonial thesis—that in "the post-imperial world all its cultures are involved in one another; none is single and pure, all are hybrid, heterogeneous, extraordinarily differentiated, and unmonolithic" (Said 1994:xxix)—"might be no less true for post-apartheid South Africa" and indeed that "from earliest colonisation to subjection under apartheid, indigenous South African cultures have experienced the whole spectrum of cultural translation" (2000:42,45). Despite the ideology of separateness and the extreme hierarchy of cultures that it desired, autobiographies such as Es'kia Mphahlele's *Down Second Avenue* and Sindiwe Magona's *To My Children's Children* show that black people were compelled to straddle "incompatible cultures" (Jacobs 2000:52) and a complex and many-layered cultural assault, intrusion, occlusion, accommodation and resistant borrowing occurred. I wish to suggest that, coming as they do from particular circumstances where a comparatively benign mix of languages and cultures could prevail, the self-translation represented in Lottering's and Nthunya's narratives is not a matter of coercion but is a movement towards a non-hierarchical linguistic interaction in which "translation [may become] a paradigm of culture contact" (Carbonell 1996:79). Their narratives bring forward a perhaps unexpected facet of the claim that "radical concepts of translation [are] emerging from ... former colonies around the world ... [and are now challenging] established European norms about what translation is and what it signifies" (Bassnett and Trivedi 1999:4). The intercultural procedures represented in the narrative of Lottering, in particular, show that her community consciously protected a reciprocal subject-to-subject translational process, recognition of which can occur more readily now that the dichotomising, subject-object (or target-source) model that once shaped metropolitan assumptions about the colonies has been challenged (Cheyfitz 1991; Niranjana 1992).

* * *

Agnes Lottering has lived most of her life between several languages but seems always to have read books in English and this suggests why english would have been a spontaneous and un-marked choice for her writing. The aspect of translation that her autobiography chiefly represents is the code-switching that was customary in interpersonal matters in her daily life: what Bakhtin (1981) calls organic translation and what, for the purposes of my discussion of her text, I have called the first level of translation. The focus in Nthunya's text is different. Although she has learned and can use many of South Africa's languages, Nthunya's autobiography indicates that once married she lived her daily life and told oral stories to her family and friends only in Sesotho. This means that she had to engage with translation and its implications most fully when she came to relate her life-story to someone who did not speak Sesotho, and so linguistic translation and generic translation (life into narrative) occur together at what I have called the second level of translation. While cultural translation is inevitably involved at both levels, that is in daily life and in textual matters, code-switching in daily life is usually a more or less habitual activity and need not engage a speaker in a conscious search for cultural connections and parallels. Therefore it is possible to suggest, without too great a simplification, that, except at moments when Lottering's autobiography presents scenes of active inquiry into intercultural matters (see below), it does not foreground translation as does Nthunya's narrative. Another way of putting this is to suggest that Lottering's narrative comes out of a history of self-translations, reflecting practices across several generations, whereas in Nthunya's text these encounters occur only at the moment of narrative production, of turning life into narrative as well as Sesotho into English. For Lottering's work, therefore, my use of 'self-translation' indicates creating a narrative of selfhood rather than auto-translation (Grutman 2001); for Nthunya's work, the idea of auto-translation is present in addition to the process of creating selfhood through narrative, for Nthunya was still thinking in Sesotho when she told her stories and translating them into english as she spoke (see below). Neither writer, however, positions herself as a "privileged cultural outpost" (Carbonell 1996:82) in relation to a reader, for they either engage in person-to-person translation in order to produce a text (Nthunya) or re-present translations that have already occurred (Lottering).

In the opening chapter of *Singing Away the Hunger: Stories of a Life in Lesotho*, Mpho Nthunya engages immediately with the second level of translation: "Making this book is a strange thing to me: in Sesotho we say *mohlolo*—a miracle, or a wonder" (1996:1), reminding her readers that she speaks and thinks in a language different from the one in which she now narrates. Her narrating began in 1992 when she kept house for a visiting American scholar, 'Limakatso' Kendall, at the University of Lesotho. As their friendship grew Nthunya began telling stories from her own and her mother's lives to Kendall who, recognising a gifted story-teller, wrote down what she heard, asked questions, and then transcribed Nthunya's material to her computer. The relationship between Nthunya (as narrator) and Kendall (as interlocutor and scribe) grows into friendship through the exchange of gifts, and Nthunya places her stories as the most precious of those gifts.[2] Kendall's "Afterword" sets out more of the process by which the book was made: the orally-oriented Nthunya "liked hearing her own words and couldn't decide if a paragraph 'worked' until she heard herself speak it" (166). When they had settled the written version of the individual stories, Kendall gave them a more or less chronological order as it seemed most rational to her. This aspect of narrative did not concern Nthunya herself, and the apparent absence of teleology (Cribb 2003), or plot, from her approach to the gathered life-stories—individual tales are strongly plotted—implies that her oral culture has given her a rather different view from the life-as-development model used by Kendall. Nthunya's sense of how her life-stories might be organised is never stated, but I assume that it is likely to derive from praise poetry and its influence on oral prose narratives. Praise poetry "advances more through the concatenation of imagery than through narrative, and the spirit of the story is more important than the plot. Oral prose narratives reflect this principle in the stringing together of independent episodes around a central character and in the 'use of parallel sets of images to embody a theme'" (Coplan 1987:12).[3]

Because Kendall does not speak Sesotho, Nthunya told her stories in english knowing that her interlocutor's language would also be that of the likely readers of her book. In Sesotho, she says, she could make "words roll like a music I am singing with my heart" whereas english left her struggling "like a car trying to start on a cold morning" (2). Kendall records that they "tried a different system" in which Nthunya narrated in Sesotho and a bilingual friend translated her words into english, but the result was not as "powerful" (167), and they both rejected it. Kendall suggests that in the method they preferred, Nthunya was not thinking in english as she told her stories to her new auditor, but still hearing them in her own language and simultaneously translating them (166). Nthunya's preference indicates that although english was required of her, her relationship to the target language was moving away from the colonial legacy of asymmetrical power relations and beginning to take on more of the "ethical intersubjectivity" (Wicomb 2002:212) that Zoë Wicomb identifies as George Steiner's (1975) standard in his study of literary translation in Europe. Besides a wish to retain control over her self-representation, an explanation for Nthunya's preference for her efforts in english may be that in oral narration, utterance is the key moment of reception. In other words, the impact of her stories on Kendall would have been immediately evident to Nthunya, enabling her to influence what was happening. My speculation is supported by Nthunya's report of what she found when she joined a story-telling group that Kendall ran in Maseru: although her command of english was not as good as that of the better-educated group members, her storytelling abilities, even in english, were superior (156). Kendall's noting that Nthunya creates "a new language in these stories" (167)[4] suggests further that Nthunya has produced a translation that does not, in Venuti's term, re-domesticate (2000) her world, but challenges the target as well as the source language. In this way, her choice of language is part of the process by which English in southern Africa is changing to english, a lingua franca that is being stripped of its colonial power to coerce the thoughts and identities of its speakers.

Nthunya also comments at the beginning of her text on the "strange[ness]" of the printed book; books and the practice of reading (especially for pleasure) are not, as she says, "part of our lives" (1) in Lesotho. Therefore she is not confident that her achievement will attain recognition from her own people, and neither can she readily imagine those readers who *will* be reached by it. She represents herself as divided and uncertain until the idea of the actual book encourages her to return, at the end of the chapter, to the question of those readers whom she herself wishes to reach. This time, she engages directly with the question of whether in translating her stories she has transgressed too far, betraying the gift that she inherited from her mother by lifting her stories out of their resonant cultural context. In this sense, her acts of self-translation have challenged the foundations of her identity as well as her narrative skills. The upshot is expressed in a simile which, in its reference to photography, crosses into a distinctly modern mode: she says that she has come to regard "this book [as] ... my album for my mother, Valeria 'M'amahlaku Sekobi Lillane, who passed away." And then she adds, in a comment that is generous even as it acknowledges that the question of readership is out of her hands: "Others can look at it if they like" (3). She is able both to assert what is hers and to release it to travel beyond her community and their innocence of books, literacy and English, into a relationship that is new in her cultural repertoire—the idea of future readers in other lands. Nthunya then concludes her reflections with what may be an intriguing conceit (to a western reader) or may be an acknowledgment of the power of her mother's Christian faith, and which also indicates both her continuing anxiety lest her bond with her mother has indeed been severed and her non-subservience to English. Her mother did not read or write in any language and so Nthunya, having participated in the transgressive miracle of creating a book, imagines another. As she puts it, she imagines that "I can give this book of English words to her, and because of the wisdom of Heaven she can read it" (3).

Agnes Lottering's book also arises out of a bond with her mother, but in her case the bond has, as she sees it, had a tragic power to shape her life. Her wish to convey her sense of living out an inherited destiny may be why in her twin narratives (she begins by relating her mother's story in the first-person in order to be able to present her own) she does not engage as directly or immediately as Nthunya does with self-translation at the second level. She feels no need to pause, as Nthunya does, to contemplate the possible impact of her narrative on her larger community, let alone on communities of readers that she does not know. Lottering's choice to write about the linguistic-cultural negotiations of her daily life in english, although such negotiations were as often conducted in isiZulu, seems to have come from her familiarity with English as a written and literary language.[5] What her narrative does bring forward, however, are certain moments in daily life when code-switching had to become conscious self-translation because cultural interactions were not working.

Lottering's venture into autobiography began after she had related parts of her life to an anthropologist, Robert Papini, at the Kwa Muhle Museum in Durban. He sent a manuscript based on interviews with her to the publishers, complete with his extensive explanatory notes, but Kwela Books preferred to publish Lottering's own telling of her story, and, after she had written her first version, asked her to flesh out her parents' part of it as much as she could. (These steps are not recounted in the text but were relayed to me by the publisher and confirmed by Lottering; what follows *is* in Lottering's narrative.) To know more about her mother's life,

Lottering sought out Irene, an older cousin whom she calls "aunt". After some persuasion the old lady told her a story which helped explain her most disturbing childhood memories: the violent rages of her father, Benjamin, and her mother's timidity. Her father was descended from Irish pioneers, the Rorke brothers, who arrived in northern KwaZulu-Natal early in the nineteenth century and who married Zulu and Swazi women, several of whom were of royal or chiefly descent. Her mother, Winnefred, belonged to the Nunn family and they too were descended from European settlers who married indigenous women (Faber 2003). Four languages were spoken on her parents' farm in the Ngome forest—English, Afrikaans, siSwati and isiZulu—and Lottering gives several indications that in this mix isiZulu tended to dominate in daily life, while at large family gatherings like her parents' wedding feast (they held a second, Christian ceremony late in life), English seems to have been regarded as the 'civilised' language to use. In these scenes, where family members compete in their anecdotes about the world beyond Ngome, an oral version of Bakhtin's sense of artistic (or novelistic) hybridity can be glimpsed: the "novelistic hybrid ... is not only double voiced ... [but] there are two socio-linguistic consciousnesses ... that come together and consciously fight it out on the territory of utterance" (1981:360). But these oral tale-tellers, living as they do between languages and cultures, do not require textuality in order to activate dialogic irony—the gathering itself calls forth the artist in them. Their speech also moves rapidly from one language to another, and this may be why, unlike Nthunya's text, Lottering's account of these gatherings does not indicate that as she writes she is translating an already told story, or set of stories, from a prior language into english. There are many words in isiZulu in her text, but they indicate that code-switching was constant at the time rather than any subsequent efforts, or failure, to find a suitable word in english.

The moments of conscious translation that Lottering represents are part of her account of the steps that her community took to smooth the way for code-switching in daily life. She remembers her parents' interactions with their Zulu neighbours as a generally happy mutual dependence but indicates that when conflict arose it necessitated the rules of exchange being re-declared. It is at these moments that the agency of self-translation is claimed, for more than linguistic shifts were needed. Self-translation had to be understood as a personal change of attitude, involving self-restraint and respect for other *mores*. For example, when Lottering's father, Benjamin, is given advice by his father about meeting the Zulu chief in order to discuss grazing rights, he is told to remember that

"The ways of the Zulu demand total respect and complete loyalty to the
elders. You have to be very, very cautious. I sometimes fear for your free
tongue. You have to learn that the Zulus have a decorous manner of speech,
and are very suspicious. Everything you say and do concerning their
welfare must be clearly understood, or else they think you are a wizard
and want to cast some sort of spell on them." (2002:87)

And such instruction could come to Benjamin equally forcefully from the
Zulu side. A few months after his father's death, he is given this
complementary guidance by the Zulu chief himself:

"Well spoken, my son of my white brother, the brave warrior who killed
a leopard with his bare hands. I've not forgotten his total regard for
humanity and respect for my people, and the love he had for the soil of
the land. Nevertheless, I must warn you about the flame that flickers in
your brain. You must learn to cool it off with spring water from the
igobongo before talking to your elders." (102)

Here the non-translation of "igobongo" (which can denote either a hollow
in the ground or an empty container) indicates the commonalities between
the two men and reminds a reader that they are both speaking isiZulu.
Advice could also come in equally forthright terms from Zulu women.
When he is preparing a feast to appease the spirit of his dead first wife and
the ancestors, Benjamin is rebuked for taking the ceremony too lightly. A
Zulu woman, Hoswayo, says:

"Oh Son of the White Chief, your own mother was a Zulu. Why then do
you mock the customs of your womb? We have listened to your father and
done some of the customs of the white man like throwing away our
isidwabas [the leather skirts of married women][6] and eating sugar and salt,
even bread and scones and tea. Why then do you so hate our customs? You
should not treat this matter lightly for it is true that the spirits don't die.
Even your white father told us that if we were bad witches our spirits
would burn in the big, big fire somewhere in the stomach of the earth."
(106)

In her sense that the cultural translations which shape ceremonies must
satisfy all the participants, Hoswayo is reiterating their ground rule for all
self-translation, and her anger indicates that if this rule were ignored then
conducting daily life would require the intervention of other agencies,
"the spirits".

Other aspects of Lottering's representation of daily life in Ngome leave it to the reader to register the complexity and instability of intercultural negotiations. Racialised epithets were often used in friendly banter on the farm: for example, Benjamin's sister tells Winnefred that her Zulu mother-in-law used to comment ironically on her white husband's ways as "savage": "'My savage mother says her white savage was like that'" (81). As at the wedding feast, these words exhibit the conscious irony, or doubled voice, which Bakhtin allocates to the novelist, and they seem to have been received as playfully denigratory. But if irony is sometimes present, the same terms could also be used in non-ironic anger. When her (white) father discovers that the unmarried Winnefred is pregnant and that her Swazi mother has planned to send the child away to be raised by her people, he explodes: "'Where do you think you are taking my child to, you stupid, stupid savage .... Do you think I want my child raised by some more savages?'" (24). It seems that this male anger, which so readily takes a racialised form, is not just disruptive of social propriety in language but is what raises barriers for Agnes at the second level of translation, in the writing of their lives. While her parents were alive, her mother's fearfulness had turned Lottering more and more against her father and she confesses to hating him at times. But then she records that when she finally heard the full story of her parents' marriage from her cousin-aunt, she returned home with a sense of relief and delight, confident that what she had heard was "such an overwhelming truth [that her] ... heart and mind [could begin] ... to understand some of the things [her] mother used to do". She was convinced that as she wrote their story, she "could not only hear the words as they spoke them—[she] could see how their mouths moved to make the sounds" (14).

Prefixing 'self' to 'translation' underlines the potential for choice or agency in transcultural autobiographical writing by colonised or once colonised people. While recognising that the self-translating subject is "*situate[ed]* ... in the context of various social, linguistic and discursive practices without *dissolving* ... into them" (Meyer 2000:101, original emphasis), I will, in the next part of this essay, backlight the question of agency by discussing moments at which the autobiographer has either chosen to leave elements of her natal culture un-translated, thereby refusing to grant a cross-cultural reader access to them, or has found herself unable to translate, perhaps because she is dealing with the ineffable and cannot articulate in her own language (let alone in another language-culture) her exact beliefs or their basis as a system. In general, adherents to a faith, or participants in a way of life, need explanation and analysis only when they have to justify their practices and beliefs to an outsider (or to themselves if doubt arises). The important point for me will be that a refusal to translate underlines the degree of agency in the sustained act of translation at the second (textual) level while an inability to translate exposes what is entailed for autobiographical subjects, and their readers, as they criss-cross between cultures in daily life.

* * *

The story that Lottering is told about her parents' marriage involves bewitchment, and it is here that the circumstances and events of her life touch most closely on those of Mpho Nthunya and here that their translational difficulties can be most directly compared. Their subject-matter means that both autobiographers are brought up against the difficult question of moving between two groups of internally coherent but incompatible belief systems.[7] Zulu and Swazi, or Sotho and Tswana, beliefs share features which are likely to be alien to the beliefs of people of European descent and this point of incommensurability is where these autobiographers' chosen and/or inevitable limits on self-translation become most evident.

In Lottering's narrative, bewitchment begins with Winnefred and continues into her own life. Winnefred is bewitched at the behest of the Zulu chief who was angered by Benjamin's intransigence when his cattle strayed into the chief's mealie fields. The chief is also silently but more deeply threatened because four daughters have been born in quick succession to Benjamin and Winnefred, whereas he has not managed to father a girl with any of his wives (2002:112-3). When Benjamin refuses to placate him a succession of disasters follows, in the last of which Winnefred hears strange laughter and sees a brightly coloured bird near the river. While pursuing these phantoms, she falls over a precipice. Three days later, she is found in a cave and it is evident that she has had sexual relations and that this may have occurred while she was, as she is when found, unconscious. Mtembu, the inyanga [diviner-healer] who has been asked by her husband to rescue her, explains the laughter of the tokoloshe,[8] the magical bird, and the chief's motives in sending them to get her "seed" (136) so as to produce daughters and then to turn her into a zombie to use against his enemies. A month after restoring her to life, Mtembu brings about what seems to be a miscarriage. Lottering writes her mother's experience from within, as a trance-like dream, using her mother's first-person voice throughout and she identifies the episode as the major reason for Benjamin's violent distrust of his wife.

It is a cultural crossing (or invasion) that leaves everyone afraid, and yet it exercises a compelling pull on Lottering's view of her own life. Some years later she falls from a tree and loses the child she is carrying. At the time, Lottering did not know about her mother's earlier bewitchment or that her mother believed her daughter fated to inherit her "womb", but her first response is to believe that a female baboon that had been hovering over her after her fall in the forest had stolen her child. Later she indicates that she no longer believes this version of events and that it came out of her troubled wish to keep both the unborn child and Pieter, her forbidden white lover. Lottering indicates how the available cultural explanations divide. When Agnes tells Pieter her version of the baboon's theft, he reminds her of what she should know as a farm child—the foetus was "still just like a thick clot of blood" (177) and could not have been stolen—and his reassurances are endorsed by her mother. On the other hand, the young Zulu woman, Tobile, who is Agnes's closest friend, supports her belief that baboons could have interfered by telling her stories about a "young girl [who] had given birth to a half-baboon child" (178) because her family had had her bewitched. Conflict between these beliefs fades as Lottering's hope that her child might still be living diminishes. As she writes, she knows that in her girlhood her emotional need led her to cross to another belief system in order to gain reassurance, but this is not the explanation that she is able to give to the more disturbing story of her mother's bewitchment.

Throughout their ordeal, Winnefred and Benjamin, and the inyanga Mtembu, speak of her bewitchment and rescue in Christian as well as animist terms, seeing it as a manifestation of evil from which God must rescue her *and* as the work of alien powers.[9] The conjunction makes some sense of events for all involved, but it leaves Winnefred with a fear-filled mystery—how can she, raised as a Roman Catholic, be affected by a belief system which lies beyond her ken. Despite its being untranslatable, her susceptibility is made plausible by several earlier scenes in which she has accepted alien beliefs because they seem to have beneficial results. For example, when Mtembu is treating her child, Winnefred says, "I listened and did as he said, half believing but with the Christian soul inside of me having doubts as to how this could possibly be" (116). When Father Jacob visits and tells the distraught parents that in order to protect their child they must use "whatever the old inyanga Mtembu told us to use, as he knew full well that you could not fight those evil happenings with herbs only" (120), he too indicates that the two systems could interact; but this view is not possible for Winnefred whose own faith has left her defenceless against malign alien beliefs. She had been taught by the Mother Superior at school "never to underestimate the devil's power" but even the memory of this advice leaves her torn: "It's as though I could hear her now .... It can't happen to me! I believe in God, I am a Catholic, not a heathen" (133). A chasm has opened that cannot be bridged by translation either in her life or in the text, for translation cannot conjure a synthesis of beliefs that does not operate for her. The potential mistake of attempting to cross from one belief-set to another is underlined when Benjamin's Zulu mother invokes the need for whole-hearted and dedicated study for anyone entering the inyanga's realm, indicating why it is so difficult completely to align and inhabit both systems. She tells Father Jacob (in terms that again seem partly ironic) that until he is re-made as a different person, he cannot participate in gathering the remedies that she is proposing to Mtembu:

> "You white people are always putting your noses where only the savage nose can smell. You do not even know how to smell out a witch. You are too inquisitive. You want to know all about the use of herbs, but have never gone to learn how to live with them in their world. You do not know where to touch and feel, nor do you know how to taste and smell. Most of all, do you know how to talk to the herbs through their own spirits? Mfundisi, you must first learn all these things. Only then your herbs will be able to cure everyone who believes in them." (143)

However right she may be, her policing of the boundary is particularly disturbing at this point, for the very crossing she prohibits has just occurred in both directions, first with terrifying consequences for Winnefred, and then to rescue her.

When Nthunya represents illness or mental disturbances such as Lottering's family experienced, she too sometimes indicates that their origins lie in bewitchment, saying that there is a systematic understanding of illness and healing that Basotho people regard as distinctively theirs, but at others she suggests that a 'western' understanding of disease is appropriate. As with Lottering's family, their cultural positioning is not predictable and makes for difficult analysis in general terms. For example, her mother, who was a devout Roman Catholic, once rose in the middle of the night to pray for protection against what she says "is coming ... [because] it is bad" (1996:80). When a bolt of lightning strikes inside their house it blackens everything but no one is harmed because, as the sangoma explains to her father the next day, "'you have got a nice person in your house who helps you ... I see her, she is holding beads'" (81). The diviner explains further that the lightning was sent by a jealous woman but "'God refused to kill you because of your wife's prayers'" (81).

In the sangoma's explanation, the two belief systems are braided together, presumably by layers of earlier translations. But in other instances Nthunya does not represent herself as living in either braided or cleanly divided strands; she refuses the option of employing "two socio-linguistic consciousnesses" (as Bakhtin puts it) and does not attempt to provide a bridging translation, or interpretation. She explains her refusal, saying that western medicine is generally held to be useless before "Basotho sickness" (111) or "sickness which is not of God" (141), and this view prevails in her account of the rapid, successive deaths of her three older sons. The hospital diagnoses the cause of death as tuberculosis but in Nthunya's eyes their deaths are brought about by her brother-in-law, Joseph, who is jealous of her family's comparative well-being. She believes that since her husband's death, Joseph, who is now the senior member of the family, has had recourse to witchcraft after he failed to impose his will on her or her sons. She understands the western medical diagnosis but dismisses it saying "[t]hey always say it's TB if they don't know what else to say" (116) and she holds to her belief that Joseph "had his ways to make it look like they died from other causes, but I always knew the cause. It was Joseph who killed them" (94). Nthunya says that one of the sangomas she consulted confirmed that Joseph was the source of her troubles and explained his motives. Although her middle son, Motlatsi, also consulted a sangoma who again identified Joseph as the culprit, it seems that neither he nor his brothers could be saved. Throughout her account of this series of bewitchments, Nthunya insists on their helplessness; at Motlatsi's funeral she sees Joseph eyeing her next son, and she says: "I knew he was going to work on Mofihli next, but there was nothing I could do" (115). It is her fatalistic acceptance of the inevitable that signals that Nthunya has gone as far as she is willing to go in cultural translation; she cannot, or will not, try to explain for readers how Joseph (or those he employed) could achieve what she believes he did.

* * *

In considering the absence of a translation of certain events in these two autobiographies which otherwise engage so vigorously with the complexities of self-translation, some comparative observations about the "anxiety .... of the borderline conditions" (Bhabha 1994:213-4) that attend them can be made. Winnefred's story is one that her biographer-daughter heard only at second-hand from her "aunt" because her mother had withheld the subject from her. Lottering's re-narration of it has to uphold her claim that she could hear her mother speak, and this intention may be why she does not question what she has been told was her mother's understanding of events. The circumstances leading to each woman's refusal to translate are different in that Winnefred was acted on by beliefs in which she did not share, while Nthunya has an inward knowledge of the practices and beliefs that she holds responsible for her losses. On the other hand, their situations are similar in that both women find themselves the victims of malign powers which have been activated in secret, and it may be because theirs is a confrontation with a malevolence working through non/super-human forces that they are unable, or avoid, or refuse, to translate their understanding of what has happened. In Nthunya's case, it is clear that her choice protects the cultural system in which she has lived, but in Winnefred's story the choice is more complex for her cultural milieu is already mixed: she had been educated at a convent school, but many members of her family on the Nunn as well as the Rorke side, particularly the women, participated in non-Christian beliefs. It is also striking that in both instances the maintenance of authority structures in the family is involved. Nthunya says directly that her sons' deaths were part of a struggle over patriarchal authority and power in her family, while Winnefred's reticence suggests that she wanted to convince Benjamin that his marital rights had not been usurped and that she was an unwilling participant in the encounter. She seems not to have succeeded. In Nthunya's case it is possible to go further with the probable reasons for her decision: placing responsibility on Joseph gathers and explains more than just her sons' deaths for it accounts for the rapidity of her loss, it draws in her brother-in-law's violent and brutal personality, and it accounts for his subsequent decline into madness. Underlying and uniting all of these factors is the point that in telling or writing of them neither narrator attempts to integrate the two belief systems in relation to which they live, or to translate their experience from one to the other.

All of the observations I have made remain outside what happened. Here Nthunya's statement about her book, "Others may read it if they like", returns to suggest that from the beginning she may have been prepared to resist the access of an outsider-reader to all of her material. In his account of an African friend's struggle against bewitchment, Adam Ashforth reflects on the difficulties he has had in understanding what he witnessed, and then in writing about it. His comments bear directly on the moment at which beliefs and epistemologies are so different that cultural translation becomes impossible, and some apply so closely to features of the narratives of Nthunya and Lottering that they warrant quoting at length. He says of the passions which either led to the use of witchcraft or were generated by it: "Whatever it was that I had witnessed, I realised I had no name for it" (2000:226). Then he says of language: "There is no pristine vocabulary of difference available to Madumo [his name for his friend] to describe his experiences with witchcraft that I could translate and then present to the world in terms familiar to the West; no language to make the words seem unique, or the effort of translation worthwhile" (244). And lastly he comments on his and his friend's radically different ways of reading the world: "It's not just a question about how events are caused but is also at root a question about meaning, about the meaning of life. At the end of the day, Madumo and I differ fundamentally over the degree of meaningfulness there is to be found in the world" (249). After outlining his western view of what is meaningful, which he calls a dwelling in comparative "emptiness" (250), Ashforth says that for Madumo "the world is full of meaning, of signs of the presence and purposes of invisible powers. To empty it of meaning would be as absurd as to empty it of air. The problem is, rather, how to interpret the signs which loom large every day" (251).

Declining to translate across a divide may seem dispiriting and even retrogressive to a postcolonial critic "in pursuit of cross-cultural mutuality", as Slemon put it (2003:11), and even more so to a South African critic in the present context of a nascent, intercultural democracy in which community-building depends on the translational creation of "mutuality". But explicit acknowledgment of the present limits to cultural translation, interpretation and ready mutuality may be an equally constructive act for the postcolonial South African critic. Doris Sommer has argued that a reader inculcated in western systems of thought (and she includes herself) should not assume a right to enter all the events and choices that inform narratives from other cultures. She refers to several texts which "resist the competent reader, intentionally" (1994:524) in order to assert the need for "our still deaf ears" to hear and respect "positions [that are] ... constructed as incommensurate or conflictive" (525). When Sommer instances Rigoberta Menchú, whose "experience with Spanish-speaking conquerors taught her not to share secrets with ill-prepared and unreliable readers" (525), she argues that this refusal is not cultural essentialism but comes out of a political and perhaps religious knowledge of what should and should not be transmitted. Sommer's reference in her phrase "our ... ears" is to an American readership which may be neocolonial in its assumptions, but her stance is equally important in postcolonial South Africa. Organic interlingual and intercultural translation will always be an uncompleted part of an ongoing process; the same must sometimes be true of the second level of translation. The difficult subject of bewitchment is a reminder that in crafting a story the writer's will to participate non-ironically in incompleteness must be understood and respected. This way, self-translation in texts will not be read only for what already makes sense, and nor will texts be too readily domesticated for premature assimilation. Venuti (2000) has warned that translation should not simply re-domesticate a text and Spivak (1992) has declared the political imperatives for observing the boundaries to translation. Their comments about the translator who is acting as a "cultural outpost" (Carbonell 1996:82) must apply equally to the self-translator and this means that the quest for cross-cultural "mutuality" cannot proceed on the understanding that translation, or access, is a right.

When Lottering, or Nthunya, steps back from liminality, the momentary silence is a forceful reminder that the readership for which, by implication, the self-translation has and has not been undertaken is not homogeneous, and especially not in postcolonial circumstances. Readers' willingness to recognise and respect "a rhetoric of refusal", especially in contexts in which we may be "used to assuming the virtues of transgressing the no-man's-zone between self and other" (Sommer 1994:533), should not be seen as grounds for disappointment (or failure) but as a necessary, however paradoxical, move towards creating the new basis of community in which postcolonial difference can be something utterly unlike colonial othering. The being and not being in two minds that such an uneven community requires seems to me well indicated by Lottering herself when, affected by the simultaneously personal and impersonal nature of autobiography, and by the ambivalence inherent in intercultural matters that are both translatable and untranslatable, she says: "I find it very hard to write this story, but I've got to put it to rest once and for all. If I read it in a book, then I'll feel as if it happened to someone else. After all, it is just a story, though it's more than that too: it's the story of my life" (2002:11).

Notes

1. In one of her self-published pamphlets promoting her herbal cures, Louisa Mvemve sketches her life story in order to explain that she has inherited and

learned her skills in diagnosis from her father and her knowledge of nursing from her mother. The pamphlet is in the National Archive in Pretoria: CAD NTS 3901 3/376 Part 1, 1915. See Burns (1996). The entry in the References is to the 2003 republication of most of this pamphlet.

2. The other major gift that Nthunya bestows on Kendall is the name 'Limakatso' meaning a bringer of good fortune and worker of miracles. Both gifts are in the realm of language.

3. In the last phrase, Coplan is quoting Scheub (1975).

4. Amplifying her observation, Kendall writes: "it isn't a unique language with its own rules, like pidgin.... It is a form of English spoken only in Lesotho, with idioms that arise from literal translation of Sesotho expressions, with a vocabulary peppered with Sesotho words, with a rhythm and with inflections all its own.... The tenses are irregular, though I notice there is a definite pattern: when she is remembering with some distance, she uses the past tense; when the memories become vivid and immediate, she shifts to the present" (Nthunya 1996:167).

5. Lottering was educated at a convent school in Eshowe and later in Durban. Much of the reading material that she mentions is European or American in origin. See Daymond (2003).

6. This word is translated earlier in Lottering's text.

7. Ashforth cautions against presuming "systematicity in ideas about witchcraft" because, particularly in urban contexts today, many cultural traditions interact and do not allow an "authoritative account of a singular 'system of belief'" (2002:126).

8. Describing the familiars of "witches", Hammond-Tooke says the tokoloshe is "a small, hairy man, about the height of a person's knee. His penis is so long that he carries it over his shoulder and he has only one buttock" (1989:75).

9. The (mis)translated term "witch" is one I have been able to avoid by following Nthunya and Lottering who use "sangoma" and "inyanga"; I have, however, had to fall back on "bewitchment".

References

Abrahams, Peter. 1954. *Tell Freedom*. London: Faber and Faber.

Ashcroft, Bill, Gareth Griffiths and Helen Tiffin. 1989. *The Empire Writes Back*. London and New York: Routledge.

Ashforth, Adam. 2000. *Madumo: A Man Bewitched*. Chicago and London: University of Chicago Press.

_____. 2002. "An Epidemic of Witchcraft? The Implications of AIDS for the Post-Apartheid State." *African Studies* 61(1):121-43.

Bakhtin, M.M. 1981. *The Dialogic Imagination*. Tr. Caryl Emerson and Michael

Holquist. Austin: University of Texas Press.

Bassnett, Susan and Harish Trivedi. 1999. "Introduction: Of Colonies, Cannibals and Vernaculars." In: S. Bassnett and H. Trivedi (eds). *Post-Colonial Translation: Theory and Practice*. London: Routledge.

Bhabha, Homi K. 1994. *The Location of Culture*. London and New York: Routledge.

Burns, Catherine. 1996. "Louisa Mvemve: A Woman's Advice to the Public on the Cure of Various Diseases." *Kronos: Journal of Cape History* 23:108-34.

Carbonell, Ovidio. 1996. "The Exotic Space of Cultural Translation." In: Roman Alvarez and M. Carmen-Africa (eds). *Translation, Power, Subversion*. Clevedon, Philadelphia, Adelaide: Multilingual Matters Ltd.

Cheyfitz, Eric. 1991. *The Poetics of Imperialism: Translation and Colonization from "The Tempest" to "Tarzan"*. New York and Oxford: Oxford University Press.

Coplan, David. 1987. "Dialectics of Tradition in South African Black Popular Theatre." *Critical Arts* 4(3): 5-27.

Cribb, Tim. 2003. "African Autobiography and the Idea of the Nation." In: Bruce Bennett, Susan Cowan, Jacqueline Lo, Satendra Nandan and Jen Webb (eds). *Resistance and Reconciliation: Writing in the Commonwealth*. ACLALS: Canberra.

Daymond, M.J. 2003. "Generic and Discursive Tensions in *Winnefred and Agnes: The True Story of Two Women* by Agnes Lottering." *Tydskrif vir Nederlands en Afrikaans* 10(2):225-41.

Daymond, M.J., Dorothy Driver, Sheila Meintjes, Leloba Molema, Chiedza Musengezi, Margie Orford and Nobantu Rasebotsa (eds). 2003. *Women Writing Africa*. New York: The Feminist Press; Johannesburg: Wits University Press.

Driver, Dorothy. 1990. "*M'a-Ngoana O Tsoare Thipa ka Bohaleng*—The Child's Mother Grabs the Sharp End of the Knife: Women as Mothers, Women as Writers." In: Martin Trump (ed.). *Rendering Things Visible: Essays on South African Literary Culture*. Johannesburg: Ravan Press.

Faber, Paul (ed.). 2003. *Group Portrait South Africa: Nine Family Histories*. Cape Town: Kwela Books.

Grutman, Rainier. 2001. "Auto-translation." In: Mona Baker (ed.). *Routledge Encyclopaedia of Translation Studies*. London: Routledge.

Hammond-Tooke, David. 1989. *Rituals and Medicines: Indigenous Healing in South Africa*. Johannesburg: Ad Donker.

Jacobs, J.U. 2000. "Cross-Cultural Translation in South African Autobiographical Writing: The Case of Sindiwe Magona." *Alternation* 7(1):41-61.

Kuzwayo, Ellen. 1985. *Call Me Woman*. London: The Women's Press.

Lottering, Agnes. 2002. *Winnefred & Agnes: The True Story of Two Women.* Cape Town: Kwela Books.

Magona, Sindiwe. 1990. *To My Children's Children.* Cape Town: David Philip.

_____. 1992. *Forced to Grow.* Cape Town: David Philip.

Mashinini, Emma. 1989. *Strikes Have Followed Me All My Life.* London: The Women's Press.

Meyer, Stephan. 2000. "Intersubjectivity and Autobiography: Feminist Critical Theory and Johnny Masilela's *Deliver Us from Evil—Scenes from a Rural Transvaal Upbringing.*" *Alternation* 7(1): 97 -124.

Modisane, Bloke. 1986 [1963]. *Blame Me on History.* Johannesburg: Ad Donker.

Mphahlele, Ezekiel. 1959. *Down Second Avenue.* London: Faber and Faber.

Mvemve, Louisa. 2003 [1916]. "A 'Little Woman's' Advice to the Public." In: M.J. Daymond et al (eds). *Women Writing Africa.* New York: The Feminist Press.

Niranjana, Tejaswini. 1992. *Siting Translation: History, Post-structuralism, and the Colonial Context.* Berkeley: University of California Press.

Nuttall, Sarah and Cheryl-Ann Michael. 2000. "Autobiographical Acts." In: S. Nuttall and C-A. Michael (eds). *Senses of Culture.* Cape Town: Oxford University Press.

Nthunya, Mpho 'M'atsepo 1996. *Singing Away the Hunger: Stories of a Life in Lesotho.* Pietermaritzburg: University of Natal Press.

Said, Edward W. 1993. *Culture and Imperialism.* London: Vintage.

Scheub, Harold. 1975. *The Xhosa Ntsomi.* Oxford: Clarendon Press.

Slemon, Stephen. 2003. "Return of the Native." In: Bruce Bennett, Susan Cowan, Jacqueline Lo, Satendra Nandan and Jen Webb (eds). *Resistance and Reconciliation: Writing in the Commonwealth.* Canberra: ACLALS.

Sommer, Doris. 1994. "Resistant Texts and Incompetent Readers." *Poetics Today* 15(4): 523-51.

Spivak, Gayatri. 1992. "The Politics of Translation." In: Michele Barrett and Anne Phillips (eds). *Destabilizing Theory: Contemporary Feminist Debates.* Stanford: Stanford University Press.

Steiner, George. 1975. *After Babel: Aspects of Language and Translation.* New York and London: Oxford University Press.

Venuti, Lawrence. 2000. "Translation, Community, Utopia." In: Lawrence Venuti (ed.). *The Translation Studies Reader.* London: Routledge.

Wicomb, Zoë. 2002. "Translation in the Yard of Africa." *Journal of Literary Studies* 18(3-4): 209-23.

Waiting for the Russians

Coetzee's *The Master of Petersburg* and the Logic of Late Postcolonialism

Monica Popescu

In Zakes Mda's novel, *The Heart of Redness* (2002), a black South African newly returned from the USA searches for a mysterious and beautiful woman, NomaRussia, whom he attempts to trace down to her small village in the Eastern Cape. Her surprising name speaks to a long tradition of imaginary relations that span continents and decades:

> NomaRussia is a very common name, one of the teachers explains. The people of this region began giving their valued daughters this name—which means Mother of the Russians—when the Russians killed Sir George Cathcart during the Crimean War in 1854. Cathcart, the teacher further explains, was the much-hated colonial governor who finally defeated the amaXhosa in the War of Mlanjeni....People got to know of the Russians for the first time. Although the British insisted that they were white people like themselves, the amaXhosa knew that it was all a lie. The Russians were a black nation.... For many months we posted men on the hills to look out for the arrival of the Russian ships. (2002:63,82-3)

I begin this essay with a movement away from its declared topic, in order to frame a larger question: what are the Russians of the latter half of the nineteenth century to a black rural community in South Africa post-1994? What ghostly dimension of selfhood do they summon up in South Africa close to the turn of the millennium? Finally, what are the gains of a fictional glide into the latter half of the previous century and into an unrelated culture, when more burning issues (democracy, equal rights, poverty and AIDS) deserve attention? This question has been persistently asked of J.M. Coetzee's novel, *The Master of Petersburg* (1994), which, with its arcane topic and geo-political distance from South Africa, puzzled many among its readership.

The puzzle reveals its extent when perceived against the political and cultural background of South Africa, which in 1994 experienced its first free elections and the long postponed dream of "one person, one vote" came true. The world was enthralled, poised between utopian and dystopian scenarios. The spectre of civil war and inter-ethnic strife seemed to have disappeared. Yet only a year before Chris Hani, secretary general of the South African Communist Party (SACP), had been assassinated. Only a year before, violence between Inkatha Freedom Party (IFP) and African National Congress (ANC) supporters was responsible for deaths in KwaZulu-Natal as well as in townships around Johannesburg. Only a year before, right-wing supporters of the Afrikaner Weerstandsbeweging (AWB) attempted to halt constitutional negotiations within the Convention for a Democratic South Africa by driving a truck into the World Trade Centre where the meetings were being held.

Despite all predictions of a bloodbath, the South African elections unfolded peacefully, and Nelson Mandela was inaugurated as president on 10 May 1994. These were not trivial local events, lost in the larger world picture. As Jacques Derrida argued in the preface to *Specters of Marx*, which he dedicated to Chris Hani, events in South Africa stand in a metonymic relation to those in the world as a whole: "At once part, cause, effect, example, what is happening there translates what takes place here, always here, wherever one is and wherever one looks, closest to home" (1994: xv). Against this political background Coetzee's novel, *The Master of Petersburg*, was greeted with astonishment at his turning away from South African realities at such a crucial time.

What motivated Coetzee to set his novel in a time and country apparently unconnected to South Africa, then on the brink of its moment of transformation, and to move further away than he had in the allegorical setting of some of his earlier novels? These earlier novels were criticised by several for their unspecific setting. Although the imperialist dynamic on the frontier in *Waiting for the Barbarians*, or the rewriting of Defoe's island narrative in *Foe*, or the imaginary Cape landscape devastated by war in *Life & Times of Michael K* were relevant to the 'colonialism of a special type' unfolding in South Africa, leftist critics especially desired a more concrete engagement with the conditions of apartheid. In *Age of Iron* Coetzee had anchored the dynamics of his novel to the township struggles of the mid- and late 1980s, only to set *The Master of Petersburg* in nineteenth-century Russia.

What rationale lies behind the plot of *The Master of Petersburg*, which takes place in 1869 in Russia and follows this fictional Fyodor Dostoevsky's return from exile in Dresden to mourn his dead stepson, Pavel? (In fact, the real Pavel outlived the real Dostoevsky.) A grieving Dostoevsky, afflicted with epilepsy, takes up residence with Pavel's former landlady, Anna Sergeyevna. In the following weeks he is offered several interpretations of his stepson's mysterious and fatal fall from a tower. The interpretations range from suicide to a fall-out with the radical revolutionary groups with whom he was associating, or police-staged murder. Investigating these possibilities brings Dostoevsky face to face with two political choices: the authoritarian state or the destructive terrorist. The former is represented by Maximov, a conservative police official, who insists on claiming for the State even the private space of fiction writing.[1] For the latter stands Sergei Nechaev, a nihilist, anarchist, and friend of Bakunin, who plans to steal the authority carried by the writer's signature and produce a pamphlet bearing Dostoevsky's name. Out of these personal and political interactions, which have no concrete outcome, Dostoevsky moves onto the brink of a new novel, *The Possessed*, which he starts writing in the last chapter of Coetzee's book.

This apparently out-of-place novel is, however, of relevance to the literary landscape of South Africa during the early 1990s. It is not a coded representation of the main political actors, as some readers have assumed. Yet it is symptomatic of the transition years, for it portrays some of their most salient features, reflecting on the position of the writer vis-à-vis a restructured field of political forces. Finally, it presents a model of connectivity that places South African culture in a special relationship to postcolonialism and the global configuration born at the end of the Cold War.

Dostoevsky's Russia: Homologies, Metonymies, and Structural Equivalences

Critical essays on *The Master of Petersburg* are few compared with the attention enjoyed by Coetzee's other novels. The handful of articles assign it to various fictional genres, some easily recognisable, others more difficult to identify. They range from semi-autobiographical text to metafictional statement (a writer imagines another author's creative processes), and from confessional fiction (Coetzee was fascinated by the 'double thoughts' inherent to guilt avowal) to political *roman à clef*.[2] Two opposing approaches stand out in these critical responses: on the one hand, some readers find the novel to be completely unrelated to what was going on in South Africa; on the other, readers apply a grid that artificially maps the political spectrum spanned by the fictional Dostoevsky and Nechaev onto political actors in contemporary South Africa.[3]

There is something clumsy about criticism that tries to read *The Master of Petersburg* as a political *roman à clef*. Instead of a one-to-one equivalence between tsarist Russia and transitional South Africa, I argue for a reading that considers the similarities between the positions of the writers in relation to the field of political forces in their countries, and the authors' ethical freedom to represent their chosen material. Instead of a *roman à clef*, we can read in Coetzee's text homologies, metonymies and structural equivalences between the geo-political and temporal spheres of tsarist Russia and contemporary South Africa.

The Master of Petersburg has been read as historiographic metafiction with a *mise-en-abyme* plot, featuring Dostoevsky on the brink of writing *The Possessed*. Coetzee places a clear intertextual mark in the title of the last chapter, "Stavrogin". This chapter releases, like a genie out of a bottle, the tormented consciousness that imagined the seduction of a young girl and left her to her subsequent suicide. Dostoevsky aficionados have been quick to catch on to the reference to Stavrogin's censored confession in *The Possessed*, incorporated in the novel only after the writer's death. For avid readers of Dostoevsky, *The Master of Petersburg* contains rewarding tidbits about the Russian author's life and writings strewn throughout the novel: Matryona, the landlady's daughter who befriends Pavel, shares her name with Matryosha, seduced by Stavrogin in *The Possessed*. Dostoevsky tells Matryona the story of Pavel's white suit—a story of compassion for a crippled girl—which recalls an explanatory story about Stavrogin's strange decision to marry the dim-witted Maria Lebyadkina.

Following intertextual clues is not the object of this essay. Yet, it is disconcerting to find out that Joseph Frank, the famous Dostoevsky scholar and bibliographer, has resented this fictionalised version of the Russian writer's life: "Coetzee is a novelist, of course, and he has the novelist's right to play with history. Still it is regrettable that he did not include a warning to his readers, many of whom will be unfamiliar with the details of Dostoevsky's biography, not to take his fiction as fact" (1995:53). And he proceeds to guide readers through the many historical truths, fallacies, and literary borrowings in Coetzee's novel.

It seems therefore that the novel has excited exactly the type of reading Coetzee has treated with suspicion, according to which a work of fiction is set side by side with historical events and measured by the stick of mimesis and power of representation. It is a relationship that places the novel in an ancillary position to history, and renders it a subtly coded narrative about the facts of history. In a lecture delivered in 1987, Coetzee expressed his rejection of the "supplementary" novel, with events checkable by history "as a child's schoolwork is checked by a schoolmistress" (1988:3). Instead, he proposed a relationship of "rivalry" between the novel and history, a relationship that does not pre-empt "the game going on between the covers of the book". Between the enunciation of this creed in 1987 and the publication of *The Master of Petersburg* in 1994, during what is usually described as the South African interregnum, from the last state of emergency to the free elections, a heated debate on the status of the arts in relation to historical contingency had been brewing in South Africa. It started off in 1984 with Njabulo S. Ndebele's call for "the rediscovery of the ordinary" and exploded in 1989 with Albie Sachs's argument against seeing "culture as a weapon of the struggle".[4] Speaking from within the ANC, Sachs was not expressing a consensus: writers supporting politically engaged texts (such as Mongane Wally Serote) were backing a literature tantamount to a South African brand of socialist realism. In this context, Coetzee's novel, *The Master of Petersburg*, arises not as a denial or rejection of the importance of the historical context, but as a claim to engage with it on one's own terms within fiction. In particular, he questions the sites and dynamic of authority and resistance in tightly controlled societies.

There are, of course, general similarities in terms of the sociopolitical situation in Russia of the 1860s and South Africa of the early 1990s. The end of apartheid and De Klerk's repeal of most of the laws on which segregationist politics was built (the Group Areas Act, the Land Acts, the Separate Amenities Act, the Population Registration Act) are comparable with the demise of serfdom in Russia in 1861. In both historical settings the abrogation of iniquitous laws did not imply the automatic empowerment of the oppressed. Historians have pointed out that the changes brought about by the Epoch of Great Reforms were superficial. In post-1994 South Africa, the ANC government realised that redressing centuries-old inequalities and widespread poverty among the black population was unlikely to be accomplished within a decade. The two historical moments share a relatively slow, although determined, rhythm of transformation.

Coetzee is aware of the different types of readerships skilled in interpreting fictional writers' voices. As he noted, "the aesopian method assumes an extraordinary community of interest between readers and writers of the kind that you might get among the embattled intelligentsia in Russia or Poland, but that you absolutely would not get in South Africa"

(1997:94). While he is aware of similarities with an imperial system, Coetzee outlines the subtle yet important differences in the field of political forces that imbricate writers and their creations. If *The Master of Petersburg* is in any way an allegory, it reflects South African political dichotomies and questions of authority rather than offering a coded identification of the main ideological positions.

The puzzle regarding Coetzee's chosen topic is compounded by the novel written by Dostoevsky around the year 1869, which is embedded in *The Master of Petersburg*. *The Possessed* is usually considered Dostoevsky's most explicit novel in terms of its political stance and is sometimes read as tantamount to a political pamphlet on Nihilism.[5] There is no sympathy in the depiction of Peter Stepanovich Verkhovensky: from the beginning he manipulates everybody's feelings, ferociously follows his political ambitions, and does not shrink from murdering Shatov, a member of the only underground cell he sets up. In this respect, Coetzee's rendering of Nechaev is toned down, and Dostoevsky's dislike of the Nihilists is transformed into a rejection of authoritarian political solutions, be they from the establishment or from the opposition. Despite its bias, however, *The Possessed* does not surrender the whole narrative to facile political mappings. At the core of the novel stands Stavrogin as an identity puzzle; his personality moves from self-confidence to self-questioning, from generosity to selfishness, from mystical belief to the freedom of atheism. The novel is sustained by a polyphony of voices. Characters embody different political positions, from mystical nationalism (Shatov) to Occidental individualism (Kirilov) and western-style liberalism (Karmazinov). The description of Stepan Trofimovich in the opening chapter, with assertions that are skilfully deflated in the lines following, is an example of Dostoevsky's mastery in building and sustaining character through the accretion of angles and incidents. Indeed, it can be argued that Coetzee's choice of Dostoevsky as the main character in his text hinges on the dialogic nature of his novels.

The perception of dialogism as the ultimate feature of Dostoevsky's novels arose from Bakhtin's *Problems of Dostoevsky's Politics*. By relinquishing the surplus of vision on the past or future trajectories of his characters, the Russian author was able to forego any claim to ultimate truth or a single, validated ethic. In his 1995 review of Joseph Frank's volume, *The Miraculous Years*, Coetzee obliquely confirms his choice of Dostoevsky as the hero of his novel because of the latter's rebellion against the constraints of political, social, and ethical points of view (2001a:114-26). Navigating between Bakhtin's and Frank's texts, Coetzee argues that the bibliographer lost "an opportunity to supply what is missing in Bakhtin, namely, a clear statement that dialogism, as exemplified in the novels of Dostoevsky is a matter not of ideological position, still less of novelistic technique, but of the most radical and intellectual courage" (123). Within his novel, Coetzee raises the problem of a writer's position and the extent of intellectual, political, and ethical freedom that an author can afford.[6]

This theme of intellectual courage, which allows a writer creative freedom, becomes important within the context of the new literature produced in South Africa after the collapse of apartheid. Seven years earlier, in his Jerusalem Prize Acceptance Speech, Coetzee had deplored the transformation of South African literature into a "literature of bondage ... unable to move from elementary relations of contestation, domination, and subjugation to the vast and complex human world that lies beyond them" (1992:98). With its insistence on contestation and domination, such a literature, Coetzee implies, becomes inadequate with the change of regime. As South Africa arguably entered its postcolonial stage in 1990, the shape of the new literature and the position inhabited by the writer in this new cultural and political climate became relevant, not only for the South African cultural arena, but in metonymic fashion, as Derrida argued (1994), it was indicative of larger global post-Cold War phenomena.

Performances of Mastery and Authority

Charting some of the themes characteristic of postcolonialism after 1990, Jean and John Comaroff speak of a movement of emphasis away from the imaginary community of the nation to smaller communities, organised, among other categories, according to age groups (2001:627-52). In South Africa after the Soweto uprising of 1976, represented in the media as a children's revolt, inter-generational tensions came to the forefront. Blaming the older generations for indirect complicity with the apartheid regime, the younger generation favoured more violent methods of opposition, organising boycotts, hunting for informers, and supporting Umkhonto we Sizwe (the military wing of the ANC), to the point that the parents half-embraced their children as saviours and half-blamed them for adopting revolutionary methods divorced from an ubuntu, or a community-sharing, philosophy. In *The Master of Petersburg* Dostoevsky dreams of Pavel's averted face; the young man's refusal to respond, from beyond the grave to the summons of the one who calls himself his father, marks the estrangement and conflict between generations.

It is obvious from his essays on Dostoevsky and Turgenev that Coetzee (2001a, 2001b) had this theme in mind when exploring Russian literature as a mirror universe to the South African condition. He outlines a parallel between Turgenev's novel, *Fathers and Sons*, and the conflict between older and younger revolutionary generations in South Africa. In *The Master of Petersburg*, Coetzee translates South Africa's intergenerational tensions into his re-imagination of the conflict in Dostoevsky's time. The fictional Dostoevsky muses on this topic:

> Is it always like this between fathers and sons: jokes masking the intense rivalry? And is that the true reason why he is bereft: because the ground of his life, the contest with his son, is gone, and his days are left empty? Not the People's Vengeance but the Vengeance of the Sons: is that what underlies revolution? (1994:108)

Fathers, sons, the people, authority, the state—these are some of the key words in Coetzee's novel on the revolutionary years in Russia, as well as in South Africa—and they come together in what Michiel Heyns has presented as a re-inscribed Oedipal triangle: father—son—state, in which rivalry over the body politic and the state replaces the quasi-erotic competition between generations (1996:81-103). The political struggle between generations (a more revolutionary age group against formerly liberal parents grown complacent) is eroticised, as the continuation of the quotation given above indicates: "Not the People's Vengeance but the Vengeance of the Sons: is what underlies revolution—fathers envying their sons their women, sons scheming to rob their father's cashboxes" (Coetzee 1994:108). Dostoevsky misreads his son's political associations for erotic hunting grounds, and the police (with the supreme father figure, Maximov, at its head) gets an erotic kick out of digging out the dirt in young revolutionaries' lives. Yet the answer is more complicated than a homoerotic competition between fathers and sons for an authority that for the moment rests with the parents, but will soon be usurped by the youngsters.

To begin with, despite the title, the father is not so much the master of the situation, and his station as an author does not automatically carry authority. For the police as well as for Nechaev and Matryona he is a simulacrum father who has failed to take proper care of his stepson. Dostoevsky gives in with equal terror and pleasure to epileptic fits in which his identity dissolves: "He knows the word I, but as he stares at it, it becomes as enigmatic as a rock in the middle of a desert" (1994:71). He explores doubling, duality of self, and duplicity, and he acknowledges his histrionic personality. Impersonation is at the heart of Coetzee's novel, and all male characters take delight in it.

Take for instance the emblematic scene of the "white suit". In an exercise of mourning, Dostoevsky puts on Pavel's misfitting suit in an attempt to inhabit his son's position and mind, to identify with him, only to tell Matryona a few minutes later that he is not the only impostor. His stepson bought the suit a few summers earlier to assume the identity of a romantic suitor. Later, Nechaev puts on the suit and acquires the allure of a son for Dostoevsky, as he tries to escape the imperial police. The white suit becomes the hallmark of identities in travesty, a *carte blanche*, a white spot in the novel which can be occupied in turn by the main characters in order to negotiate their political allegiances and relations of domination. As a *carte blanche* it marks the void of identity, a mask without content, revealing the shifting grounds of social, political, and gender identity, and reinscribing or ascribing filiation. It opens up a potential of infinite reversals of authority and filiation: the father can turn out to be "a faded copy of the son" (1994:64).

Dostoevsky's signature can be forged and Nechaev has no qualms about taking over Dostoevsky's author function and using it for his own political purposes. Furthermore, the voice of the people that Nechaev claims constantly to be hearing and to which he purports to attune his actions may turn out to be his own voice disguised. Yet simulacrum in *The Master of Petersburg* does not designate so much a poststructuralist/ postmodern perspective, as it marks Coetzee's awareness of a fanning out of sources of authority, and of degrees of political authenticity. As I shall argue later, it anchors a novel apparently unrelated to the South African situation to reformulated questions of identity and authority characteristic in the early 1990s in that country.

Sartorial metaphors occupy an important position in this novel. As Pavel, Dostoevsky, and Nechaev don it, the white suit collapses apparently radical differences. In its revelation of the soft grounds of identity and the mobility of political positionings, the white suit becomes a grotesque mask. Instead of healing the gap through the process of mourning, it carries a message about identity which beyond its firmest claims at authenticity remains performative: "but now, looking in the mirror, he sees only a seedy imposture and, beyond that, something surreptitious and obscene, something that belongs behind locked doors and curtained windows of rooms where men in wigs and skirts bare their rumps" (1994:71). This last mark of transvestism is a reminder that the transformed Oedipal triangle, father—son—fatherland, represents a subversion of the cult of masculinity and virility on which authoritarian and patriarchal states, such as the Russian Empire and South Africa of the apartheid years, rely. Dostoevsky first encounters Nechaev cross-dressed and made-up as a woman and identifies him after the latter insists on his dislike of effeminate behaviour. As soon as it is offered, any identity statement is immediately denied or reversed.

The conclusions follow. First, authority is hollowed out, as it is grounded on imposture; the very notion of authority comes under scrutiny. Dostoevsky, the literary authority whom both Nechaev and the police attempt to co-opt in order to buttress their political position, is a master of histrionics, doubling, and duplicity. Second, Dostoevsky as protagonist refuses to side either with the nostalgic reading of authority and tradition offered by Maximov (that they live in an age when the children rise against the fathers; therefore, it is the duty of fathers to teach and enforce the social law) or with the revolutionary reading of authority professed by Nechaev (that the voice of the people demands a radical transformation of society). While the historical Dostoevsky had become a champion of the Orthodox Church and had adopted a conservative political outlook by the 1860s, the character presented by Coetzee does not sympathise fully with the Nihilism of the revolutionary youth or with the conservative discourse of empire.

On this point as on many others the character in the novel differs from the real-life author. Unfortunately, the older Dostoevsky represented in the novel has been interpreted as Coetzee's own failure to offer due tribute to the generation of the Soweto uprising and the ANC freedom fighters which came to power after the elections of 1994. This is a serious charge against a writer whose first novel after the end of apartheid raised great expectations. Derek Attridge confesses that he is "disturbed" that the novel "presents a vision of the writing process, and more generally of creativity, of inventiveness ... that sets it against the ethical realm, as having nothing to do with ethics, or with human responsibility" (1996:36) and he compares *The Master of Petersburg* with *Age of Iron* in which Coetzee proposed "a certain kind of human responsibility" (1996:36). However, we should note the differences between the sociopolitical backgrounds against which the two novels were written. *Age of Iron* was published at the end of the Emergency and reflects back on the years of struggle. It was inconceivable to be a writer opposing the apartheid regime and not propose "a certain kind of human responsibility". *The Master of Petersburg* was written when the democratic forces were advancing towards majority rule, the ANC had entered negotiations with the government, and the binaries of the apartheid years (reinforced by the dichotomies of the Cold War) were giving way to more complex ways of viewing power and political authority.

This political landscape determined Coetzee's fresh analysis of the position of a writer in relation to the field of political forces. This new positioning emerged in his article, "Erasmus: Madness and Rivalry", first published in 1992 (Coetzee 1996). Coetzee is fascinated by the "extraordinary resistance in the Erasmian text to being read into and made part of another discourse" (103). Opening up a link from Erasmus, to Huizinga, to Zweig, Coetzee takes delight in *The Praise of Folly* in "its jocoserious abnegation of big-phallus status, its evasive (non)position inside/outside the play— just as its weakness lies in its power to grow, to propagate itself, to beget Erasmians" (103), one of whom Coetzee implies himself to be. In the explosive situation of the early 1990s Coetzee's refusal to align his writing with the democratic forces could have been interpreted in a reductionist way.

Rather than read the novel as a betrayal by a writer of whom so much was expected, could we perhaps interpret it as a sign of Coetzee's discomfort to align the ethics of his novel with those of the victims of yesterday because they are the winners of today? Against the betrayal argument, I contend that Coetzee's refusal to incline his novel in the direction of the young revolutionaries presents the reader with new definitions of authority, commensurate not only with the situation in the 1860s in Russia but also with the 1990s in South Africa. The early 1990s have brought about a hitherto unimagined fragmentation of the political field, previously separated into coherent pro- and anti-apartheid camps. Within the National Party, tensions were appearing between F.W. de Klerk and the more conservative members. The latter were convinced that by releasing Mandela and unbanning the anti-apartheid parties, De Klerk had set the country on a fast track to black rule and economic collapse. The Conservative Party, led by A.P. Treurnicht, accused the president of betraying the Afrikaner volk. Extremist factions such as the neo-Nazi AWB were threatening to derail negotiations between the government and a coalition of the ANC, UDF (United Democratic Front), and Cosatu (Congress of South African Trade Unions). There was continual violence and conflict between the IFP and the ANC, as the former refused until the eleventh hour to join the process leading to democratic elections. Potential disagreement between the ANC and the SACP also emerged, since the former was moving away from the economic platform that advocated a socialist economy. At the same time, the early 1990s saw a coming together of political forces at the negotiation table and the birth of the Convention for a Democratic South Africa. Unlikely alliances were also formed, as Mangosuthu Buthelezi's IFP joined forces with the AWB under the slogan of protection for minorities in an ANC-dominated South Africa. And the majority of the Coloured population removed its support from the ANC, granted during the 1980s, to vote for the National Party in the 1994 elections. All these newly emerging faction lines and alliances modified the binaries of the apartheid years. This reconfiguration of the political field brings to the foreground notions of versatility, ambiguity and hybridity.

Returning to the novel, we should not forget that 'mastery' does not stand only for a position of power and authority, or only for literary craftsmanship, but also for skilfulness and versatility: "What a charlatan!" exclaims Doestoevsky about Nechaev, "yet he no longer knows where the mastery lies—whether he is playing with Nechaev or Nechaev with him" (1994:190). Finally, Coetzee's novel invokes a rethinking of the boundaries of social, political and gender identity through excess. There is a climactic scene, following the quotation above, in which Dostoevky observes that "all the barriers seem to be crumbling at once: the barrier on tears, the barrier on laughter". According to Kevin Platt, there is a category of literary texts which emerges in times of social and political turmoil and which, instead of looking backwards with nostalgia at the world that is vanishing or looking forward with anticipation at the new social order, collapses visions of past and future in simultaneity. Instead of making sense of the revolutionary times and instating epistemological order, such texts "make nonsense", so that, through the evocation of laughter and tears, they force the reader into an abandonment of commonplace historical meaning, and open up a new understanding. This category of texts, which Platt terms "revolutionary grotesque", is characteristic of the "Epoch of Great Reforms" (1855-1874), when the tame revolution from above clashed with the radical doctrines of Nihilists. This time-frame "presents a picture overflowing with ambiguity and irony" (Platt 1997:67), and with its soft and permeable notions of authority seems to have appealed to Coetzee's post-1990 sensibility. Instead of dismissing *The Master of Petersburg* as irrelevant to the great changes in South Africa, or as eschewing political and ethical questions, or as presenting in code the political actors of 1994, I read it as demarcating Coetzee's new, historically-determined position on writing in relation to the field of political forces.

To return to Coetzee's metaphor of the game between the covers of the book, *The Master of Petersburg* allows him to define fiction writing as operating independently, without losing sight of historical contingency. While stepping sideways from the South African scene, Coetzee actually pitches his game to refer obliquely to the sociopolitical background, to redefine authority and wrench it from its traditional loci. At the same time, he sketches out features of the early 1990s, such as a drawn-out temporal dimension characterised by the anxiety of waiting and a collapse of coherently forward or backward teleological gazes into a protracted present.

Transition Time and the Logic of Late Postcolonialism

The periodisation of postcolonial literature and theory carries significant weight in defining the moment at which Coetzee's text was published. I have labelled the third and most recent time-frame in the history of the discipline *late postcolonialism*. This marks the advent of a new horizon in South African and global culture.[7] The first two stages are already well described: the anti-colonial moment emerged out of the Bandung movement and the struggle of the former colonies to gain independence; the postcolonial stage looked beyond the economic and political fields to outline the lasting effects of cultural colonisation. These two moments are defined in relation to the political events that shaped them: the decolonisation struggle in the wake of World War II and the crystallisation of Cold War dichotomies starting with the 1960s.

In a conversation with John Comaroff, Homi Bhabha argued in favour of inserting the 1960s as a delineating period in the trajectory of the discipline. His argument focused on the revolts within the education system, the contestation of the canon, and the rise of structuralism and poststructuralism as systems of thought (2002:15-46). We can add the transformations in the political field: the concretisation of Cold War dichotomies with the erection of the Berlin Wall in 1961, as well as the contestation of traditional Marxist tenets in the wake of knowledge about Stalin's atrocities and Soviet intervention in Hungary and Czechoslovakia. The third stage, that of late postcolonialism, is shaped by the collapse of communist regimes in Eastern Europe and the emergence of global capitalism. Late postcolonialism marks the waning of the theoretical euphoria of earlier stages and a new historical period.

The belatedness rendered by its name is connected to the late arrival of this moment for countries like South Africa and Namibia. Late postcolonialism recognises the protracted dimension of waiting for the moment of liberation. It foregrounds an anxiety about the arrival of the moment of freedom as well as disquiet for what lies beyond. At the same time, late postcolonialism marks a transformation, a death of sorts of what characterised the earlier stages of the discipline, as it challenges Marxism and poststructuralism alike as tools insufficient for the definition of the historical present and past or for shaping a relation with the future. Yet the spectres of Marx and the ghosts of a poststructuralist intellectual tradition haunt late postcolonialism. Postcolonialism is not rendered irrelevant; it metamorphoses itself into a late postcolonialism, in which it is both present and absent, both relevant and surpassed. The previous paradigms bequeath some of their elements, and glimpses of their rhetoric still flash up. The temporality of late postcolonialism allows moments of synchronicity of the three different stages.

The South African 'transition' offers a key to the understanding of this new stage of postcolonialism in which the euphoria of liberation is tempered by the threat of neo-colonialism. At the same time, Marxism, which fuelled the decolonisation process, must be adjusted after the collapse of the Soviet bloc. This liminal temporal dimension shatters the teleological understanding of history and hybridises and complicates time. The movement forward is complicated and deflected by processes of analysis, mirroring, and coexistence with alternative ideologies.[8]

An important characteristic of this time-frame is, as I have pointed out, the protracted dimension of waiting. South Africa moved from the sphere of Emergency to expectancy.[9] Critics have been quick to spot the theme of waiting in *The Master of Petersburg*: like a modern Orpheus, Dostoevsky is waiting for a sign from his stepson from beyond the grave. Infused with a sense of mysticism, he is waiting for God to address him and direct him; and finally he is waiting for the creative impulse to take a clear direction and grow into a new novel, *The Possessed*.[10] In an emblematic scene in the novel, Dostoevsky wakes up to a call that he thinks to be the voice of his dead stepson, but turns out to be the howling of a dog. By twists of reasoning and paradoxes, he sets out the theme of expectation of the unknown:

> If he expects his son to come as a thief in the night, and listens only for the call of the thief, he will never see him. If he expects his son to speak in the voice of the unexpected, he will never hear him. As long as he expects what he does not expect, what he does not expect will not come. Therefore—paradox within paradox, darkness swaddled in darkness—he must answer to what he does not expect. (Coetzee 1994:80)

This scene has been read as characteristic of Dostoevsky's attitude towards writing, as he opens himself up to inspiration that might arrive in new forms (Attridge 1996:27). I would like to push this reading further and embed it in the literary context of the 1990s in South Africa. The movement away from a politically committed form of literature to an exploration of the manifold realities of the transition, beyond the binaries imposed by the Cold War and the apartheid setting, implies an opening towards a new literary landscape, with new genres and new sources of inspiration. It is a literary landscape in which the new may come in the form of a haunting theme, of something old and half-forgotten, yet different.

It is in this context that I return to the title of this essay: "Waiting for the Russians". On the one hand, it is a pun on the title of Coetzee's earlier novel, *Waiting for the Barbarians,* and the persistence of the theme of Beckettian waiting in his writing. At the same time, it points to the reshaping of an older topography of cultural inspiration (the Russian and more recently the Soviet theme). By placing his novel in Russia, Coetzee has dipped into an older thematic and stylistic reservoir: leftist politicised literature in South Africa under the apartheid regime was influenced in tone and topic by socialist realism. The time-frame of this novel is unexpected, yet the clash between authoritarian state and underground organised dissent, and between milder and more radical revolutionary practices is rendered relevant to the South African experience. The startling quality of the Russian theme resides in its spectrality. With Coetzee's novel, Russian culture makes an unexpected comeback.

In its Soviet form, Russian culture was demonised in apartheid South Africa as the absolute other of the Christian nationalist values of Afrikanerdom, while it was praised by freedom fighters. An episode from Coetzee's memoir *Boyhood* testifies to the strength and coerciveness of dichotomies imposed by the Cold War and reshaped by the apartheid culture. The young John Coetzee discovered with stupefaction that certain dichotomies were heavily coded and polarised:

> When the Russians and the Americans were first set before him as antagonists between whom he had to choose ("Who do you like, Smuts or Malan? Who do you like, Superman or Captain Marvel? Who do you like, the Russians or the Americans?"), he chose the Russians as he chose the Romans: because he likes the letter r, particularly the capital R, the strongest of all letters.... Then came the realization, from the disapproval of his parents, from the puzzlement of his friends, from what they reported when they told their own parents about him: liking the Russians was not part of the game, it was not allowed. (1998:27-8)

The child Coetzee stubbornly insisted on having his own private rules for the game, unrestricted by the politicised dichotomies of the historical contingency.

What unpredictably returns with Coetzee's novel is an uncanny cultural tradition that dislodges public attention from South Africa's pursuit to gain membership to the new global financial and cultural economy. At the beginning of the 1990s, mainstream ANC theses moved away from leftist ideology and things of Soviet inspiration and launched a discourse of integration and democracy. The return of 'the Russians', in this fictional guise, becomes culturally significant beyond South African literature of the transition, and is relevant to postcolonial studies as a whole. Using a Russian theme, Coetzee moves laterally from the vertical structures of postcolonialism to explore the horizontal structures between less visible cultures of late postcolonialism.

Since their inception, postcolonial studies have honed their work of resistance and decolonisation against imperial forces past and present. Postcolonial writing, both creative and scholarly, has taken on the task of writing back, reversing hierarchies, proving the biased nature of ethical, aesthetic, and political judgments originating in the metropolis, reciprocating the glance. And necessarily and imperatively so. Yet in its strategy, it has focused on the vertical axis between the metropolis and the colony, even when promoting hybridity and in-betweenness as liberating subject positions. With his unexpected topic, Coetzee opens up a triangulation, in which post-apartheid (and postcolonial culture) is no longer perceived *only* as part of the vertical relationship with the Western world, but is also involved in complex interrelations with other marginal cultures. The uncanny, unexpected arrival of the Russians as the topic of Coetzee's 1994 novel places transition culture in South Africa in a richer, more nuanced global picture.

Notes

1. The methodical censorship apparatus that the Russian imperial police deploys in Coetzee's fiction is indexical of the repressive laws formulated in apartheid South Africa, and which the writer explored in his collection of essays *Giving Offense* (1996).
2. See Pienaar (1995), Scanlan (1997), Aldeman (1999), Lawlan (1998).
3. The ideological difference between Russian Nihilists and Umkhonto we Sizwe, the armed branch of the ANC, is too great to be overlooked. Derek Attridge sees that Nechaev "can hardly be read as a salute to the fighting

members of the ANC and the South African Communist Party" (1996:26). In humanising Nechaev, Coetzee is unlikely to be drawing a parallel with the anti-apartheid revolutionary youth that emerged in the 1976 uprising.

4. See Ndebele (1994) and Sachs (1998).
5. Critics agree that Dostoevsky wrote the novel under the impact of Nechaev's trial and the details about the murder of the student Ivanov, material that the writer kept almost unchanged in his novel (Walicki 1979:322).
6. Sue Kossew points out that both Dostoevsky and Coetzee have been accused of not being sufficiently politically committed (1996:78).
7. Other periodisations have been offered. Jean and John Comaroff proposed the independence of India as the start of the decolonisation period and the year 1989 as the triumph of neoliberal global capitalism (2001). David Scott argued for a Gramscian interregnum called "after postcoloniality", which succeeded the anti-colonial and postcolonial moments (1999).
8. See also Monica Popescu (2003).
9. The first State of Emergency was imposed on July 21, 1985, and lasted until March 1986. It was reimposed on June 12 of the same year and then renewed annually until 1990.
10. Derek Attridge argues that most of Coetzee's novels occur within a temporality of the "messianic", which he describes according to Derrida's parameters from *Specters of Marx*: a "dessert-like messianism (without content and without identifiable messiah)" (1996:27). These ideas are developed in Attridge's book *J.M. Coetzee and the Ethics of Reading* where he says of *The Master of Petersburg*: "It doesn't speak to us of South Africa, but it speaks of the role of literature, of art, in a country like South Africa, a country struggling to be born anew. It is not a reassuring account" (2005:133).

References

Aldeman, Gary. 1999. "Stalking Stavrogin: J.M. Coetzee's *The Master of Petersburg* and the Writing of *The Possessed.*" *Journal of Modern Literature* 23(2):351-7.

Attridge, Derek. 1996."Expecting the Unexpected in Coetzee's *Master of Petersburg* and Derrida's Recent Writings." In: Ruth Robbins, John Brannigan and Julian Wolfreys (eds). *Applying to Derrida*. New York: St Martin's Press: 21-40.

————. 2005. *J.M. Coetzee and the Ethics of Reading*. Chicago: University of Chicago Press; Pietermaritzburg: University of KwaZulu-Natal Press.

Bhabha, Homi and John Comaroff. 2002. "Speaking of Postcoloniality, in the Continuous Present: A Conversation." In: David Theo Goldberg and Ato Quayson (eds). *Relocating Postcolonialism*. Oxford: Blackwell: 15-46.

Coetzee, J.M. 1982. *Waiting for the Barbarians*. New York: Penguin.

—————. 1988. "The Novel Today." Upstream 6(1):2-5.

—————. 1990. *Age of Iron*. New York: Random House.

—————. 1992a. "Confession and Double Thoughts: Tolstoy, Rousseau, Dostoevsky." In: David Attwell (ed.). *Doubling the Point: Essays and Interviews*. Cambridge: Harvard University Press: 251-93.

—————. 1992b. "Jerusalem Prize Acceptance Speech." In: David Attwell (ed.). *Doubling the Point*. Cambridge: Harvard University Press: 96-9.

—————. 1994. *The Master of Petersburg*. New York: Viking.

—————. 1996. "Erasmus: Madness and Rivalry." In: *Giving Offense: Essays on Censorship*. Chicago: University of Chicago Press: 83-103.

—————. 1997. "Voice and Trajectory: Interview with Joanna Scott." *Salmagundi* (Spring-Summer):114-15.

—————. 1998. *Boyhood: Scenes from Provincial Life*. London: Vintage.

—————. 2001a. "Dostoevsky: The Miraculous Years." In: *Stranger Shores: Literary Essays 1986-1999*. New York: Viking: 114-26.

—————. 2001b. "Gordimer and Turgenev." In: *Stranger Shores*. New York: Viking: 219-31.

Comaroff, Jean and John Comaroff. 2001. "Naturing the Nation: Aliens, Apocalypse and the Postcolonial State." *Journal of Southern African Studies* 27(3):627-52.

Derrida, Jacques. 1994. *Specters of Marx: The State of Debt, the Work of Mourning, and the New International*. New York: Routledge.

Dostoevsky, Fyodor. 1970 [1872]. *The Possessed*. London: Heinemann.

Frank, Joseph. 1995. "The Rebel." *The New Republic* 213(16):53-6.

Heyns, Michiel. 1996. "Fathers and Sons: Structures of Erotic Patriarchy in Afrikaans Writing of the Emergency." *Ariel* 27:81-103.

Kossew, Sue. 1996. "The Anxiety of Authorship: J.M. Coetzee's *The Master of Petersburg* (1994) and Andre Brink's *On the Contrary* (1993)." *English in Africa* 23(1):67-88.

Lawlan, Rachael. 1998. "*The Master of Petersburg*: Confession and Double Thoughts in Coetzee and Dostoevsky." *Ariel* 29(2):131-55.

Mda, Zakes. 2002. *The Heart of Redness*. New York: Farrar, Straus and Giroux.

Ndebele, Njabulo S. 1994. "The Rediscovery of the Ordinary: Some New Writings in South Africa." In: *South African Literature and Culture: Rediscovery of the Ordinary*. Manchester: Manchester University Press: 41-59.

Pienaar, Hans. 1995. "Coetzee's Solidarity of Silence: A Strange, Humbling, and Sometimes Chilling Tale of Fame, Literature, and Privacy." *Sidelines* 2:47-59.

Popescu, Monica. 2003. "Translations: Lenin's Statues, Post-communism and Post-apartheid." *Yale Journal of Criticism* 16(2):406-23.

Sachs, Albie. 1998. "Preparing Ourselves for Freedom." In: Derek Attridge and Rosemary Jolly (eds). *Writing South Africa: Literature, Apartheid, and Democracy, 1970-1995*. Cambridge: Cambridge University Press: 239-48.

Scanlan, Margaret. 1997. "Incriminating Documents: Nechaev and Dostoevsky in J.M. Coetzee's *The Master of Petersburg*." *Philological Quarterly* 76(4):463-77.

Scott, David. 1999. *Refashioning Futures: Criticism after Postcoloniality*. Princeton: Princeton University Press.

Walicki, Andrzej. 1979. *A History of Russian Thought from the Enlightenment to Marxism*. Stanford: Stanford University Press.

DEPLORATIONS

COETZEE, COSTELLO AND DOUBLING THE N

MICHAEL GREEN

... although the houses founded in temperate zones have generally been a success, the Cistercian Rule has never been properly lived in the tropics. So many mitigations are required that the life is unrecognisable. The monks of Leopoldville in the Belgian Congo, Beagle Bay in northern Australia, and the monks of Brazil rapidly lost their true Cistercian character. The climate had simply twisted their Rule out of shape. For that matter, it is easy to see how poorly the Rule of St Benedict is adapted to the Southern Hemisphere, where everything, as they say, is upside down. Since the seasons are reversed, Lent falls in harvest time, and the monks have to fast when they need to eat; then, in compensation, they have plenty to eat when they could easily fast. (Merton 1962)

Postcoloniality is the condition of what we might ungenerously call a comprador intellegentsia: a relatively small, Western-style, Western trained group of writers and thinkers, who mediate the trade in cultural commodities of world capitalism at the periphery. In the West they are known through the Africa they offer; their compatriots know them both through the West they present to Africa and through the Africa they have invented for the world, for each other, and for Africa. (Appiah 1996)

"One of the more startling disjunctures between text and referent in recent South African writing occurs at the moment when Sister Bridget, 'sister by blood' (2003:124) to J.M. Coetzee's eponymous protagonist in *Elizabeth Costello* and Administrator of the Hospital of the Blessed Mary on the Hill, Marianhill, dismisses Elizabeth's suggestion of a 'Greek' model for art and life in Africa. Pointing out that this is just what had occurred to the early colonialists—'educated Europeans, men from England with public-school educations behind them' (2003:140)—when they first came in contact with the Zulus, Sister Bridget declares, "'Well, the Zulus knew better." She waves a hand towards the window,' we are then told, 'towards the hospital buildings baking under the sun, towards the dirt road winding into the barren hills', and continues: "'This is reality: the reality of Zululand, the reality of Africa. It is the reality now and the reality of the future as far as we can see it'" (2003:141).

"What is startling about Sister Bridget's gesture is that the landscape outside the windows of Mariannhill—for Coetzee's 'Marianhill' cannot help but allude to this actual site—differs significantly from the one described here. The hospital is there, and the hills too, but the hills around Mariannhill are anything but 'barren'. Covered now with informal housing rapidly being transformed into a low-cost formal housing estate, they are set off still by the remainder of the intensely cultivated land for which the monastery that gives Mariannhill its name was famous from its earliest days. The monastery was renowned too for its expertly constructed roads and bridges, far better built than those of the colony of Natal in general at the time of its founding, and their contemporary legacy is the tarred, busy, multi-laned M1, which can scarcely be described as 'winding' as it cuts its brutal way between the industrial parks which have sprung up around Mariannhill and the predominantly black residential areas formed as locations for labour during the apartheid years.

"Now the point I wish to make in noting this is not one of simple counterfactualisation. *Elizabeth Costello* is a work of fiction, perhaps even a novel. It has, at least, a fictional protagonist, and the settings of the 'Eight Lessons' into which her experiences are divided are presented in modes that vary from what the implied author—who appears only in 'Lesson 1: Realism'[1]—calls 'moderate realism' ('supply the particulars, allow the significations to emerge of themselves' (2003:4)) to a (internally contested) 'tissue of allegory' (196). In this context, Coetzee's misspelling of 'Marianhill'—one 'n' instead of two—can be read as a clear signal that he claims for *Elizabeth Costello* what Nathaniel Hawthorne, in defending *The House of the Seven Gables* as 'A Romance', called 'a certain latitude' (1851:ii) from the mimetic fidelity expected of a novel.[2] This allows us to note the missing 'n' in the name Coetzee invokes for his fictional 'mission station' in terms of appropriate seriousness, central in fact to the mode in which Coetzee works, rather than as a simple spelling mistake, 'checkable by history (as a child's schoolwork is checked by a schoolmistress)' (1988:3).[3]

"In the same vein we could account, too, for the blatant inaccuracies in the way in which the mission hospital is positioned geographically: Mariannhill—two n's—is not, as described, 'in rural Zululand' (2003:116) at all, but firmly positioned within the province of KwaZulu-Natal, with the

rapidly expanding light-industrial centre of Pinetown now pressing right
up against it. Far from being in 'the sticks in Zululand' (124), it is just 23
kilometres from the centre of Durban and 63 from Pietermaritzburg. The
hospital (in actuality St Mary's Hospital) is the only Level One District
hospital attending to public sector patients between these two major
metropolitan centres, and serves a community of over seven hundred and
fifty thousand people.

"Dedicated as it is to the healthcare needs of the 'poorest of the poor',[4]
most of the fifteen thousand patients treated at St Mary's annually come
from peri-urban, even rural areas, and so—to continue with our rather
pedantic checking—we could concede something to Coetzee as far as the
'rural' nature of his setting is concerned. Seventy-five percent of the
hospital's patients are women and children, putting it at the forefront of
the fight against HIV/AIDS, and so the latitude Coetzee claims in having
Sister Bridget concentrate the energies of the hospital 'more and more on
the plight of children born infected' (116) is also not that far off the mark.
We could complain, however, that Sister Bridget's 'great innovation' of
having 'native doctors'—'traditional healers', that is—'work besides
doctors of Western medicine' (134) is a lot further from the mark. Apart
from a rather tentative and not particularly successful invitation put out
to traditional healers in the early 1990s, St Mary's has not experimented
much in this direction. Eighty percent of the hospital's operational
funding is obtained from the Department of Health, and so its administrators
are careful to follow the guidelines and protocols for dealing with HIV/
AIDS set by the province of KwaZulu-Natal.[5] Historically, too, Mariannhill
saw itself as engaged in a long and 'single-handed fight with the dark
powers of witchcraft' (1950:76), as Francis Schimlek put it in his book,
published by the Mariannhill Mission Press, *Medicine Versus Witchcraft*.
But the point I wish to make is that none of the fictionalising freedom
Coetzee takes with these details has the same scandalising effect as Sister
Bridget's wave at the hills that serve to locate her.

"Why is this? Why indeed should any of the localising details
concerning the institution touched on so far be in the least pertinent if we
accord fiction in general its usual conventions, let alone the kind of ludic
and elliptical work for which Coetzee has been so celebrated?

"Perhaps this is the moment to speak to the title of my talk today. It is
taken, quite appropriately I think for so Catholic a project, from an
apocryphal Costello story. Published in the *New York Review of Books* the
year after the appearance of *Elizabeth Costello*, 'As a Woman Grows
Older' makes up for the lapse Adam Mars-Jones notes with disapproval

in his review of the novel—'It's announced that Elizabeth plans to visit her daughter in Nice after a conference, but the visit isn't referred to again' (2003)—and one is forced to wonder if its belated appearance doesn't signal the possibility of an actual forthcoming publication entitled *'The Opinions of Elizabeth Costello,* revised edition'.

"(I might add as an aside that I once asked Professor Coetzee, after he had given one of Costello's early and yet-to-be-published Lessons at a conference in Krakow in 2001, if Elizabeth Costello was building up to something bigger. His reply was that she was running out of steam.)

"In any event, it is in this supplementary story that I find a word that some may (or is that 'might', Elizabeth?) apply to Sister Bridget's gesture. '"*Deplore*",' says Costello to John, her 'good and dutiful son':

> 'a word one does not hear much nowadays. No one with any sense *deplores*, not unless they want to be a figure of fun. An interdicted word, an interdicted activity. So what is one to do? Does one keep them all pent up, one's deplorations…? I deplore what the world is coming to. I deplore the course of history. From my heart I deplore it…. But the detail, John, the detail! It is not just the grand sweep of history that I deplore, it is the detail…. It is details … that exasperate me….' (15)

"Indeed. And it is the detail, not the grand sweep of Sister Bridget's argument through the history of the humanities, that prevents some of us (fortunately not nearly enough of us to worry Secker & Warburg's offices in London and New York, not even those in Sydney and Auckland) from being able to take the wave of her hand lightly.

"It is a simple fact, difficult to accord any weight I know in a realm of discourse dedicated to interrogating anything like 'a simple fact', that it is impossible for anyone even vaguely familiar with Mariannhill—yes, with two n's—not to see Sister Bridget's appeal to reality (an appeal upon which her entire argument rests) as little short of—well, 'amusing' is, I am afraid, the word that comes to mind. Put bluntly, the mismatch between her appeal and the details of its – yes, I will claim this, knowing just how naïve it must sound—'extratextual' referent (for so it is claimed to be, even within the text of the fiction) is too obvious to be treated as ironic, even if the text did point us this way (which it doesn't). It can only come across, for those acquainted with the hills of Mariannhill, as, quite simply, *wrong*—and the implied author's clear lack of awareness of this is what gives the moment its comic effect. For in the very instant that Sister Bridget invokes a physical setting in support of her position—let me quote again the point that carries the day for her in her argument with her sister so that it is fresh in our minds: "'This is *reality*: the *reality* of Zululand, the *reality* of Africa. It is the *reality* now and the *reality* of the future as far as we can see it'"— what is actually conjured up for certain readers is a demonstrable unreality, a non-reality, if you will, that is not even a meaningful counter-reality. What used to be called, no less, a howler.

"And so, what do we have here? A little in-joke for pedants of the particular, a rather crass giggle that can all too easily be turned back on the lack of sophistication amongst the locals? A minor point of relevance only to a minuscule audience? To be met by a mildly irritated shrug from the author's representatives (for we know from the long history of his notorious reticence that he will not respond himself to any point concerning his writing) who will no doubt say that he could have called his—and who else's is it, finally?—hospital on its mission station 'in the sticks' (even this local colloquialism is put into the mouth of a character, after all) anything he liked? Take away not just the 'n' but the whole name, pick any other entirely invented appellation, make sure only to distance the signifier from (the idea of) the signified—would this change the Lesson in any particular way?

"But Coetzee *did* choose to load the name of his hospital with the overtones of Mariannhill, and we must pause for a moment to ask why. Certainly the nature of the argument given to Sister Bridget relies, as I have said, on the grounding of her ideas in a specific location, just as her sister Elizabeth's 'Lesson'—'the humanities teach us humanity' (151)—needs to be accompanied by the story of its being acted out in its more individualised Australian setting. The hills of 'Marianhill', then, take on the fictional version of the specific and the actual, that is, they are intended as contributions towards the verisimilitude many reviewers find all too thin in this 'novel of ideas'. (In this case I suppose we could, if we wished, put down the blatant inaccuracy the name conjures up instead to Coetzee's characterisation of his younger self, 'All his life he has lacked interest in his environment, physical or social. He lives wherever he finds himself, turned inward' (1998:393).)

"At another level, the use of the name and setting of 'Marianhill' could be taken as an example of the way in which Coetzee's 'postmodern' fictional strategies must be understood, as David Attwell has argued, 'in the light of his postcoloniality' (1993:20). Attwell was taking on the full blast of the early Leftist charges of 'philosophical idealism' levelled at Coetzee when he made this argument, and so the problem, as he says, 'can be defined sharply: is the turn towards textuality in Coetzee a turning away from history?' (17). His answer to this: '*situational* metafiction' (2003:3, my emphasis)—'a mode of fiction that draws attention to the historicity of discourses, to the way subjects are positioned within and by them, and, finally, to the interpretive process, with its acts of contestation and appropriation' (1993:20). This is well put, but Attwell also characterises the problem as 'primarily ... a question of *reference*' (17, his emphasis), and we must ask ourselves on this occasion what the implications are for a reference made in a work of fiction—however much it is 'split', or 'cleft', or 'suspended' (17-18), however much we recognise the work of fiction to be the very condition for the gesture of referentuality—when the thing to which it refers resists, refuses, denies that gesture.

"'Kafka's ape is embedded in life. It is the embeddedness that is important, not the life,' (2003:32) Elizabeth says to the long-suffering John. Is it worth noting at this point that this is, too, Coetzee's own first name? Perhaps so, if we may take a chance on the identity of the implied author of Lesson 1, whose longest appearance is devoted to the conviction that for Realism, 'the notion of *embodying* turns out to be pivotal':

> Realism has never been comfortable with ideas. It could not be otherwise: realism is premised on the idea that ideas have no autonomous existence, can exist only in things. So when it needs to debate ideas, as here, realism is driven to invent situations—walks in the countryside, conversations— in which characters give voice to contending ideas and thereby in a certain sense embody them. (9)

"It is precisely the emergence of the 'author' meditating on the very form 'he' is using that, of course, in a fine twist distances *Elizabeth Costello* from the realm of realism. But neither this twist, nor the twist that Sister Bridget's argument is, finally, not proven conclusively by her appeal to the real, does away with the unfortunate effect that one of the elements crucial to the 'embedding' and 'embodying' of Lesson 5 has at just the precise moment when the invocation of the specific really matters.

"In none of the other Lessons does the local impinge in any serious sense, so much so that the work as a whole takes on something of the air of Costello's aspirations as a novelist. This is best caught in the moment when John tells the chairman of the jury that "'his mother will be disappointed ... if she learns that the Stowe Award is hers only because 1995 has been decreed to be the year of Australia'". She wants to be "'the best'", he says, "'not the best Australian, not the best Australian woman, just the best'" (8).

"'Lectures often begin with light-hearted remarks whose purpose is to set the audience at ease,' says Costello in her lecture in Part One of 'Lesson

3: The Lives of Animals' (62) just before—of course—making certain no one in the audience will take her opening remarks in that way.

"I must apologise for neglecting this convention of public speech myself, but let me perhaps make up for it now by saying that it is possible that Coetzee, to the degree that he shares Costello's opinions, must have been equally disappointed to find himself called, on the dust jacket of *Elizabeth Costello*, only 'One of the best novelists alive'.

"Thank you, thank you....

"But we must for the moment take Costello's dislike of being evaluated within so circumscribed a list of possible candidates seriously. John too is concerned 'that his mother not be treated as a Mickey Mouse postcolonial writer' (9). The Disneyland image has a lot to say about where the interest in the literary turn of the 'post-colonial' is really centred. But it is another issue to do with the national and the postcolonial that interests me here. Coetzee, strongly associated as he is with things South African despite or perhaps because of his parodic, allegorical, and pre-emptive interrogation of them, compounds the problems of his status as a postcolonial writer by recasting his own concerns—via Costello—as those of a writer who is Australian 'by birth' (1). I will not be so crude as to comment in any way on Coetzee's literal translation of himself to Australia, but the suggestion that these concerns remain the same be they those of an Australian, a South African, or, by implication, a writer from any of the multiple conditions that may be described primarily in terms of their experience of colonialism, could be seen as troubling at a time when there is a renewed interest in the specificities of postcolonial literary practices.

"Certainly Coetzee's 'postcolonialism' is not of what Biodun Jeyifo calls the 'normative and proleptic' type (1990:53); that is to say, he is quite obviously not a writer or, for that matter, a critic, 'who speaks to, or for, or in the name of a post-independent nation-state'. The very thought of any such will-to-identity in his work is negated by the force with which he inhabits the second kind of postcoloniality identified by Jeyifo, that is the 'interstitial or liminal': 'an ambivalent mode of self-fashioning of the writer or critic which is neither First World nor Third World, neither securely and smugly metropolitan, nor assertively and combatively Third-worldist. The very terms which express the orientation of this school of postcolonial self-representation are revealing: diasporic, exilic, hybrid, in-between, cosmopolitan,' says Jeyifo (53), who names Coetzee specifically as one of its paradigmatic figures.

"One can well imagine how much Coetzee would deplore being assigned

to any school, but some of the terms Jeyifo lists here could be applied to
Elizabeth Costello—could be, that is, until they are rarefied beyond even
the international wanderings that form the settings for the earlier lessons
and we are carried finally into a realm where 'All is allegory' (2003:229): a
realm from which Elizabeth, Lady Chandos (who signs herself 'Elizabeth
C.'), begs in her letter to Francis Bacon to be rescued. Much of Elizabeth's
failing power in 'Lesson 8: At the Gate' is spent in trying to prevent her
judges from turning all she says into allegory. After recalling the 'death'
and 'rebirth' of the frogs in the mud of the Dulgannon river—'I am
speaking now of one river in particular now,' she reminds them—she
insists that 'the life cycle of the frog may sound allegorical, but to the frogs
themselves it is no allegory, it is the thing itself, the only thing' (217). She
is forced, despite this, to leave open the option that, as one of her judges
puts it, '"these Australian frogs ... embody the spirit of life'—even as she
cries out within herself, '*I am worth better than that*'" (218-9). To her own
surprise, however, imagined densely and sympathetically, the coming
back to life of the frogs does become something 'that she can believe in'—
'she can believe in that,' she says, 'if she concentrates closely enough,
word by word' (220). For here the frogs of the river Dulgannon take on the
'different kind of being-in-the-world' Costello says Ted Hughes is feeling
towards in his Jaguar poems:

> 'in these poems we know the jaguar not from the way he seems but from
> the way he moves. The body is as the body moves, or as the currents of
> life move within it. The poems ask us to imagine our way into that way
> of moving, to inhabit that body.
>   'With Hughes it is a matter—I emphasize—not of inhabiting another
> mind but of inhabiting another body. (95-6)

"A strange point to lie at the centre of Coetzee's most—fictionally
speaking—disembodied, disembedded work. For all his emphasis on
Costello's ageing body, each of the Lessons has an air of the lost
physicality of her three nights in a row with Emmanuel Egudu; his voice,
it turns out in the sting in the tale of 'Lesson 2', once made her shudder
too, throwing doubt back across her rejection of 'The Novel in Africa' as
'an oral novel, a novel that has kept touch with the human voice and hence
with the human body, a novel that is not disembodied like the Western
novel but speaks the body and the body's truth...' (53). All Elizabeth has
now, however, to protect her from the 'contagion' of 'saying one thing
always for another' (228), from yielding in her exhaustion 'to the figures'
(229), is her frogs, 'Because they exist,' she says—'the Dulgannon and its

mudflats are real, the frogs are real. They exist whether or not I tell you about them, whether or not I believe in them… it is because of their indifference to me that I believe in them' (217).

"One cannot but be struck by this appeal to the real—the Dulgannon, she insists, 'is not negligible. You will find it on most maps' (218)—and Sister Bridget's wave. I am not qualified to say if a similar kind of referential disjuncture comes into play at this point but, either way, we are put into the position of having to query the *national* contexts of these two very specific appeals to reality.

"In a way, 'The Humanities in Africa', split as it is specifically between South Africa and Australia, stages just such a query, as much in its various versions as in the playoff of Marianhill and Melbourne that characterises what we must assume is the finalised form in *Elizabeth Costello*. Like most of the other Lessons, 'The Humanities in Africa' has appeared in print before. In this case, however, the text itself has differed quite drastically in its three different outings, although it must be said that 'Marianhill' remains consistent—consistently 'wrong', that is—through all three, from its parallel German/English text in *The Humanities in Africa/Die Geisteswissenschaftern in Afrika* to its remarkable inclusion in *The Best Australian Stories 2002* (few South Africans, indeed, and not many Australians, were ready for this), to the combination of these two versions in 'Lesson 5' of *Elizabeth Costello*. It is the Australian version which should teach us the most about being wary of pinning 'The Humanities in Africa' to Africa, south or otherwise: not because of its more heavily accented Australianness, in which Sister Bridget's lecture disappears to be displaced by Elizabeth Costello's more sexually intimate performance of the meaning of 'humanity' upon the voiceless, dying body of Mr Phillips in a Melbourne 'old folks' home' (151), but because of the lesson the collection of stories itself has for African writers.

"'The whole volume,' writes Margaret Lenta in 'Reading Australia', 'is evidence [that] Australians, unlike ourselves, feel entitled to be interested in anything, anywhere' (2003:n.p.). Thus, whilst 'Australia itself is not neglected', 'there are stories dealing with sexual confidences on a French beach, a chilly Easter on an English canal, an unspecified location where werewolves interact with men'—all of which demonstrate Costello's argument in 'Lesson 2: The Novel in Africa', that what African writers can learn from Australian writers is to get out 'of the habit of writing for strangers' (51), something Australian writers were able to learn how to do 'when our market, our Australian market, decided that it could support a home-grown literature' (52). It is precisely the maturity of a national market that allows a writer, in Costello's view, to go on to international—no, something beyond that, not just international greatness, but greatness, pure and simple and unspecified. For the African writer, however, says Elizabeth, the question still is, 'Why are there so many African novelists around and yet no African novel worth speaking of?' (50). And the answer? 'Exoticism. Exoticism and its seductions' (51).

"This point, properly explained, silences even Egudu, but it also prompts us to ask, cautiously, a further question: given the kind of emptying of its local significance that Mariannhill undergoes in 'The Humanities in Africa', what role other than an 'exotic' role could 'Marianhill' be identified as playing in its fictionalisation? I return again to the fact that Coetzee *did* choose to name his hospital after Mariannhill, but is he in this simply 'performing his Africanness'? Providing some local colour? And this not very successfully, in the case of Sister Bridget's wave, which, as I have said, disqualifies some of us, purely on the basis of our local knowledge, from participating in the willing suspension required by the 'universalising' of fiction.

"Now it may be said—and I am sure this has occurred to you pretty forcefully by now—that I am hanging far too much on one momentarily uplifted hand. Let me go on to say, then, that while it is not inimical to Coetzee's fictional project to anything like the same degree, the point we are dealing with now does require us to note that Marianhill can only serve its purpose in the fiction by a similar, although more conventionally acceptable, distanciation from anything like its historical reality. By this I mean, following Costello, its ability to 'exist whether or not I tell you about [it], whether or not I believe in [it]'. Drained of all local particulars, geographic and historic (I shall return to the latter shortly), does Mariannhill not become little more than a seductive setting for an argument that—despite Sister Bridget's gesture, or rather because of it, and its failure to connect a specific reality to a general argument—remains entirely in the realm of ideas: ideas that are given little purchase on their setting or, more importantly, marked by the refusal of their referent to be appropriated within those ideas?

"Now I must make it clear that I am not, in asking this, attempting to reinstate what Coetzee once called the 'the appropriating appetite of the discourse of history' or 'the colonisation of the novel by the discourse of history' (1988:2). I am encouraged, rather, in this line of thought by Costello's response in Part Two of 'The Lives of Animals' to a question from the floor concerning Swift which I think we may lift from its place in her larger argument without losing its force. First, Costello gives a counter reading to *A Modest Proposal* that suggests that Swift may be being more literal than is generally accepted; this she concludes with the words, 'If you want Swift to be a dark ironist rather than a facile pamphleteer, you might examine the premises that make his fable so easy to digest' (2003:101). Here, again, we run into *Elizabeth Costello*/Elizabeth Costello's almost obsessive concern with the collapsing back of what the fiction has established as 'real' into parable or fable or allegory, figures in fact of any kind.

"When she turns to Gulliver, Elizabeth modulates this concern—which is, as we have seen, ultimately a concern of one kind or another with the referent—more explicitly into the historical, more specifically the colonial historical: 'What has always puzzled me about *Gulliver's Travels*,' she says,

'and this is a perspective you might expect from an ex-colonial – is that Gulliver always travels alone. Gulliver goes on voyages of exploration to unknown lands, but he does not come ashore with an armed party, *as happened in reality*, and Swift's book says nothing about what would normally have come after Gulliver's pioneering efforts: follow-up expeditions, expeditions to colonize Lilliput or the island of the Houyhnhnms.

'The question I ask is: What if Gulliver and an armed expedition were to land, shoot a few Yahoos when they became threatening, and then shoot and eat a horse for food? What would that do to Swift's somewhat too neat, somewhat too disembodied, somewhat too unhistorical fable?' (102, original emphasis)

"What indeed? And what would the equivalent effect be of playing off something of what *happened* to Mariannhill *in reality* against Coetzee's (forgive me) '"somewhat too neat, somewhat too disembodied, somewhat too unhistorical fable"'? What would happen to the fictionalisation of Mariannhill if our concern was, as it is for Sister Bridget in her lecture on the humanities in Africa, 'to be historically accurate'? (120).

"The conventions of presenting a paper—to say nothing of my own poor powers—preclude me from achieving anything like this effect, but let us at least note that the subject of the address Sister Bridget gives on the occasion of having an honorary degree conferred upon her for her work at *Marianhill*—the betrayal of the humanities by secular rationality—does not tie in with the fervently-fought internal battles (of which St Mary's hospital itself is a contested result) that historically tore *Mariannhill* apart. That history is silenced by the present that Coetzee creates, and while there can be no requirement that Coetzee does anything other than what he has done, one can lament the loss incurred, the potential undone.

"I say a history that is silenced, and that brings me to the first of the ways in which Mariannhill could have spoken back to—well, to whom, exactly? The fictional author, the implied author, someone identified in the world as 'J.M. Coetzee'? Perhaps 'to what?' is the better question—the ways in which Mariannhill could have spoken back to the fictional effect of 'The Humanities in Africa'.

"Founded in 1880, Mariannhill was originally a Cistercian house, more specifically the Cistercians of the Strict Observance, or, as they are popularly known, the Trappists. Now the Trappist Order is a contemplative Order. The contemplative life, as set out in the Rule of St Benedict, involves withdrawal from the world, solitude, prayer, fasting, manual work and, above all, silence. Even standing together uselessly is considered a breach of silence. The recitation of the Divine Office ranks first amongst the duties of the monks; beginning just after midnight, this takes up seven hours a day. A strict vegetarian diet is followed—as a penance, not because eating meat is considered wrong in itself—and extensive periods of fasting. The daily timetable set for the monks organises the use of every minute, and every aspect of their lives is carefully regulated by the one thousand eight hundred and two paragraphs of the Order's *Regulations*. These set out the prescribed behaviour for every likely occurrence in monastic life, holding at bay all unnecessary cares and disturbing influences so that neither anxiety nor insecurity can interfere with striving towards a state of constant union with God.

"Trappists are not unconcerned with the spreading of God's word, of course, but their Constitutions and Statutes forbid missionary activity. As Constitution 31 puts it, 'it is the contemplative life itself that is their way of participating in the mission of Christ and his Church'; therefore 'they cannot be called upon to render assistance in the various pastoral ministries or in any external activity, no matter how urgent the needs of the active apostolate'. But if the Trappist life is strictly a contemplative one, what was a branch of the Order doing landing on the south-eastern coast of Africa in 1878? Bishop Ricards of Port Elizabeth had decided that the silent example of the Trappists would succeed where conventional missionaries, Catholics and Protestants alike, had so remarkably failed in his Vicariate. Being Irish himself, he attempted without success to recruit Irish Trappists for his project, and it was the Austrian Franz Pfanner who finally brought a small band of monks to Dunbrody, the site Ricards had chosen for them. To this day, both the monks and nuns associated with

Mariannhill are almost exclusively of Austrian or east European extraction, and so while Sister Bridget's Irishness—emphasised by her religious name's heavy Irish associations—would have warmed Bishop Ricard's heart, it is a distinct anachronism within the context of Mariannhill.

"In any event, Pfanner fell out repeatedly with Ricards, and left the Eastern Cape in 1880 to found Mariannhill in Natal. Various accounts are given for the choice of this name, ranging from the Cistercian tradition of dedicating their monasteries to Mary to the fact that by a strange coincidence Maria Anna had been the name of both Pfanner's mother, who died in childbirth, and his beloved stepmother. To this we may add that Pfanner had been a deeply controversial figure at Maria Wald, the monastery near Cologne where he had become a Trappist, and he spent increasing amounts of time alone outside the cloister in the hills that sheltered the monastery—the Marianne Hills. His choice of name then for his new foundation was intended, I believe, to express something of his own peculiar take on the strict observances of the Trappists, and any alteration to that name risks missing this point.

"At first his monastery flourished, with its farms, roads, and buildings soon taking on the features of a small town. We should note that the complex did not include a hospital as such, however, as Franz was a staunch follower of the water cures popular in Germany and would have nothing to do with 'English doctors ... and alopathy with expensive and poisonous medicines' (Roos 1983:70).

"In 1885 Mariannhill was elevated to the status of an Abbey (with Pfanner as its first Abbot), and by 1887 its success was such that it 'had become numerically the largest abbey in the world' (Brain 1975:173). This numerical success was, however, a result of the monks being drawn ever-increasingly into the active apostolate. It began with their giving in to requests by native chiefs for schools for their children (occasionally allowed within the Trappist Order), and soon developed into wholesale missionary work. Even though Pfanner tried to keep within the spirit of the Cistercian Order by avoiding hasty evangelism in favour of the natives coming of their own accord to the impressive monastic estates, the contemplative life was under serious threat at Mariannhill.

"This was not helped by Pfanner's taking to the medium of print in order, initially, to win support and alms for his work. His letters and articles were soon a regular feature in even the secular press of Natal, so much so that one editorial in the *Natal Mercury* began, 'The Abbot of Mariannhill, though a devout Trappist, cannot be said to exemplify the rule of silence imposed upon the brethren of his Order. In the Press, at any rate, he is one of the most communicative of men. He is ready at all times for a joust in the arena of controversy' (September 19, 1889).

"Pfanner's work expanded along with his reputation. A vast network of stations was developed, stretching up to the Drakensberg and then around the southern tip of the colony of Natal and into East Griqualand. In order for these stations to operate as missions, however, more and more dispensations from the Rule of St Benedict and the Regulations of the Order had to be given. As one of the more astute historians of Mariannhill puts it,

> Solitude and withdrawal from the world are opposed to the needs of a missionary. A missionary locked up in his enclosure cannot fulfil his duties even though he may pray and sing psalms all day long. A missionary must go out. The task imposed upon him by his Master is to teach, to baptise, and to go after erring sheep. Silence falls away by itself. (Roos 1983:11)

"Such activity caused tension and hostility between those monks who wished to remain within the 'regular' religious life of a Trappist and those who had given themselves over to the freer life of the missionary. One way in which Pfanner attempted to alleviate this was by asking for an Order of Sisters who could take over most of the active mission work. When this was refused, he formed his own association of women helpers. He organised them along lines so close to those of a religious Congregation that it was not long before they were formally accepted as such. And so the Sisters of the Precious Blood—Coetzee's 'Sisters of the Marion Order'—came into being. In their fictionalisation, however, what is lost is the desperate fight Pfanner had to put up to prevent them being turned into Trappestines, as limited in their access to missionary work as his own monks were meant to be. The addition of the word 'Missionary' to their name when they became an independent congregation in 1906 is a direct result of this struggle.[6]

"The conflict between contemplatives and missionaries was brought to a head during the Canonical Visitation of 1892. The report of the Visitator led ultimately to Pfanner's deposition. He retired to one of the most distant of the stations he had established (although he never ceased to involve himself in the affairs of Mariannhill, even under the most severe proscriptions) and years of unsuccessful attempts by a number of other Abbots to combine the contemplative and apostolic ideals followed. Pfanner himself believed almost to the last that they could be combined— that to be a good missionary, in fact, one must be a good monk—but the monastery he founded was separated by decree from the Order of the Trappists in 1909 (the year of his death), and became, eventually, the Congregation of Mariannhill Missionaries.

"When, then, the text of 'The Humanities in Africa' refers to Sister Bridget as a 'medical *missionary*' and 'Marianhill' as a '*station*' (even in the heyday of the missions, Mariannhill was never a station but the motherhouse), these casual references suppress, however unintentionally, however much with another project altogether in mind, a whole series of micronarratives in the history of colonialism that could in themselves do much to unsettle the rapidly sedimenting grand narratives of decolonisation. And while Sister Bridget—or, more appropriately now, *Blanche*, as Elizabeth ever more insistently falls back on calling her—invokes what we are meant to see as a crucially flawed grand narrative for 'the humanities in Africa', it is rather alarming that the local, the specific, the *human* story that is meant to modify at least, if not counter in some binary way, her story, is not drawn from something closer to hand, something more material, more intimate for Mariannhill.

"Perhaps I am beginning to carp now, and I know I am not being fair at all to the project that *Elizabeth Costello* represents, but I do this out of respect for the welter of stories that tumble out of a situated, specific sense of Mariannhill. The absence of the giant figure—in all senses of that word—of Pfanner alone reduces the mission work of Mariannhill to a given of postcolonial historiography, blurring it into the tropes attendant upon Protestant mission activity which seem so to inform Sister Bridget's missionary attitudes and erasing even further the desperately under-researched Catholic—let alone Trappist—approaches to apostolic work in the colonies. Telling idiosyncrasies thus simply disappear. Even the hospital that Sister Bridget administers was only able to come into being (under the pressure of the 'Spanish Influenza' epidemic of 1918) once the influence of Pfanner's attitudes to medical treatment had begun to wane.

"And what of the celebrated A.T. Bryant, who came to South Africa to join the community of Mariannhill? Amongst the most fervent of the missionaries, he refused to complete his novitiate (this had been shortened so that he could work as a teacher and missionary) when ordered to do so by the Visitor. He left Mariannhill and offered himself as a Familiar to the Oblates on the Bluff, eventually being transferred to Zululand where he could indulge himself to the full in studying and writing about the Zulu 'before the white man came'. The lost irony of this pre-eminent spokesperson for the history and the language of the Zulus having begun his religious life as an observer of silence flattens out into a far more direct and brutal act of silencing when it is extended, as it should be, to include the story of Father Edward Muller Kece Mnganga. He was the first black priest—secular priest, note, and assistant priest only at that; no blacks were allowed to enter the monastery for many more years—to emerge from Mariannhill. After being trained and ordained in Rome, Mnganga was sent to join Bryant at Ebuhleni. Bryant's claims to a superior knowledge of the Zulu and constant interference with Mnganga's educational and mission work led to a physical altercation, the result of which was that Mnganga was placed in a government asylum in Pietermaritzburg. There he was quickly found not to be mentally deranged, but he refused to leave until the 'men who put him there'—the Bishop and Bryant—came to collect him. He was to wait for the next seventeen years.[7]

"And then there are the stories associated with Mariannhill that Coetzee does, briefly and obliquely, touch upon. The 'retired' and disabled sculptor, Joseph, whose endlessly and exactly repeated 'Gothic' images of Christ crucified become the focus of Elizabeth's argument with her sister over the proper models for African art and life, could have been modelled on any one of the black artists connected with the Studio of Liturgical Art set up by Sister Pientia Selhorst at Mariannhill in the early 1950s. (One of the sculptors there was in fact named Joseph, Joseph Dhlamini.) Features of 'Joseph's' work as presented by Coetzee, however, echo the work of the most famous of these artists, Ruben Xulu, although Xulu did go on both to vary his style and subject-matter, and to exhibit his carvings. He lived on various Catholic missions, visiting and working at Mariannhill quite regularly until, in 1985, his throat was slashed and his stomach ripped open by an unknown assailant who left him to bleed to death on the monastery grounds.

"Xulu had been, what is more, traumatised by some mysterious event when he was seven years old which resulted in the life-long loss of his hearing and impaired his ability to speak so he was unable even to cry out for help at the time of the attack[8]—figure enough, one would think, figure 'embedded' in the physical, the historical, for the suffering that Sister Bridget says the Zulus look for in '"their gospel, their Christ"' (2003:144).

"From the patronising heights of this reminder to Elizabeth, she goes on to pronounce that '"ordinary people do not want the Greeks. They do not want the realm of pure forms"' (144). Again, one is tempted to say, indeed: and what else but the most rarefied of forms is your sweep through the history of the humanities?

"This, in effect, is precisely what Elizabeth Costello goes on to do in the letter to Blanche that makes up much of Part IX of the version of 'The

Humanities in Africa' included in the novel (Part VI in the version published in *The Best Australian Stories 2002*). The 'story' (2004:148) she tells there of baring her breasts to the aged and ill Mr Phillips makes the point that, 'In all our talk about humanism and the humanities there was one word we both skirted: *humanity*' (150). Out of her realisation that the pose she has adopted in her modelling for his painting is derived *'From the* Greeks... from the Greeks and from what the generations of Renaissance painters made of the Greeks' (149) comes Elizabeth's rejoinder to her sister's last words to her on her South African visit: 'The humanities teach us humanity.... That is what you forgot to say. That is what the Greeks teach us, Blanche, the right Greeks. Think about it' (151).

It is this understanding that gives a much heavier ironic weight than is apparent at the time to the only response Elizabeth is capable of making as she parts from her sister: '"So: Thou hast triumphed again, O pale Galilean"' (2003:145). This irony (not given anything like its full dimensions in the version of 'The Humanities in Africa' that does not include the Australian section) entirely undercuts any sense of Sister Bridget having, as Attwell and others would have it, the 'last word'[9]—so much so that we are also made aware just how much Sister Bridget, despite the undoubted forcefulness of character granted to her, joins the rather thin and limited array of interlocutors set up to keep in play, technically at least, the various positions adopted by Costello in the different Lessons. Too perfunctory to perform this function in a serious fictional sense, they all take on some of the unconvincing character of Sister Bridget's wave.

"To suggest that it would have been more appropriate to look for a response in the physical, historical 'embeddedness' of Ruben Xulu, say— one silenced artist speaking, as it were, to another, as Mr Phillips's laryngectomy calls up through sheer contingency Xulu's vocal impairment and its place in the violence of his end—is to force the point beyond any reasonable application. But the lingering nature of this entirely accidental conjuncture between the local archive and the fictional project does bring home the degree to which it is left to Costello *herself* to convince us of the positions she adopts in the 'Lessons', rather than Costello as a character engaging meaningfully (not so much in the 'realistic' sense set up for dismissal from the first, but in an 'embedded' way) with other characters or the particular settings the novel invokes.

"And so we must turn our attention from Sister Bridget's last word and its supporting gesture to the position taken by Elizabeth in this Lesson. Is this, we must ask, more compelling when it comes to the issue of the nature and status of the Humanities in Africa?

"In attempting to answer this, we must acknowledge that the rather neat rejoinder in Elizabeth's letter is, quite properly, not the end of the story. It is troubled further by 'what she does not write, what she has no intention of writing', that is, 'how the story proceeds' (2004:151). The more overt conjunction of death and sexuality that follows her posing for Mr Phillips carries Elizabeth from humanity to *eros, agape*, even *caritas*, but these too are left hanging as questions as she passes beyond any neat conclusion at all to the question of why she cannot write of this incident, and the question behind that:

> *Blanche, dear Blanche*, she thinks, *why is there this bar between us? Why can we not speak to each other straight and bare, as people ought who are on the brink of passing? ... Sister of my youth, do not die in a foreign field and leave me without an answer!* (155)

"The end of the story, then, and the conclusion to 'Lesson 5: The Humanities in Africa', is a question, not so much an open question as an unanswered question. Left to thought, un-communicated, the question takes us beyond the Humanities, Africa, the Humanities in Africa, the Humanities in Australia too, for that matter; it directs us instead to the concluding Lesson (beyond which hovers, of course, a 'Postscript'), 'Lesson 8: At the Gate'.

"In this Lesson Elizabeth puts her primary conviction as a writer, the conviction—belief, if you will—that, as a writer, it 'is not her profession to believe, just to write' (2003:194). This (turning as it does on her argument regarding the frogs of the Dulgannon which we have touched upon already) we may be prepared to grant her—on the condition that she truly does *not* believe, truly *'maintain[s] beliefs only provisionally'* (195). What we cannot allow the author is carrying the game by a kind of self-emptying or (to stay with the Greeks) what Terry Eagleton called, when writing so long ago of some forms of deconstruction, *kenosis*: achieving victory, that is, by being the first to get rid of all one's cards and sitting with empty hands (1983:147).

"With this proviso in mind, let us take Coetzee too at face value—remembering how 'truth' is problematised in autobiography no less than (secular) confession by the double-bind of questions of self-deception and the problem of closure (1992:252)—when he says, 'my difficulty is precisely with the project of stating positions, taking positions' (205). Let us take seriously the formal devices by which he seeks to achieve, as he sees Erasmus doing in *The Praise of Folly*, 'a position not simply impartial between ... rivals but also, by self-definition, off the stage of rivalry altogether, a *nonposition*' (1996:84, his emphasis).

"In order to do so we must follow, as Coetzee does, the direction Foucault is forced to take in the face of Derrida's challenges to his 'archaeology of silence' in *Madness and Civilization* (1967:x). In response to Derrida's observation that the discourse of an archaeology of madness can only belong to reason, just as its investigation is dependent upon the very judicial record that denounces madness, Foucault concedes that 'the philosopher trying to enter madness *inside* of thought can do so only as a fictional project'. As to the next question, 'would such a fiction lie inside of philosophy?' (1996:87), we must surely follow, as does Coetzee in his essay, 'Erasmus: Madness and Rivalry', Shoshana Felman when she states,

> in the play of forces underlying the relationship between philosophy and fiction, literature and madness, the crucial problem is that of the subject's place, of his position with respect to the delusion. And the position of the subject is not defined by what he says, nor by what he talks about, but by the place—unknown to him—from which he speaks. (1985:50; cited in Coetzee 1996:87)

"The implication here—no, the *demand*—is, that the strategy of fiction in such a project truly undermines any sense of the place or position of its author; in short, that there is something excessive to it beyond any neat critical formulation that may explain it as a strategy, anymore than the place—or, rather, *nonplace*[10]—from which it is generated may be explained from somewhere outside, beyond that place.

"Any suspicion—and I believe it is this suspicion that lies behind the more sceptical responses to both Coetzee's fictionalised 'autobiographies' and *Elizabeth Costello*—that this nonpositioning is too canny, too sure of its own uncertainty, undercuts the whole enterprise.

"It is this suspicion that informs Peter Singer's contribution to the 'Reflections' included in *The Lives of Animals*. The animal-rights philosopher concludes a fictionally re-created exchange with his daughter regarding the weakness of many of Coetzee's arguments with the words,

> 'But *are* they Coetzee's arguments? That's just the point – that's why I don't know how to go about responding to this so-called lecture. They are *Costello*'s arguments. Coetzee's fictional device enables him to distance himself from them. And he has this character, Norma, Costello's daughter-in-law, who makes all the obvious objections to what Coetzee is saying. It's a marvellous device, really. Costello can blithely criticize

the use of reason, or the need to have any clear principles or proscriptions, without Coetzee really committing himself to these claims. Maybe he really shares Norma's very proper doubts about them. Coetzee doesn't even have to worry too much about getting the structure of the lecture right. When he notices that it is starting to ramble, he just has Norma say that Costello is rambling.' (1999:91)

"To this his daughter replies: '"Pretty tricky. Not an easy thing to reply to. But why don't you try the same trick in response?"'. It is largely Singer's lack of skill as a writer of fiction that prevents us from entering the truly vertiginous zones of Coetzee when he in turn responds, '*Me?* When have I ever written fiction?' The device is too obvious and not nearly well turned enough as a closing strategy to keep the game in play.

"But it does prepare us for the final move necessary for this presentation. This is to say that the issue is really not how Coetzee is positioned in relation to these texts, but how the reader is positioned by them. I have tried to speak to an instant in *Elizabeth Costello* when at least one small, highly circumscribed group of readers is disqualified from participating in the text's negotiations with its referents, and I have tried to suggest possible stories emanating from the historicity of Coetzee's imagined setting in 'The Humanities in Africa' that would, in another, hypothetical, fictional project, give back the kind of discursive materiality lost in that instant.

"I have done this, I repeat, not as a referential corrective of some sort, or as an exercise in historicism, materialism, or any of their varied combinations, but with a view to testing the effects of a particular kind of fictional approach against a specific sense of audience. I take Attwell's point when, commenting on the kind of 'embeddedness' Costello has in mind in her reference to 'Kafka's ape', he writes,

> Costello shifts attention here from the relation between the word and the world—the traditional emphasis in debates about reference—to the relation between the self and the word. She argues, in effect, that while we may have given up on realism's illusionism, this does not mean the end of desire. She argues that we are invested in the acts of apprehension which carry that desire and connect us to the being of others. Costello—and at this point, I would argue, we could add Coetzee—shifts the debate about reference from the heuristic and phenomenological to the ontological and ethical. (2002:20),

but I am left to wonder about both the ontology and the ethics of a mode of writing that excludes, at a particular moment, the investment of a specific section of the community of its readership.

"As for the 'fictional project' behind that reference (understood now as an 'investment in an act of apprehension', a 'desire that connects us') – well, upon what grounds other than those of fictionalising oneself into being does a reader ever engage with... a text, I nearly said. Yet surely the heartfelt centre of *Elizabeth Costello* is to remind us that a sympathetic imagining—'embodiment', fullness, the sensation of being—is necessary for, vital to, the understanding of panthers, sheep, and frogs, and every sort of otherness. Every sort of otherness including, as Sister Bridget's wave does not, the actual life erupting in those hills, so far from being barren, surrounding Mariannhill. For it is the richness and complexity of that life, finally, that counters the grand generalisations of her gesture rather than the more-or-less pat individualised response (all the more pat for remaining within her sister's terms) that Elizabeth belatededly includes in her letter. More importantly, it is that life—that life that 'exists whether or not I tell you about [it], whether or not I believe in [it]'—that sustains Elizabeth's much more heart-felt nonpositioning, that gives her 'the place—unknown to [her]—from which [she] speaks.'

"As for that most tenuous of lines intersecting this place, that line between speaking of and for so deftly dealt with throughout Coetzee's oeuvre, well, that is another question for another occasion. For the moment we can leave it, I think, to the form it took in the history of Mariannhill—with its past restored through the recovery of its 'n'—which, oddly enough, echoes Elizabeth Costello's difficulties with the writing of the consistently silent Paul West. The Trappists, writes Father Francis Schimlek of the Congregation of Mariannhill Missionaries, 'with St Paul, maintained that in a pagan community things were happening of which a good Christian best know nothing, speak nothing, and still less have them printed on paper for everybody to read.... Let the dead bury their dead, and be done with this problem. *Vanitas vanitatum*—"Our duty is to preach the Gospel of Christ," they said, "and not to investigate the convictions and practices of witchdoctors and their followers. It is hard enough as it is"' (1950:11-12).

"Hard enough, indeed. Still, to such, be they contemplative monks in their closed community lost in prayer for the world outside or writers at their desks struggling to find the appropriate form for the one specific, indifferent detail in which they can believe, precisely because it does not believe in them, let us commend the hills of Mariannhill.

"Thank you."

146 Michael Green

Notes

1. Primarily to remind us, I suppose, that the author is one of the key effects generated by his or her fiction.
2. Paul Rich is not alone in identifying "a partial restoration to the romance mode through the idiom of literary post-modernism" (1984:133), although he is amongst the very few to have traced this romantic strain in South African fiction—the critical evaluation of which certainly has been, as he puts it, "mainly dictated by the norms of literary realism" (1984:120).
3. Jane Poyner (2003), for example—the only other critic I have read so far to have noticed the change of spelling—is only prepared to allow that "Coetzee (perhaps deliberately) misspells Mariannhill".
4. St Mary's Hospital Website: http://www.stmarys.co.za/
5. Information obtained in an interview with Sister Regina Bachmann in November 2004.
6. See Sr. M. Annette Buschgerd, *For A Great Price: The Story of the Missionary Sisters of the Precious Blood* (Reimlingen: Mariannhill Mission Press, 1990).
7. All the official histories of Mariannhill circumvent Mnganga's story in one way or another. Something approaching the full account only emerges from the oral sources used by George Sombe Mukuka for his D.Phil. dissertation, "The Establishment of the Black Catholic Clergy in South Africa from 1887 to 1957". See pp.142-64 and Appendices.
8. See Cormick (1993:11-21).
9. See Attwell (2002:23). This paper was first presented in the same year that *The Best Australian Stories* was released, a year before *Elizabeth Costello* was published; Attwell would thus have been working with the version published in *The Humanities in Africa/ Die Geisteswissenschaften in Afrika*. Anton van der Hoven's reading—"Coetzee chooses to end the story with Sister Bridget pointedly, even obsessively, hammering home her belief that her sister Elizabeth is mistaken" (2003:95)—is cut short in much the same way, if to different effect.
10. Not to be blurred into a Utopian position.

References

Appiah, Kwame Anthony and Henry Louis Gates (eds). 1996. *Identities.* Chicago: University of Chicago Press.

Attwell, David. 1993. *J.M. Coetzee: South Africa and the Politics of Writing.* Cape Town: David Philip.

_____. 2002. "The Life and Times of Elizabeth Costello: J.M. Coetzee and the Public Sphere." Conference: J.M. Coetzee and the Ethics of Intellectual

Practice, 26-27 April. University of Warwick.

Brain, J.B. 1975. *Catholic Beginnings in Natal and Beyond*. Durban: T.W. Griggs & Co.

_____. 1982. *Catholics in Natal II: 1886-1925*. Durban: Archdiocese of Durban.

Brown, William Eric. 1960. *The Catholic Church in South Africa: From its Origins to the Present Day*. London: Burns and Oates.

Coetzee, J.M. 1988. "The Novel Today." *Upstream* 6(1):2-5.

_____. 1993. *Doubling the Point: Essays and Interviews*. Cambridge: Harvard University Press.

_____. 1996. *Giving Offense: Essays on Censorship*. Chicago and London: The University of Chicago Press.

_____. 1999. *The Lives of Animals*. The Tanner Lectures. Princeton: Princeton University Press.

_____. 2001. *The Humanities in Africa/Die Geisteswissenschaften in Afrika*. Munich: Carl Friedrich von Siemens Stiftung.

_____. 2002. "The Humanities in Africa." In: Peter Craven (ed.), *The Best Australian Stories 2002*. Melbourne: Black Inc., 101-19.

_____. 2003. *Elizabeth Costello*. London: Secker and Warburg.

_____. 2004. "As a Woman Grows Older." *The New York Review of Books* 51(1):15.

1990. Constitutions and Statutes of the Monks of the Cistercian Order of the Strict Observance. Rome: Cistercian Order of the Strict Observance.

Cormick, Dina. 1993. *Bernard Gcwensa and Ruben Xulu: Christian Artists of Natal*. Pretoria: Academia.

Derrida, Jacques. 1978. "Cogito and the History of Madness." In: *Writing and Difference*. Trans. Alan Bass. Chicago: University of Chicago Press.

Dischl, Fr. Marcel CMM. 1982. *Transkei for Christ: A History of the Catholic Church in the Transkeian Territories*. Mariannhill: Mariannhill Mission Press.

Eagleton, Terry. 1983. *Literary Theory: An Introduction*. Oxford: Blackwell.

Gamble, Helen. 1982. *Mariannhill: A Century of Prayer and Work*. Mariannhill: Mariannhill Mission Press.

Felman, Shoshana. 1985. *Writing and Madness*. Trans. Martha N. Evans and Shoshana Felman. Ithaca, N.Y.: Cornell University Press.

Foucault, Michel. 1967. *Madness and Civilization*. Trans. Richard Howard. New York: Random House.

Hawthorne, Nathaniel. 1851. *The House of the Seven Gables: A Romance*. Boston: Ticknor, Reed, and Fields.

Jeyifo, Biodun. 1990. "For Chinua Achebe: The Resilience of Obierika." In: Kirstin Holst Petersen and Anna Rutherford (eds). *Chinua Achebe: A Celebration*. Oxford and Plymouth, NH: Heinemann and Dangaroo: 51-70.

Lenta, Margaret. 2003. "Reading Australia." *The Sunday Independent* (9 March).

Mars-Jones, Adam. 2003. Review of *Elizabeth Costello*. *The Observer* (14 September).

Merton, Thomas. 1962 [1949]. *The Waters of Siloe*. New York: Image Books.

Mukuka, George Sombe. 2000. "The Establishment of the Black Catholic Clergy in South Africa from 1887 to 1957." University of Natal, Pietermaritzburg. Unpublished D.Phil. thesis.

Poyner, Jane. 2003. "'The Lives of J.M. Coetzee': Writer/Critic/Citizen?" *Law, Social Justice & Global Development Journal* 2003(2). <http://elj.warwick.ac.uk/global/issue/2003-2/poyner.html>

Rich, Paul. 1984. "Romance and the Development of the South African Novel." In: Landeg White and Tim Couzens (eds). *Literature and Society in South Africa*. Cape Town: Maskew Miller Longman: 120-37.

Roos, Fr. Anton. 1983 [1961]. *Mariannhill: Between Two Ideals*. Trans. Sr. M. Adelgisa Herrmann. Mariannhill: Mariannhill Mission Press.

Schimlek, Francis. 1950. *Medicine Versus Witchcraft*. Mariannhill: Mariannhill Mission Press.

Singer, Peter. 1999. "Reflections." In: *J.M. Coetzee: The Lives of Animals*. Edited by Amy Gutman. Princeton: Princeton University Press: 85-91.

Van der Hoven, Anton. 2003. "The Triumph of Method: J.M. Coetzee, the Humanities, South Africa." *Pretexts: Literary and Cultural Studies* 12(1):85-96.

"Which World? Whose World?"

Postcolonialising Gordimer

Ileana Dimitriu

As a writer and public intellectual, Nadine Gordimer—for over four decades—responded comprehensively to the South African social context, while critics and readers alike acknowledged her as an uncompromising anti-apartheid spokesperson. In the early 1990s, after the demise of institutional apartheid, there was uncertainty as to what the position of this writer would be under the new dispensation. Would her preoccupations in her fiction retain interest and significance? Would her work be of less relevance in a society seeking to return to the challenges of civil life? In her first two 'post-apartheid' novels—*None to Accompany Me* (1994) and *The House Gun* (1998)—Gordimer remained preoccupied with the South African scene, albeit in a more variegated way. Along with other critics, I have noted Gordimer's post-1990 engagement with the concept of the civil imaginary and her new concerns with the private life as more independent of, and not inextricably linked to, the public domain (Dimitriu 2000; 2001). These new tendencies can be seen, in retrospect, to signal a kind of liberation from the burden of excessive social responsibility within large historical events.

Gordimer's two more recent two works of fiction—the novel, *The Pickup* (2001), and the short-story collection, *Loot* (2003)—suggest a shift of emphasis in her writing. She seems to have renounced her exclusive focus on South Africa which, in the past, she considered to have been "*the* example, the epitome of cultural isolation"(1999:212). Now that writers feel less moral pressure to engage with a repressive social context, she is keen to offer literary replies to an important question: "How, in national specificity, does each country go about moving *beyond* itself, to procreate a culture that will benefit self and others?" It is a question to which she attempts to give an answer in the tellingly titled essay, "Living on a Frontierless Land: Cultural Globalization" (1999:212), an essay which presents a new aspect of Gordimer's writerly profile. What are new are her excursions beyond the national question: her aspiration to step beyond cultural isolation and enter a larger, 'post-ideological' world scene.

The important point is that in seeking to extend her compass beyond South Africa, Gordimer avoids what might be a temptation for the writer who turns from the peripheries of the ex-colony or postcolony—that is to turn, or return, to the imaginative and literary circles of the northern hemisphere, where reputations continue to reside or be made. Gordimer has, after all, the status of a Nobel Prize winner. She has also, throughout her career, embraced not only the politics of writing, but also her artistic debt to the great European tradition of thought and fiction. It is to her credit, therefore, that she seeks—in her latest essays and fiction—to look at, and beyond, South Africa in ways newly pertinent to a post-apartheid dispensation. She takes an interest in what I term here "significant peripheries", by which I mean that Gordimer looks beyond the local to cognate socio-cultural paradigms at other margins of the world. She does not focus on centres or metropoles, a drive which might have been a legitimate compensation given her past over-investment in the local scene. Rather, she seeks to show that there are no clear boundaries between metropoles and margins, and that it is necessary to adjust global interests to a series of intersecting margins. Gordimer conceptualises 'margins and centres' as global networks of many margins in diverse locations, including the 'margins-in-centres'. In this way, she aligns herself with recent postcolonial re-thinking of peripheries, that is, peripheries in relation to one another, as illustrated by Ania Loomba's comments on new models for describing the relationship between national and transnational forces:

> ... While we cannot gloss over the real differences between our various locations across the globe, and between the histories and realities we analyze, it is equally *important to forge connections between the differently positioned subjects of the new empire ['world order']* ... *reconciling the demands of local archives and conditions with broader paradigms* of colonial and postcolonial history. (2005:14, 28, my emphases)

Such a perception of significant peripheries is mostly implied, but at times explicitly defined, in Gordimer's recent commentaries. I shall start, therefore, by pointing to new tendencies in her critical thinking, as reflected in her latest collection of essays, *Living in Hope and History: Notes from Our Century* (1999). In comparison with the tone of the previous essay collections, which focused on South African literary and social stringencies, the latest collection signals Gordimer's need to rejoin the world, both as cultural commentator and literary artist. In the essay, "Our Century", for example, she reflects on humanity's technological, political and cultural achievements and failures in the last hundred years. Her focus is on complex networks of cultures, so that when she talks about South Africa, she does so in terms of world-force intersections and exchanges. Aware that the destiny of no country is free of sweeping tendencies worldwide, she explores the dimensions of "living on a frontierless land", and how this inescapable condition affects one's relationship with one's home base. She is a proponent of what Nederveen Pieterse calls "critical globalism" (1995), a process which she neither endorses nor dismisses. While she ponders her own understanding of 'glocalization' in political and economic terms—as in the essay "The Frontierless Land: Cultural Globalization" (as mentioned above)—she does so in order to gauge useful analogies for the globalisation of culture. She talks, for example, of "the ethics of mutual enrichment" in "the expansion of ideas" by drawing an analogy with the trade-exchange-rate. She is aware of the danger of any new orthodoxy in artistic expression worldwide, of 'universal' blandness and 'market-realism', and suggests that a writer's/artist's "aim [is] *to value the differences*, bring them into play across aesthetic frontiers and thus disprove the long-held sovereignty of national and political divisions over the development of human potential" (1999: 209). She envisages the play of artistic differences as circular and receptive of change.

Gordimer's ideas of cultural globalisation are pursued in the essay, "The Status of the Writer in the World Today: Which World? Whose World?" She insists here on the need for writers' vigilance against any political rationalisation or intimidation meant to corrupt their 'search for truth', even when derived from African inspirations. Negritude, for example, is regarded as an anachronism; it has exhausted its necessary initial momentum, while Mbeki's African renaissance should not be accepted as an essentialist veneration of the past, but rather as an invitation to be receptive to a larger world:

> The nurture of our writers, our literature, is a priority which should *not create for us a closed-shop African 'world literature', a cultural exclusivity, even post-colonial*, that has kept us in an ante-room of self-styled 'world literatures'. Let our chosen status in the world be that of writers who *seek exchanges of the creative imagination,* ways of thinking and writing, of fulfilling the role of repository of people's ethos, by opening it out,

> bringing to it a *vital mixture of individuals and peoples re-creating themselves.* (1999:28, my emphases)

This is a bold 'post-apartheid/ post-Cold War' voice. Gordimer states her artistic right to freedom of expression, her voice vigilant against any form of intimidation or censorship—whether old or new—including current tendencies in mainstream political circles to impose new kinds of social and cultural conformity. On an earlier occasion, when addressing the Pan African Writers Association in 1997, she said:

> So we have lost that status of what one might call national engagement. ... And I ask myself and you: Do we writers seek, need that nature of status, the writer as politician, statesperson? Is it not thrust upon us, as a patriotic duty outside the particular gifts that we have to offer? ... As the cultural arm of liberation struggles, we met the demands of our time in that era. That was our national status. We have yet to be recognized with a status commensurate with respect for the primacy of the well-earned role of *writer-as-writer* in the post-colonial era. (1999:22)

Here Gordimer again stresses the need—after apartheid in South Africa, after independence in the rest of Africa—for writers to resist any political agendas that might infringe upon their freedom of expression. She suggests that there is no need to fear the various cultural intersections, exchanges and networks; no need to fear mixing with foreign cultures, as "all civilisations—including China and Japan—have been the result of intersections and clashes". And, quoting the Congolese writer, Henri Lopès, she foregrounds "'the interchange of ideas, of solutions to a common existence [for] every civilisation is born of a forgotten mixture, every race is a variety of mixtures that is ignored'" (1999:28).

Gordimer also encourages conversations among African writers, as well as between African and South American writers, the latter of whose writings—because of recognisable societal challenges in racially mixed and economically unequal societies—might offer valuable comparative perspectives. She is careful, nevertheless, to point out that the revival of social and artistic confidence among post-independent writers should not exclude

> our freedom of access to, and appropriation of, European and North American literary culture. I believe we have passed the stage, in the majority of our countries, of finding Shakespeare and Dostoevsky, Voltaire and Melville, 'irrelevant'. I believe that, as writers and readers, all literature, of whatever origin, *belongs* to us. There *is* an acceptable

'world literature' in this sense; one great library to which it would be a folly of self-deprivation to throw away our membership cards. (1999:26)

In some ways, Gordimer has always had an interest in a concept of world literature. She has always acknowledged the influence of the great classics on her writing. A change of emphasis is apparent, however, in the last decade. Inspired by Edward Said's work in the early 1990s, now Gordimer confesses to

> placing a new concept of 'world literature' alongside the one I had posited with my eyes fixed on Euro-North America as the literary navel-of-the-world. In the all-encompassing sense of the term 'world', can any of our literatures be claimed definitively as 'world' literature? Which world? Whose world? (1999:18)

The point is that there are different perspectives on the world, which derive from different positions, localities and contexts. These perspectives are—in the words of Vilashini Cooppan—"locally inflected and globally mobile" (2001:33); or, to borrow a phrase from Vinay Dharwadker, "a montage of overlapping maps in motion" (2001:3). In other words, world literature is never a bland, sanitised concept; rather it is one anchored in complex 'localised' circumstances. The notion of 'localised cosmopolitanism', as advocated by Bruce Robbins, is a useful conceptual tool for our discussion:

> No one is or ever can be a cosmopolitan in the sense of belonging nowhere ... .The interest of the term cosmopolitanism is located, then, not in its full theoretical extension, where it becomes a paranoid fantasy of ubiquity and omniscience, but rather (paradoxically) in its local applications. (1998:260)

Far from being a rootless cosmopolitan, Gordimer—for all her global aspirations and achievements—is multiply linked to events both at home and abroad; indeed, as anti-apartheid spokesperson for most of her literary career, she appealed to audiences both local and international. She has continued to do so, while in her more recent works—which I mentioned above, as well as in the aims of her anthology of international short stories, *Telling Tales* (2004)—she has occupied increasingly multiple positions in relation to the concepts 'home' and 'abroad'.

What I am suggesting is that Gordimer is an established figure in world literature, but on her own terms. Just as she remains vigilant concerning new post-independence impositions locally, so she refuses to subscribe to a totalising cultural globalism. Hers is an aspiration to hold a "membership card" of world literature, 'postcolonialising style'. This apparently paradoxical tendency has become increasingly pronounced in the last few years. With the moral pressure eased for an exclusive focus on things South African, Gordimer uses her newly-found artistic freedom not to turn to any bland universalism, but to enter more fully into the circuit of significant postcolonial peripheries, beyond her locality. The subtitle of my article, "Postcolonialising Gordimer", therefore, is deliberately ambiguous. On the one hand, it follows the train of thought in Gordimer's recent critical essays, to suggest new emphases in the author's literary preoccupations: she looks *beyond* the local to various significant margins that are reminiscent of home-as-margin. On the other hand, the subtitle suggests a need to analyse Gordimer *through* postcolonial interpretative lenses.

The issue of 'Gordimer and postcolonialism' needs initial clarification. Let me start by asking: is what I am suggesting nothing more than that Gordimer has absorbed—in a somewhat impressionistic way—what in literary criticism is already in danger of becoming a new orthodoxy: 'postcolonialism'? In the past, Gordimer was seen as either a localised literary activist (anti-apartheid spokesperson) or—in the tradition of European realism—as a world writer (Nobel prize winner). The difficulty of linking Gordimer to postcolonialism lies partly in the configuration of the term postcolonialism itself, which continues to be an eclectic critical practice and, therefore, difficult to define. The term may refer to a systematic preoccupation with the *concrete experience* of colonialism and its effects on contemporary society, both in the ex-colonies and in global developments that impact on the grim economic realities of postcolonial societies. But postcolonialism also involves *speech acts* that connect material conditions to discursive identifications of race/identity, place/dislocation, migration/exile, hybridity/liminality, centre/margin, etc. There is a tension, then, between *postcolonial practice* (and the activism it invokes) and *postcolonial theory* or the engagement with concrete experience via the analyses of texts.

It is this type of tension between concrete particulars and rhetorical enunciations that prompts a critic like Ato Quayson to try to avoid any binary separation of *theory* and *practice,* and perceive postcolonialism instead as *process*. The term has the advantage of removing 'postcolonialism' from the chronological implication of 'after colonialism', where the prefix suggests that the colonial inheritance has been superseded by another set of circumstances. As Quayson says:

It is important to highlight instead a notion of coming-into-being. ... My aim is to give a steady methodological grounding to what I describe as *postcolonialising discourse*. Though deriving essentially from postcolonial theory, *postcolonialising is meant to suggest creative ways of viewing* a variety of cultural, political and social realities, both in the West and elsewhere, *via a postcolonial prism of interpretation*. (2000:11,21, my emphases)

To see postcolonialism as a process of "coming-into-being", rather than as a measurably objective social reality unfolding according to chronological markers, suggests the critic's willingness to explore the phenomenon in its complex intertwining with global—both social and cultural—tendencies: "the emphasis is on looking awry at ... the dominant modalities of analysing particular social issues" (Quayson 2000:21). The important shift here is to grant the interpreter an active role in the making of a postcolonial field of understanding. We receive—a reception aesthetic is involved—various conditions or expressions as postcolonial, as an ongoing process of shaping a global dimension. Thus, centres are seen to have within them their own peripheries; by the same token, peripheries may be more or less significant, depending on how one focuses the interpretative lens.

In fact, attempts to locate postcolonialism as a continuing process—as a condition and concept of continuing relevance in a globalising world—characterise several recent debates. Peter Childs and Patrick Williams, for example, go so far as to point to a reality beyond current postcolonialism, to '*post*-postcolonialism': a future that is embedded in contemporary postcolonialising processes of coming-into-being and of struggle against the current legacy of colonialism. It is an intimation only, an "anticipatory discourse" of things to come, prompting in the critic the need to "recognize that the [post-post-] condition which it names does not yet exist, but work nevertheless to bring it about" (1997:7). Or, to put it differently, it is important to augment one's analysis of the past with "the rapidly mutating present, thus, in a sense, trying to anticipate the future" (Loomba 2005: 14). Although this critical stance is still in its incipience, it already offers a useful insight into the need to focus on the interpretative 'process' rather than on any binarism, whether of 'practice' *vs* 'theory', or of postcolonial 'materiality' *vs* its 'linguistic' turn.

The change to process-based enquiry also implies a shifting away from limits of postcolonialism as past-oriented field (with the prefix 'post' referring either to 'after independence' or to 'after colonialism began'). Instead, we are pointed to the future, and beyond the usual contradictions.

Seeing postcolonialism as 'process of postcolonialising' means engaging with it epistemologically, that is, by focusing on the significant issues integral to the formation of the global world order after colonialism. In this way, postcolonial issues become the "critical strain posed within and against, as well as antecedent to, dominant notions of globalization ... [becoming] the historical conscience—and consciousness—of the very discourse of globalization" (Loomba 2005:14,15). Last but not least, postcolonialism seen as on-going process means reaching beyond one's locality and expressing "the desire to perceive cognate or parallel realities within seemingly disparate contexts [while drawing] on a notion of the centrality of colonialism for understanding the formation of the contemporary world" (Quayson 2000:10).

This returns me to the title of my essay. As I have mentioned, the ambiguity in the title indicates not only an attempt to analyse Gordimer through a postcolonial prism of interpretation, but also a new emphasis in Gordimer's literary preoccupations: her "looking *awry*" (to echo Žižek, 1991)—beyond the local, in pursuit of cognate social paradigms—at new edges and significant peripheries elsewhere. It is a tendency, to reiterate further, that does not suggest an escapist drive, but an exploration of the locality (South Africa) in relation to multiple networks of, and intersections with, other margins of the world, whether 'third-world-margins' or 'margins-in-centres'.

* * *

The shift is particularly noticeable in Gordimer's *The Pickup* (2001), her first novel to imbue the locality with significant global resonance. The novel unfolds in two locations, in South Africa and North Africa, while both these 'peripheries' are qualified by global allure and constraint: it is in the US, for example, that the migrant character Abdu hopes finally to seek his destiny; it is to her mother's US connections that Julie turns to secure Abdu his precious identity card. All this is symbolic of the fact that South Africa has emerged from its isolation to seek a role on the African continent. Gordimer presents South Africa today as both a microcosm of world forces and a country collectively seeking a better understanding of itself. By placing part of the action in North Africa, she offers a skilful way of exploring new post-apartheid issues at home through a 'distant reading' of the local, particularly of the politics of identity and belonging, or—as I have just suggested—home and exile, or emigration and immigration.

This short novel represents an abrupt juxtaposition of what may strike one as two novels in one. It could have been two separate short stories: the one dealing with the dreams and realities of illegal immigration, the other dealing with the dreams and realities of escape against the background of an unnamed desert country, indeed the desert itself. Having been expelled from his first imagined mecca (South Africa), Abdu, the 'illegal', seeks another destination, whereas Julie, his South African wife, finds contentment in an unnamed North African state, Abdu's home country. There is no apparent reason why Gordimer should remove the protagonists from the familiar South African setting. Is it to suggest Julie's avoidance of the challenging transformation in her own country, including the need to 'transform' relationships with her white, conservative parents? Is the novel a parable: the result of the author's unease in dealing with local circumstances? Or is it—as suggested by Sue Kossew (2003)—a commentary on globalism and its 'asymmetrical' opportunities of access to the so-called First World?

Gordimer presents the reader with the impact of liminality and exile on one's sense of identity and belonging, on one's relationships. The novel is about conditions of dislocation in post-ideological times: it is an exploration of how immigration, as well as emigration, affects the sense of self in human interaction. As Gordimer said in an interview (Kossew 2001:55-61), she has been preoccupied with the new, post-apartheid phenomenon of illegal immigration to her country, and the reactions of resentment and xenophobia that it usually provokes. Gordimer reveals Abdu's psychological turmoil and internal contestation of the presupposed monolithic 'centre', the continual movement and interchange between different mind-states and hypostases of the self, or what Homi Bhabha refers to as liminality, "this interstitial passage between fixed identities" (1994:4). The particular form that liminality takes in the first part of this novel is the 'underground' of illegal immigration to South Africa:

> He [Abdu] must go underground. There is a world underground this city, in all cities, the only place for those of us who can't live, haven't the means, not just money, the statutory means to conform to what others call the world. Underground. That darkness is the only freedom for him. (2001:58-9)

This is a post-apartheid world of unfixed identities. Abdu is an individual whose silences, at first, seem to be eloquent signs of self-confidence: his silence speaks of his own underlying convictions about survival in a material world. His is the search of the nomad, who forever hunts for greater opportunities while knowing that he has nothing to lose. Illegal immigration is thus presented—to Julie's immature self—as testing the individual's emotional capacity to survive uncertainty, as something akin to romance.

The second part of the novel deals with the emigration of two characters from South Africa to Abdu's unnamed home village, somewhere in North Africa. Here, Gordimer uses a novelistic technique reminiscent of *July's People* (1981): by shifting the perspective to another plane of reality, the reader gains better perspective on the central story. Significantly, the couple emigrate from one periphery to another, and not to the metropolis; in this way, by seeking familiar patterns elsewhere, Gordimer offers a defamiliarisation of the local, a distant reading from the periphery's many interactions and exchanges with global forces. Julie needs to leave her home in South Africa and emigrate to a place similar to the one she has left behind—a world of severe discrepancies—in order to see the real character of her place of origin. Julie has a realisation of the fact that she is now a stranger to herself, to her familiar ways, that she is as her new family now see her:

> that girl, that woman had lived all her life in the eyes of black people, where she comes from, but never had had from them this kind of consciousness of self: so that was what home was. She was aware of this with an intrigued detachment ... if she was strangely new to [Abdu's family], she was also strangely new to herself. (2001:117)

Julie begins to ponder the old ways of her privileged life as a rich businessman's daughter in the northern suburbs of Johannesburg and, before meeting Abdu, her leftish life-style as an independent young woman. What she then thought to be emancipated multiculturalism and the embrace of diversity in a new South Africa, she now sees in a different light: "we were playing at reality; it was a doll's house, the cottage; a game, the El-Ay Café" (164). Her insights deepen as she is constantly exposed, in the North African state, to extreme forms of poverty, which she had somehow failed fully to absorb back at home, in South Africa. She now sees "the normal state of lassitude in the extremes of poverty ... the shacks where goats were tethered and women squatted in their black garb like crows brought down wounded ... a dead sheep lying bloated in a shroud of flies" (132). At the same time as she is forced to look at the poverty around her, she learns about the humiliation of inefficient bureaucracy: "never before had she shuffled along in a queue in hope to gain a right – that had been the history of blacks in her country" (202). The roles are now reversed, and Julie is "like one who has [metaphorically] to settle for the underbelly of a car" (143), just as Abdu had to do literally as an illegal motor mechanic in her home country.

But if postcolonialism is a material condition that Julie—blinded by her privileged upbringing—did not see at home, it is also, as Quayson says, a process of its condition. The material conditions also have metaphoric and psychological value: postcolonialism has, over the decades, deeply scarred Abdu as an all-encompassing condition, and, on Julie's entering an intercultural marriage, the scars begin to leave their mark on Julie's mental universe. As with various other inter-/multicultural phenomena—terms associated with the American melting pot—this particular intercultural partnership suggests an asymmetrical world of skewed power relations. When Abdu takes her to the local market, Julie finds alongside traditional merchandise kitschy plastic utensils "decorated with flower patterns of organic ostentation that seemed tactless in a desert village" (126): all wares that the First World—through its multinational sweatshops—has "dumped" here, and which the locals are eager to buy because "they don't break so soon" (126). Julie also comes to experience the impact that the global circulation of new technological forms of communication has on the Third World. Instead of a muezzin announcing prayer time from the top of the mosque, "'there's now a recording and a loudspeaker ... that is what we have in the miracle of technology in our place'" (125), Abdu says sarcastically. Abdu and his friends would prefer "change with a voice over the internet, not from the minaret, a voice demanding to be heard by the financial gods of the world" (176). Julie comes to understand that these people desire global technology even as they resent its offerings to their conditions of asymmetrical access.

As she learns about the younger generation's response to westernisation, Julie can see that Abdu and his companions, who all share a similar educational background, are critically aware of global interactions and exchanges in the Third World, of what Raymond Williams referred to as the dialectic of "residuality" and "emergence" (1977): a dynamic that produces a mutation in which traditional and progressive ideas or practices are reconfigured into new perspectives and modalities. The generation that cherishes "Nike boots, cellphones, TV consoles, hi-fi and video equipment" (203) is, at the same time, aware that important changes have to be made for these status symbols to be truly affordable and integrated into everyday life. Abdu regularly meets like-minded young men, unemployed/unemployable graduates, who have also "been returned [from the West] like dead letters—illegals have no fixed address, no identity" (176). Back home, they keep talking about politics and pondering various solutions for the overcoming of economic discrepancies:

> These young men want change, not the rewards of Heaven. ... To catch up! With elections that are not rigged up or declared void when the government's opposition wins; hard bargains with the West made from a position of counter-power, not foot-kissing, arse-licking servitude (they bring the right vocabulary from the West, whatever else they were denied). (176)

Having been exposed to the West through illegal immigration, or through the West's own invasion of the local market-place, the young educated generation of North Africans thinks in terms of meaningful exchanges and interactions—the need to "cross-fertilize Islam with the world, if the ideals of Islam are to survive" (177)—rather than of rigid traditionalism: "... total Islamization, against world powers—what a mad dream" (177). They understand the complex interactions between the global and the local not in mechanistic terms, not as rigid polarities, but in terms of irregular boundaries, as well as unpredictable disjunctures and overlaps: i.e. "fractally" and "polythetically", as Arjun Appadurai refers to the complex dialectic between the local and the global. In using these terms, Appadurai explains how the collective identities in the Third World are constantly shaped by western images, what he calls "the ethnoscapes, technoscapes, financescapes, mediascapes and ideoscapes" (1993:305) that are brought back home by the returning migrants from the West.

While Julie becomes a keen observer of these collective identities, she also feels a sense of profound alienation. She is thus forced to consider another type of dislocation: that of the internal exile in solitary communion with the North African desert. She experiences a sense of localised alienation and *Unheimlichkeit* ["the uncanny"]—to evoke both Freud's and Heidegger's term, literally translated as "not-at-home-ness"—which has the potential, paradoxically, to unleash regenerative psychic energies. Indeed, we participate in Julie's growth and redefinition of self, in her struggle to come to terms with a new culture, a new language, and a new religion. In the process, she learns—like Gordimer's Vera Stark before her—that 'none can accompany her' on the journey towards a new sense of identity; in fact, nothing but the desert, which becomes a character in its own right. The desert is an echo of, and companion to, Julie as she challenges her old secure white South African experience of love, location and independence: "The desert. No seasons of bloom and decay. Just the endless turn of night and day. Out of time" (172). For Julie, the vastness of the desert provokes a longing for self-knowledge, for the reassessment of her past. Contrasted with the silent effect of the desert on her, Julie's early privilege in South Africa seems frivolous and insignificant.

Apart from its being offered as support for introspection and self-knowledge, the desert may also be interpreted as embodying Julie's scepticism about the meta-narratives of sociopolitical totalities, whether South African, North American, Australian (or North African, for that matter): the desert is outside of any social space, including that of the North African village itself. This is an indirect, authorial way of expressing doubt about the ultimate validity of any single system of reference, whether local or global. It may also suggest Gordimer's own sense of exhaustion with political overdetermination, or her disenchantment perhaps with more recent social configurations, both locally and internationally. In short, the desert is itself a multivalent, hybrid device in the mental exploration of the material conditions, as it opens new awareness in Julie of an increasingly sterile relationship between her husband and herself. It is also a sobering reminder of the psychological damage that has been inflicted on Abdu by global neocolonialism. His is the personality of the 'other', scarred by cynicism and mistrust after his encounters with the symbolic 'Other', the *'grand-autre'*—to evoke Lacan (1968)—in whose gaze he can see only a relentlessly repeated rejection-cum-annihilation of self. Both Julie and Abdu wish to find a home in exile, to be integrated and accepted in a different social space. But Gordimer presents Abdu's damage as beyond healing. As she points out in an essay, poverty—apart from its socio-economic disfigurations—has also had psychologically disempowering effects on the disenfranchised. It is important, she says, to "harness the negatives of social resentment into vital partnerships for change" (1999:186). Abdu, however, is presented as unable to change: he has lost his ability to love—sex is to him something apart from love—and cannot reciprocate Julie's feelings in genuine intimacy.

To use the Other/other binarism once more, Abdu is bitter about what he perceives to be his being 'othered', and starts resenting Julie herself for refusing to support his securing access to the [global] Other that has been so inaccessible to him. He is even prepared to be an exile again, as this is the closest he can get to the gaze of the mythical Other and its seductive appeal of material advancement. As she has an intimate knowledge of the western mentality with its social and psychological hierarchies, Julie is realistic about the difficulties her husband is almost certain to encounter in the United States. She is, therefore, not prepared to join him when he "return[s] to the same new-old humiliations that await him, doing the dirty work they don't want to do" (266). The couple are unable to go beyond, or process, their diverse views and background experiences, unable to open up to what they are each prepared to endure in the future. They can only pursue their different needs and ideals by going their separate ways: the final irony of the relationship resides in its sacrifice and loss. In this relationship, cultural "diversity" cannot translate into a mature acceptance of "difference"—to use Bhabha's (1994) terms; a fixed and predetermined diversity of views and mentalities cannot be overcome; diversity cannot be transformed into meaningful understanding of, and respect for, otherness.

The novel ends with a perplexing reversal of roles. Abdu, the illegal immigrant to South Africa, proves to be the eternal nomad, but one who no longer manifests his earlier dignity. Tragically, he is a phenomenon of the 1990s: a global mercenary condemned by history forever to be seeking opportunities elsewhere. Julie, previously a spoilt daughter, manages to transform her claustrophobic life not by substituting one place of privilege for another, but by turning her back on materialistic pursuits and global metanarratives, such as emigration and immigration. Instead, she embarks on a journey of self-discovery that proves to have no boundaries other than those imposed upon her by her own inner dedication. Rejecting what she comes to regard as the superficial landscapes of global opportunities, she identifies the map of her own inner life as a new country of exploration. Intriguingly, she does not wish to emigrate to the United States, but neither does she choose to repatriate herself to South Africa.

One may say, of course, that Julie's privileged upbringing permits her the luxury of her decisions. *The Pickup*, however, is not a moral tale. Gordimer is not judgmental of Julie, but permits her her own struggles of belonging and belief in the importance of internal exile. To her credit, neither is Gordimer judgmental of Abdu. He is compelled by circumstance to seek his own location and journey on to the allure of the United States. If the migrant is the product of neocolonialism, he is also the product of the postcolonial condition: that time after apartheid, after the ideological binaries of the recent past.

* * *

Gordimer has continued, since *The Pickup* (2001), to show interest in the dynamics of the local and the global, of the global beyond the local. Her collection of short stories, *Loot* (2003), is an explicit engagement with this new tendency in her artistic vision, her new focus on (dis)location,

place and displacement in South Africa and the world today. What strikes
the reader at a first glance is the multiplicity of locales—more stories
are set outside South Africa than inside the country—and the fact that
eight of the ten stories relate to issues of global politics.

The thrust of the 2003 collection is identity and belonging in conditions
of post-apartheid and post-Cold War indeterminacy and liminality,
particularly as applied to exile, deracination and dislocation in the world
today. It is significant that the title story, "Loot"—which, as is usual
with Gordimer's short-story collections, sets the tone of the volume as
a whole—is situated outside of South Africa. The story refers to a real
incident that took place in Chile, an earthquake at sea having provoked
a tsunami. Gordimer makes use of this geo-physical context to reflect
on the consequences of extreme situations on the human psyche. Human
greed—in the looting of the objects exposed by the receding sea—is shown
to have no boundaries as it 'contaminates' people across all national and
social barriers; no one escapes the temptation to grab hold of some object,
whether needed or not, and everyone has his/ her price in material ways.
Gordimer reveals the frailty of all human convictions in extraordinary
circumstances: she even manages to introduce an allusion to the time of
political uprisings, when "the ordinary opportunity of looting shops was
routine to people" (4). No one is spared Gordimer's cynical gaze: looting
and death by drowning are presented as the ultimate levellers. (Is Gordimer
too a looter, looting a human tragedy as a subject of her art?)

The story, "Loot", is a reminder of Gordimer's long-standing
preoccupations with identity, betrayal, and disenchantment in human
interaction. These themes were also strongly represented in her previous
short-story collection, *Jump* (1991), where she was fully absorbed by
the social climate of the late 1980s, the last stage of apartheid before its
disintegration. In that collection, all the stories were set in South Africa,
and she combined the motif of underground and guerilla struggle in the
public and private life with symptoms of morbidity, broken promises, and
unstable allegiances. The current collection is not free of these motifs, but
as the writer's context has become less politically extreme, she now feels
freer to apply her motifs beyond the locality. Concomitantly, Gordimer
has become more contemplative in her latest storytelling endeavours.
Here too comparisons may be entertained with those earlier stories in
which she stressed existentialist ideas: individual responsibility and free
will; choice and the 'nausea' of choice; the indeterminacy and uncertainty
of life and death. *Loot* combines essential traits of the earlier and the
later collections, while bringing to both a new touch: her opening to the

world, to global perspectives, to 'the ethics of beyond'.

"Visiting George" is situated in London and looks at the phenomenon of South African exile and dislocation. It is a meditation on an old comrade of the struggle years, who was in exile in England during apartheid; someone who decided not to return to South Africa after 1990. His are ethical dilemmas that require decisions and choices no longer circumscribed by the struggle binaries of 'us and them'. The narrator muses on George's profound disappointment with the Left and especially with so-called communism in the ex-Soviet Union:

> He had left the Party after a visit to the old Soviet Union in the Fifties when he was taken round collective pig farms. But I was thinking now—perhaps only thinking now—we all have our point of no return in political loyalty, and the stink of pigs is as good as, say, the disillusion of corruption. (2003:70)

Gordimer does not, in this short story, elaborate on the corruption of, and her own disenchantment with, the now defunct communist system, but she does so in a critical essay where she reflects on the "now fallen star, the red star". It is in her non-fiction that she fully analyses "the tragedy of the Russian attempt to improve our human lot" and "*this sense of abandonment* that the collapse of the Soviet Union brings to our century", since "the ideals of socialism have been betrayed and desecrated in many countries" (1999:226-7). Gordimer is profoundly affected by the trajectory of the Soviet Union because she had believed that communism could have been a solution to overcoming the corruptions of colonialism:

> My personal sense of the defining events of our century is dominated by two: the fall of Communism and the end of colonialism. And the two extraordinary developments are linked subjectively, even contradictorily, for me, since ... I looked to the Left as a solution to the oppression of the poor, in my home country and the world. (1999:225)

It is not surprising, therefore, that Gordimer pursues the saga of the "fallen star, the red star" in more than one short story, for example in the last, untitled story in the novella, "Karma", which is part of *Loot*.

This story unfolds against the background of the general economic and ideological collapse of the Soviet Union in the early 1990s. The Soviet Union is presented mockingly, as a form of 'enlightened' patriarchy, with tyrants and "Government fathers providing" for everyone (214). We look at this sinister social scene through the eyes of a young woman,

Elena, whose childhood and young adulthood were marred by a social system that was unable to translate its own 'grand narrative' into lived experience. Caught up in a schizoid routine—one that included endless food queues as well as regular State ballet shows—Elena grows up hoping to be free one day. When the change comes—the disintegration of the Soviet Union—most social structures collapse and millions of citizens, formerly employed by the State, find themselves pauperised:

> Old people [were] begging in the streets; they were everywhere, old men in the remnants of their respectable functionaries' or clerks' suits, old women with the bewildered faces of former housewives, shamed under shawls. (220)

A bankrupt country cannot offer Elena, who dreams of becoming a teacher, a better chance in life than that of being a chambermaid. When her own grandmother starts begging at street corners, Elena starts an affair with an Italian businessman, who helps her out of the country and "saves her from the chaos in Russia" (224). Once in Italy, she agrees to enter into a marriage of convenience (to a butcher), so that she can cease being an illegal immigrant and obtain citizenship. Trapped in an unwanted pregnancy—"a healthy Russian woman become an Italian wife" and "no morning sickness" in her pregnancy (229)—Elena has an illuminating insight into the new kind of unfreedom of the post-communist aftermath. She visits a cattle-breeding installation, where she sees the animals chained by the leg:

> The bulk of each animal is contained—just—by the bars of a heavy stall; it cannot turn round. It can only eat, at this end of its body. Eat, eat. The butcher owner tells her: at six months, ready for slaughter. Prime. ... She is swollen with horror, her body feels the iron bars enclosing her, the bars are before her eyes, she cannot turn about ... . She does not know where it comes from, this knowledge—happening to her—of how it is for them, beasts born dumb as a human being can be made dumbly unable to free itself ... and there is now, here, a child inside her seeded by the owner of these beasts in iron bars. (231)

Elena's epiphanic experience echoes that of George when visiting the "collective pig farm" in the Soviet Union, as quoted above. While George's illuminating moment prompts him to leave the Communist Party, Elena's prompts her to abort her unwanted child, even at the cost of jeopardising her legal status in the West. Gordimer's disappointment with the trajectory of "the red star" is profoundly underscored in these actions.

Another aspect of illegal immigration—as global phenomenon—is presented in "Homage", which takes place in an unnamed metropolis, and whose protagonist is also nameless: "*I am nobody*; no country counts me in its census, the name they gave me doesn't exist; nobody did what was done" (136). This person has been paid to assassinate a politician. He has no official identity, no papers, no name, "no face": "This city has never seen my face. Only the back of a man leaping up the steps" (138) after an assassination. The protagonist calls to mind Abdu, "the *nobody* Abdu" of *The Pickup*, who too has to endure an identity-less existence. Whether in Johannesburg or in any other big city of the world, the pain of clandestine existence is similar: it involves an annihilation of identity and a silencing of self. The unnamed and 'silent' protagonist of "Homage" says:

> All the time I was being pushed out of one country into another, I was afraid, afraid of having no papers, afraid of being questioned, afraid of being hungry, but now I had nothing to be afraid of. I still have nothing to fear. *I don't speak.* (137)

The story ends in anti-climax, with the 'silent' illegal finding a desperate way of reclaiming his voice, his self. He feels an urge to take a bunch of roses to the burial place of the man whom he has killed. The assassinated man has a name, while his killer has no name. By bringing homage to the dead man with a name, a somebody, the nobody-alien also perversely and tragically claims his identity, his right to have a voice and a name, even in death: "Today I bought a cheap bunch of roses held by an elastic band wound tight ... and laid it there, ... where my name is buried with him" (139). The nobody, although alive, has no life; his name is buried alongside the lifeless body of him who had a name, an identity. This is the desperate silence of the disenfranchised.

Such a life-and-death dynamic is also explored in "An Emissary", which places side by side the—generically named—"Northern hemisphere" and the "Southern hemisphere", in terms of the various playgrounds/ places for escapade used by an adulterous couple. While the first part deals with the North, the second is placed in an unnamed location in the Southern hemisphere, where the couple go on a holiday, only to meet their deaths by malaria. Gordimer's use of generic place indicators is deliberate: her intention seems to be to alert public sensitivity, through the metaphor of transmission, to the fact that in a global order the rich North and the poor South are linked in a complex relation: something which the G8 in its poverty-alleviation discussions is now forced to confront. The story is introduced by what appears to be an extract from a health brochure warning of malaria: "'Malarial mosquitoes can even stow away on international flights—just ask unsuspecting victims near airports in Germany, Paris and São Paulo'"(143). We see Gordimer, the literary activist, at work here and, as in the stories analysed above, in this story she hints at an issue of global significance, being willing to go beyond her immediate locality and contemplate the Southern hemisphere as a 'significant periphery'.

While most stories in *Loot* are situated in locations around the world and illustrate circumstances of 'significant peripheries', other stories are located in a post-1990 southern Africa. Of these I shall focus on "Mission Statement", as it best encapsulates recent issues of identity in the region. With the story taking place in an unnamed African state, most probably Zambia in its southern African brand of "global localisation" (Gordimer 1999: 207), "Mission Statement" offers a complex engagement with issues of place and displacement. It is against the background of land appropriation that the interracial relationship between Roberta Blayne and Gladwell Chabruma occurs, and this may be interpreted as an illustration of the 'postcolonial body' as concept: a crucial site for inscription, identity representation, and discursive control.

Roberta, whose grandfather was a colonial copper-mine manager, has grown up abroad, and returns here—to the 'home' of her childhood and memory—as a development officer; she is on a mission with "a plan for the country to enter globalisation" (11). She is subconsciously drawn by a desire to explore her family 'roots', only to find that the meaning of life does not reside in the past, but in the present, which happens to unfold elsewhere, far away from her roots. The need to explore and purge her family's suppressed colonial past is prompted by her own dislocated existence. As a member of the mobile international NGO network, whose work takes her to various places without the need to establish lasting bonds, she feels the call of a mythical land of origin, not only as ephemeral visual experience but also as lasting 'presence'. This echoes Dennis Lee's concept of home as longing for a recognisable spatial 'cadence', or pattern: a "'presence', both outside myself and inside my body opening out and trying to get into words" (1974:397). Roberta is only accustomed to the presence-cum-erasure pattern of her diasporic condition. When she moves from country to country, therefore, she is quick (in a superficial way) to adjust to the new surroundings; whenever she occupies yet another hotel room, for example, she finds it easy, as "she was accustomed to this kind of takeover. Whatever *lingering presence* of others was *quickly erased* by hers"(10) [my emphases].

Intriguingly, she processes her largely subconscious need for the 'cadence' of a home in a physical relationship with a black man through whom she comes to revisit old family guilt. The remainders of Buffalo Mine, which used to belong to her grandfather, encapsulate the colonial legacy of ruthless exploitation, which haunts Roberta; while she initially still hopes that the traces of the past would, eventually, be completely erased from her memory, she ends up by finding out that certain psychological traces persist, even though many inscriptions have been 'overwritten'. Her private experience mirrors the process of collective cultural experiences that are accretions of many layers of colonial practices and "spatial histories" as "palimpsests" (Carter 1987). She finds out how intimately 'place' with its traces and overwritings—the old mine of the past, Gladwell's farm of the present—informs the development of her own sense of self and belonging.

Complete erasure of guilt proves to be impossible for Roberta. She cannot liberate herself from the ghosts of collective white guilt. But neither is her black lover capable of erasing vestiges of his own personal or cultural history when he—from Roberta's point of view—"dredg[es] up into his life some remnant [a wife] from the past" (65). The couple prove unable to stand the test of different traditions merging—Williams's "residuality" and "emergence"—for even if Gladwell tells Roberta that it is part of his tradition to accept a polygamous arrangement, this is not the case in her tradition. One cannot escape Gordimer's subtle mockery of Gladwell's opportunistic invoking of polygamy when he himself takes advantage of a western life-style. In short—and to her credit—the author is neither prepared to offer idealised versions of the 'other' nor to suggest some 'politically correct' happy ending. Roberta leaves southern Africa to become "again a member of an aid agency's personnel, walking away barefoot" (66) and empty-handed. The burdens of an overdetermined place and past are too painful for her, and she chooses to give up her quest for belonging and return to her itinerant work existence.

* * *

Do we perceive, in *The Pickup* and *Loot*, Gordimer as a world writer? A postcolonial writer? A postcolonialising world writer? I suggest the last of these categories: a writer of neither centre nor periphery, but one inhabiting significant peripheries of becoming: 'post-postcolonial' processes of new adjustments between the old formulations of North and South. A recognition of, and response to, complex new relationships among the various edges of the world have been reinforced recently by Gordimer in an unexpected project: she has edited an activist-inspired collection of short stories, *Telling Tales* (2004), for which she approached twenty-one well-known contemporary world writers whose work she admires, writers from both North and South, including five Nobel prize-winners. She asked them each to offer a short story without receiving royalties, so that the profits from the sale of *Telling Tales* could be donated to the HIV/AIDS global fund. As Gordimer states in her Introduction: "We decided that we too should wish to give something of our ability, as imaginative writers, to contribute in our way to the fight against this disease from which no country, no individual, is safely isolated" (2004:1). The artist literally steps out of the ivory tower into the market place: the imaginative contribution is sold, then donated, as words become a material object, a book. By attending to both postcolonial discourse and materiality, Gordimer is 'postcolonialising', in Quayson's sense. Is this a further instance of Gordimer, the artist and activist, seeking a new role after apartheid: an affirmative project which enhances her artistic integrity?

References

Appadurai, Arjun. 1993. "Disjuncture and Difference in the Global Cultural Economy." In: P. Williams and L. Chrisman (eds). *Colonial Discourse and Postcolonial Theory: A Reader*. London: Harvester Wheatsheaf: 305-23.

Bhabha, Homi K. 1994. *The Location of Culture*. London: Routledge.

Carter, Paul. 1987. *The Road to Botany Bay*. London: Faber and Faber.

Childs, Peter and Patrick Williams. 1997. *An Introductory Guide to Postcolonial Literature*. New York: Prentice-Hall.

Cooppan, Vilashini. 2001. "World Literature and Global Theory: Comparative Literature for the New Millennium." *Symplokē* 9(1):15-43.

Damrosch, David. 2003. *What is World Literature?* Princeton and Oxford: Princeton University Press.

Dimitriu, Ileana. 2000. *Art of Conscience: Re-reading Nadine Gordimer*. Timisoara: Hestia.

_____. 2001. "A New Sense of Social Space: Gordimer's Civil Imaginary." In: R. Wilson and C. van Maltzan (eds). *Spaces and Crossings: Essays on Literature and Culture in Africa and Beyond*. Frankfurt am Main; New York; Oxford: Peter Lang: 335-48.

_____. 2002. "The Civil Imaginary in Gordimer's First Novels." *English in Africa* 29(1): 27-54.

Dharwadker, Vinay (ed.). 2001. *Cosmopolitan Geographies: New Locations in Literature and Culture*. New York: Routledge.

Gordimer, Nadine. 1998. *The House Gun*. Cape Town: David Philip.

_____. 1999. *Living in Hope and History: Notes from Our Century*. Cape Town: David Philip.

_____. 2001. *The Pickup*. Cape Town: David Philip.

_____. 2003. *Loot*. Cape Town: David Philip.

_____. 2004. *Telling Tales*. London: Bloomsbury.

Gurr, Andrew. 1981. *Writers in Exile: The Identity of Home in Modern Literature*. Brighton: Harvester.

Kossew, Sue. 2001. "Living in Hope: An Interview with Nadine Gordimer." *Commonwealth: Essays and Studies* 23(2):55-61.

_____. 2003. "Beyond the National: Exile and Belonging in Nadine Gordimer's *The Pickup*." *Scrutiny 2* 8(1):21-6.

Lacan, Jacques. 1968. *The Language of the Self: The Function of Language in Psychoanalysis*. Translated from the French by A. Wilden. Baltimore, MD: Johns Hopkins University Press.

Lee, Dennis. 1995 [1974]. "Cadence, Country, Silence: Writing in Colonial Space." In: B. Ashcroft et al. 1995. *The Postcolonial Studies Reader*. London: Routledge: 397-401.

Loomba, Ania et al. (eds). "Beyond What? An Introduction." In: *Postcolonial Studies and Beyond*. Durham and London: Duke University Press: 1-38.

Nederveen Pieterse, J. 1995. *The Development of Development Theory: Towards Critical Globalism*. The Hague: Institute of Social Science.

Quayson, Ato. 2000. *Postcolonialism: Theory, Practice or Process?*. Cambridge: Polity.

Robbins, Bruce. 1998. "Comparative Cosmopolitanisms." In: P. Cheah and B. Robbins (eds). *Cosmopolitics: Thinking and Feeling Beyond the Nation*. Minneapolis: University of Minnesota Press: 246-64.

Williams, Raymond. 1977. *Marxism and Literature*. Oxford: Oxford University Press.

Williams, Patrick and Laura Chrisman. 1994. *Colonial Discourse and Postcolonial Theory: A Reader*. London: Harvester Wheatsheaf.

Žižek, Slavoj. 1991. *Looking Awry. An Introduction to Jacques Lacan through Popular Culture*. Cambridge, MA: MIT Press.

Barbara Adair's *In Tangier We Killed the Blue Parrot*

A Queer Reading

Cheryl Stobie

[F]amily life and the intimate sphere are areas that are very much fundamental to the nation-state's sovereignty. The area of international migration of sexual dissidents brings to the fore questions of national identity, citizenship and belonging. (Binnie 2004)

The study of the postcolonial nationalisms of the so-called Third World continues to be quasi-uniformly based on the presupposition of an unexamined totalising signifier: universalised heterosexuality. (Bacchetta 1999)

Let us now imagine reintroducing into the politico-sexual field ... *a touch of sentimentality*: would that not be the ultimate transgression? The transgression of transgression itself? For, after all, that would be love: which would return: *but in another place*. (Barthes 1975)

In 2004 Johannesburg-based human-rights law lecturer, Barbara Adair, published *In Tangier We Killed the Blue Parrot*. This novel is set in a symbolically resonant space, Tangier, Morocco, and employs techniques of intertextuality to fictionalise the lives of Jane and Paul Bowles, American writers who were part of the expatriate community in Tangier for some time in the middle of the twentieth century. Also included as characters are a number of Western literary figures, such as William Burroughs and Gertrude Stein, and a number of Moroccan characters, some of whom are purely fictional, and others of whom are based on historical figures. The novel explores the unconventional marriage of the Bowleses, both of whom were bisexual, and their love affairs with Moroccans of the same sex as themselves. It also incorporates, unmarked, parts of the Bowleses' fictional texts.

Few South African readers would come to the novel with much prior knowledge of the Bowleses, yet the text is clearly marketed by Jacana, a local press, as of significance to a South African readership. In addition, before the main text begins, the author sketches out the genesis of the novel in a brief preface, dated 1993, which provides a clear optic through which to read the ensuing fictionalised account. In the preface the author, Barbara Adair, is sitting in the Café Hafa in Tangier, on the threshold of being able to view the Straits of Gibraltar; she is grateful to be travelling in Africa after the lifting of travel restrictions on South Africans following the unbanning of the ANC and the move towards democracy. A young hustler approaches her and tells her that Paul Bowles is in the café. Whether the old man who has been pointed out to her is indeed Paul Bowles she does not ascertain; their connection is a purely imaginative one, leading to the writing of the novel. The stimulus for the writing of the text thus occurs on the cusp of the transition to democracy in South Africa, and the changing sociopolitical landscape over the next eleven years which it took to bring the book before a reading public provides the implicit focus for interpretation. Adair laconically comments:

> It feels strange to be sitting in a café in Tangier. For years South Africans have been unable to travel to other countries in Africa. Now for the first time, with the announcement of the release of political prisoners and the unbanning of the African National Congress, we can travel. Is it for this reason that I welcome political change in my country or can I muster other reasons for my hopefulness? But as I sit in this café I am grateful. (2004a:n.p.)

The author positions herself as a tourist engaging with another African country's culture as a result of the imminent shift to democracy. Yet her motives are unclear, even to herself. Her 'imprisonment' within South Africa has affected her, as a privileged white South African, far less than her compatriots who have borne the travails of oppression, disempowerment and literal imprisonment. Adair's question as to whether she can "muster other reasons for my hopefulness" suggests an awareness—possibly including a degree of cynicism—of her ethically compromised position, and raises general questions for South African readers about the continuing burdens of binarised systems, such as apartheid, in a transitional national imaginary. Adair's question directs the reader to respond to the text as a meditation on the significance of the dissolution of some systemic boundaries, such as the ability to travel, and the liberalisation of censorship of sexually explicit material, but it also foregrounds the place to be occupied by former colonisers in the new nation-state.

In terms of content and style, the novel itself blurs conventional binary categories. Most importantly, it allows questions to be asked about the interface between queer theory and postcolonialism in contemporary post-apartheid South Africa as compared with a similar liminal, transitional space in mid-twentieth century Tangier, which William Burroughs referred to as the "Interzone" (Mullins 2002:4). Just as democratic South African literature and theoretics are exploring the implications of a transitional, newly democratic, multiple society with Constitutional guarantees in terms of sexuality as well as race, the Interzone was a similar interstitial space of developing contradictory and contesting discourses: "Suspended between nations, cultures, and languages, the Interzone is a place of intermediacy and ambiguity, a place that remains outside standard narratives of nationhood and identity" (Mullins 2002:3).

This essay rests theoretically on a growing body of work on the Interzone between queer theory and postcolonial theory (Bell and Valentine 1995; Lambevski 1999; Povinelli and Chauncey 1999; Alderson and Anderson 2000; Patton and Sánchez-Eppler 2000; Hawley 2001; and with a specifically South African focus Elder 1995; Hoad 1999; Barnard 2001; Epprecht 2004). Queer theorists critique homophobia in postcolonial discourse, while postcolonial theorists "decry gay/lesbian studies as 'white' and 'elitist'" (Hawley 2001:1). Jon Binnie summarises the hazards inherent in this conceptual terrain, individually and collectively:

> While significant in challenging the ethnocentricity of lesbian and gay studies, postcolonialism is in danger of producing a theoretical purity and universalism where alternative ways of conceptualising the relationships between sexual dissidence, globalization and national identity are squeezed out. The universalising tendencies of postcolonial theory combined with the elitist tendencies of queer theory mean that bringing them together is dangerous. (2004:148)

In order to avoid these pitfalls, instead of focusing on identity-based lesbian and gay studies, I rely on queer theory's examination of forms of behaviour or writing which reject the power of heteronormativity and propose instead a fluid zone of possibilities. Further, to ground the discussion in the specific, material and corporeal, rather than the merely theoretical or the elitist, I use as particular exemplars of queer theory textual representations of bisexuality.

In this piece bisexuality refers to "the sexual or intensely emotional, although not necessarily concurrent or equal, attraction of an individual to members of more than one gender" (James 1996:218). The trope of bisexuality is a particularly apposite means of gauging shifts within the body politic of South Africa, as this sexuality functions as a marker of change or instability, and embodies a set of social signifiers and anxieties about boundaries, appetite, commitment and health (Eadie 1997). In the post-apartheid South African context there has been a burgeoning of texts which employ this trope. The shift between apartheid-era censorship and post-apartheid exploration of the implications of bisexuality is revealed by juxtaposing the banning of the camp (and lily-white) *The Rocky Horror Picture Show* soon after its appearance on the cinema screens of South Africa in 1975 (dir. Jim Sharman) with the uncontroversial screening on M-Net of the locally-made, bilingual short film, "Me, My Husband and His Boyfriend" in 2005 (dir. Nomakhomazi Dyosopu), starring an exclusively black cast.

The cultural and sexual encounters which are represented in many post-apartheid texts are coded as racial meeting-grounds, and I evoke (post)colonialism to problematise the treatment of racial difference, and to enquire into the representation of the 'other' in the fiction of Jane and Paul Bowles, as well as in Barbara Adair's novel. In order to respond to *In Tangier We Killed the Blue Parrot* in an appropriately receptive manner, I explore issues of liminality and hybridity as a means of analysing the representation of gendered, sexualised and racially inflected bodies in various spaces in the novel. In particular I focus on one character who embodies the concept of surprise, and I tease out various implications following from her unique status in the text. I touch on some implications of a South African author's choice, at this historical juncture, to write a novel about life in Tangier, and the significance of this postcolonial dialogue. I consider ways in which this text is embedded in its own cultural matrix, and ways in which it offers a re-framed Interzone for South Africa some ten years after independence.

The notional zone for my enquiry, in postcolonial terms, is Homi Bhabha's Third Space, where the binary ideological system of colonialism is revealed to be subject to productive ruptures, contradictions and transitions. Bhabha adapts the concept of the liminal to cultural hybridity. Expanding on his concept of the Third Space, a cultural space of transformation, he claims:

> ...the theoretical recognition of the split-space of enunciation may open the way to conceptualizing an *inter*national culture, based not on the

exoticism of multiculturalism or the *diversity* of cultures, but on the inscription and articulation of culture's *hybridity*. To that end we should remember that it is the 'inter'—the cutting edge of translation and negotiation, the *in-between* space—that carries the burden of the meaning of culture. It makes it possible to begin envisaging national, anti-nationalist histories of the 'people'. And by exploring this Third Space, we may elude the politics of polarity and emerge as the others of our selves. (1994:38-9)

This liminal or third space discussed by Bhabha is exploratory, non-hierarchical and humble. This "in-between" space of "translation and negotiation" in ideal terms constitutes the body politic of post-apartheid South Africa, although within the predominantly Africanist agenda of the ANC under Thabo Mbeki issues involving sexuality and gender have been handled with defensiveness, anxiety and hostility. Mbeki's characteristic denialism employs a binarist action/reaction paradigm, rather than allowing for dialogue within a broader framework.

Marjorie Garber examines the possibilities of a similar imaginary space to Bhabha's in terms of the body, gendered subjectivity and queer sexuality. In this context she comments:

The 'third' is that which questions binary thinking and introduces crisis.... [T]he 'third' is a mode of articulation, a way of describing a space of possibility. Three puts in question the idea of one: of identity, self-sufficiency, self-knowledge.... [The third] reconfigures the relationships between the original pair, and puts into question identities previously conceived as stable, unchallengeable, grounded and 'known'. (1992:11,13)

Garber's term, "space of possibility", makes it clear that while the third space opens up the potential for different, previously unimagined, transgressive or subversive experiences, perceptions or readings, these are not inevitable or simply automatically produced by the context. Any such event is contingent, partial, tentative or volatile. Garber follows up her insights on the third to a consideration of the applicability of the concept specifically to bisexuality:

The question of whether someone was 'really' straight or 'really' gay misrecognises the nature of sexuality, which is fluid, not fixed, a narrative that changes over time rather than a fixed identity, however complex. The erotic discovery of bisexuality is the fact that it reveals sexuality to be a process of growth, transformation, and surprise, not a stable and knowable state of being. (1995:65-6)

Although, misleadingly, often not flagged as bisexual,[1] the lives of the Bowleses have previously been explored by biographers such as Millicent Dillon (1988) and Christopher Sawyer-Lauçanno (1989). Paul Bowles was born in New York in 1910. He initially received recognition as a composer, but over the course of his long life he achieved a reputation as a novelist, short-story and travel writer, a translator of fiction by a number of Moroccans, and a collector of Moroccan folk music. He had relationships with men and women before he met Jane Auer in 1937. She was born in New York in 1917, and had had a number of affairs with women when they met. They agreed to a non-monogamous and bisexual marriage. They married in 1938, and their sexual relationship with each other lasted a few years, after which they led separate sexual lives, although the marriage endured as a primary emotional relationship (Dillon 1988:43,223). They travelled in South America, where Jane Bowles's novel *Two Serious Ladies* (1943) was set, and in 1947 settled in Morocco. She suffered from writer's block and ill-health, and died in 1973. Paul Bowles died in Tangier in 1999.

In addition to the biographical coverage of their lives, both Jane and Paul Bowles creatively re-worked aspects of their lives in fictional form, and raised issues connected to sexuality and relations with racial 'others'. Jane Bowles's persistent thematic concerns are the exploration of women's fluid sexual desires and their striving for autonomy within a system of mandatory binary sexuality. Race and class can also be discerned operating in this economy, especially with regard to travel to 'exotic' locales. Marcy Jane Knopf comments:

> Many of Bowles's characters travel to other places to seek positions of power and experience desires through their power over 'others'. This dynamic may reflect Bowles's own position as a white, privileged woman; nevertheless, it represents a complicated web of erotic relationships that are inseparable from the politics of power. (1996:155)

Knopf goes on to comment, "[b]oth Jane and Paul Bowles's writing is heavily problematic in its representations of colonialist relationships and colonialism in general" (163).

Jane and Paul Bowles spent most of their married life together in the city of Tangier, William Burroughs's Interzone. The term is an abbreviation for the International Zone. It is also a shorthand for a specific text written by Burroughs, a place which generated it, and a style of writing about issues of sexuality, race and nation which avoids easy binaries, and, while implicated in its own ideologies, simultaneously attempts to critique them, as in the cases of *Two Serious Ladies* or Paul Bowles's best known novel,

The Sheltering Sky (1990). Before proceeding to examine Barbara Adair's usage of this Interzone, it is necessary to contextualise it in literal terms.

Tangier is a prime example of a liminal city. Geographically sited slantwise, at the north-western corner of Africa, its east-west axis lies between the Atlantic Ocean and the Mediterranean, and on a north-south axis it functions as a portal to and from Africa. Historically it was the site of a series of invasions over the centuries, and a contact zone for three major religions: Islam, Christianity, and Judaism. For most of the period between 1923 and 1956 it was designated an International Zone, governed by representatives from eight European countries, including Great Britain, France and Spain, and later also including the United States (Pickford 2004:2). This cultural hub acquired a reputation for decadence. The International Zone had a weak and fragmented administration, and as laws were not stringently enforced illegal activity, including commerce in sex and drugs, flourished (Mullins 2002: 4). As Mullins comments,

> Sexual tourists have long been and continue to be drawn to Tangier. As a border town between North Africa and Europe, it is a site where cultures, sexualities, bodies, fantasies, and politics meet and emerge more complex for having encountered one another there. (x)

This Interzone is a Third Space in terms of national belonging, cultures and languages, an interstitial space of contradiction, multiplicity and possibility, a space which fostered the creation of fiction which explored new conceptions of nation and subjectivity. Mullins epitomises Interzone literature as contesting "totalizing narratives of nationality and also of language, culture, identity, and sexuality" (5). While Mullins's specific focus is on sex between men, I would argue that bisexuality, which is obsessively re-worked in the fiction of Jane and Paul Bowles, is an even better example of a Third Space of sexuality.

* * *

Like its setting, the form of *In Tangier We Killed the Blue Parrot* is complex. Aside from the 1993 preface, there are two other time schemes in the text. The bulk of the text unfolds in a truncated and fictionalised version of the lives of the Bowleses in 1949 and for a few years after this date. Some sections are in free indirect narration, while others (signalled by italics) are in first-person narration. The main narrators are the characters Paul and Jane Bowles; Paul's narration occupies some fifty per cent more space than Jane's. The italicised sections do not have the narrators' names attached to them, but the reader has to deduce from the context which character is using first-person narration. In the first and last chapters of the text the focaliser is Belquassim, Paul's intimate friend. Belquassim is not based on an actual individual: the name is taken from a minor and racially stereotyped character in the actual Paul Bowles's novel, *The Sheltering Sky*, although the two characters are very different from each other. The framing chapters of *In Tangier We Killed the Blue Parrot* are set some fifteen years after the bulk of the text. The first chapter opens with Belquassim raising his glass in a toast to salute his memories of Paul and Jane in the previous years, and musing: "'The telling of a memory makes the story, the story that is more exotic than the experience. What happened itself is not real, only the story is real. The real adventure. And it can never be repeated. And he had never told this story before'" (2004a:1).

Belquassim's salute naturalises the triangular relationship between the three characters, thereby disrupting the conventional "politics of Noah's Ark" narrative (Hogeland 1994:18-21), which demonises triangulation. Belquassim's words signal a textual privileging of discourse, narrative and interpretation over the claims of factual history. They also suggest that the subsequent free indirect narration which comprises each alternate chapter will be primarily focalised through the character of Belquassim, who, of the four main characters, is the only one who is purely (and doubly) fictional. The fourth character in the scheme is Cherifa, based on a Moroccan woman who was a lover of Jane Bowles.

The unconventional marriage between the characters, Paul and Jane, is perceived by Paul in the imagery of harbours and, significantly, a city:

> For Jane I am her harbour, for me, Jane is my harbour. Everyone else is just one of the small ports that we call into along the way. We always come back to our common city. It may be a city that will destroy us in the end, but we will come back anyway. We will come back always, because—I can't call it love for that is just a word .... We come back to each other because, maybe, we fill each other's emptiness. But it is a relationship that is difficult to sustain. It cannot last. (Adair 2004a:46)

As in post-apartheid South Africa, intimate connections are being reconfigured. Physical and emotional relationships are conceived in terms of spatial metaphors, which reveal the anxiety associated with paradigm shifts. A twenty-first century South African reader would perceive the implied comparisons between the dilemmas of these characters, exploring the lived realities of two bisexuals who are polyamorous yet emotionally committed to each other, in an unconventional marriage. These issues resonate with current South African debates about homophobia, about broadening the concept of marriage to include same-sex unions, and about honest negotiations with sexual partners in a context of multiple partners, traditional polygyny, rampant HIV/Aids, and the widespread sexual abuse of women and children.

While Adair uses several locales in Morocco in different chapters, the main setting is Tangier. She provides a number of narratives which briefly relate key moments in her history of Moroccan cities, particularly Tangier. These serve to reveal that the city, like contemporary South African cities, is fragmented and fosters a wide variety of actions and interpretations. The Moroccan city in the past of the novel represents both a source of needed money and employment, and the plundering of people's treasured ancient artefacts and tangible connection with their heritage. On the other hand, however, the city offers a relative Eden for those suffering under the burden of colonialism. This implies that Tangier is no static, utopian zone of purity, but a site of constant process, subject to multiple historical and ideological forces, and unreliable in its provision of benefits.

In a particularly shocking and poignant story in the novel, the city is represented as a battle zone during the local uprisings against the French colonialists. Paul admires those who are protesting, commenting:

> This is the sound of people who want to be free, free from the French who won't let them walk on their stinking bourgeois boulevards without being sneered at. And they think that if they are free of the French, the Boulevard Pasteur is called the Avenue Mohammed V, they will be free from hunger and from nihilism. They won't you know, but it doesn't matter, what matters is their movement, their need to destroy those that they perceive are the cause of this wanton poverty and squalor. We are all its cause. We all want to destroy. I can't think of purity any more, it sickens me. (96)

The central episode in this story of revolt is when a young fleeing boy is shot by a French guard, and a woman cradling the boy in his death throes is also shot in the back of the head in cold blood. Such renditions of the Moroccan city are comparable with the history of South African cities, under apartheid ideological zones of racial 'purity', and after 1994 subject to progressive change and inclusivity, yet also problematic locations of expectation and exploitation, seen for instance in the proliferation of squatter camps, the increasing presence of Aids-orphaned street children, and escalating protests against poverty, unemployment, slow delivery of housing and services, and widespread corruption.

Yet alongside this failure to give succour to its inhabitants, the city of Tangier offers a tantalising contact zone for a range of people who would not otherwise interact. It is represented as a quintessentially liminal space. In Paul's words:

> *Last night was interesting. Jane, Bill and I went to the Hotel Mirador. I love the bar in the hotel. It has a desperate quality to it. The bar itself is set against the windows, which are long and reach to the floor. Someone who sits there is forced to look out, and what does he see through those windows? The mountain ranges of Spain. It's almost as if we can never get away, any of us. Something else is always there looming large, but not close enough to reach out and touch. The mountain range across the sea halts our movement. And the sea in between engulfs. The bar is always full of expatriates and young boys. It really does have the feel of the International Zone, Tangier, owned by no one, least of all by its indigenous people. The bar is a mini replica of Tangier, local boys mixing with foreigners, all of whom have no real existence. The boys because they have left their culture and their homes to sell sex for money, and the foreigners because the very reason we all came to Tangier was to be outside of that world which is supposed to give us meaning. No-one in that bar has any essential identity, we all just exist. (20-1)*

The sharp juxtapositions of literal and symbolic spaces represented in this passage range in scale from the architecturally liminal, the windows in a hotel, that is, a space of temporary habitation which is not home, to the grand scale of the national, colonial and international. In the heyday of the International Zone of Tangier in the 1950s, foreigners numbered almost half the city's population (Ellingham et al 2001:79), spurring a process of hybridisation. The microcosm which Adair chooses to represent the city and its interactions is appropriately enough the bar, which for Muslims is an emblem of deculturation and sin. As a result of the Qur'anic prohibition on alcohol, "as a Moroccan, if you went into the bars it meant one thing: you and Faust, the same pact, the inevitable consequences. The bar was the line that separated one world from another" (Adair 2004a:13-4). The bar is also represented in the novel as a space of conviviality, loss of inhibition and control, altered states of consciousness, and the blurring of traditional barriers such as difference in age. This space cannot be perceived as a carnivalesque zone where pleasures are freely indulged in, as the carnival is by definition a rare occurrence which serves to offer temporary escape from the status quo, while serving ultimately to bolster it. The bar, in contrast, is a permanent liminal site, where some power relations are softened, while others such as class and economic privilege remain intact in the offering of sexual services by boys.

A South African readership would consider what sites and opportunities are available for meaningful contact between previously segregated strata of society, and to what extent the dissolution of boundaries involves interactions beyond the merely economic, fleeting or trivial. Further, the question arises as to what the implications are of a dialectic which straddles the fault-lines between tradition and modernity, the local and the global, the individual and the community, the queer and the straight worlds, the hedonistic and the ethical, the devout and the secular, consumerism and corruption.

Although Belquassim has gained a love of European culture, especially literature, through his association with Paul, his sense of displacement and deculturation are evident. Both in his own cultural surroundings and in foreign ones Belquassim feels displaced and sinful, and regards himself as a conduit of corruption. Belquassim's loss of connection to his past is also signalled by his relationship with his mother. He knows that she lives on "[t]he outer edges of the International Zone where they had no place or space or culture" (74), yet he has forgotten exactly where her dwelling is, and abrogates his filial duties.

The character Jane, too, muses about Tangier and the complex ethical questions which it raises with regard to power relations:

> *I love this city—even the name, Tangier, has a ring to it. And the International Zone. I cannot rationalize its existence politically. No one who thinks, I believe, can ever rationalize colonialism in any form. It is only the faceless patriot who believes in the right of conquest and subjugation. Or is it sometimes I am not certain colonising others? Perhaps we all do it without recognizing what it is. Am I colonising Cherifa, or is she colonising me? But I love the city for that lack of morality that it has. No one, at least no one of the expatriates imposes a judgement upon anything or anyone. Everyone is somehow outside of social morality. I can move from the streets of the souks where women sit day after day working, selling, bartering, to the cafés where the men are permanently stoned on hash or majoun, to the places where the expatriates get drunk. And everyone just carries on living; it is as if they know that judgement here is of no force and effect and so it just passes them by.* (24-5)

Despite Jane's principled questions about colonisation, when it comes down to questions of sexual appetite and power she is clearly in a morally compromised position with regard to Cherifa, although she rationalises away her culpability by reference to the city's lack of morality, which supposedly exonerates her own actions. Yet the partisanship of her view is revealed by the shift from "the city" as an entity which is amoral, to the expatriates who eschew judgement. She is shrewd enough to note the parallels between the intoxications indulged in by Moroccan men and expatriates, regardless of gender, while Moroccan women are perceived as suffering the double jeopardy of race and gender, and yet her relationship with Cherifa is represented as exploitative, just as the sexual-colonialist desire between the historical Jane and Cherifa "was troubled by complicated issues of race and class differences" (Knopf 1996:164).

Race and class differences are still present as unexamined issues in Adair's novel, thereby perpetuating some degree of gender inequity and othering of Cherifa; this othering is substantially different from the alienation experienced by the character Belquassim. Belquassim and Cherifa are presented as structural counterparts of each other by virtue of their attachments to Paul and Jane. Belquassim's hybridity and angst are narrated from a position of interiority, and his character and opinions are developed over the course of the text, while Cherifa is represented rarely, and only from the outside; no sections of the text are mediated through her consciousness, and what representation there is is largely from a hostile perspective. Furthermore, she is a static character, conveyed primarily through a series of stereotypes. The first account of her in the text is typical; Belquassim comments:

> "Jane ... had persuaded herself that she was in love with a woman who sold herbs and other medicines in the market. Her name was Cherifa. Cherifa, tall, heavy and dark. She would cover herself with a *djellaba* and *haik* during the day. At home, in the evenings, she would wear a white cotton shirt and faded blue jeans. Her long brown fingers that she used to sift the millet, the long dark fingers...". Belquassim imagined how they penetrated Jane's body, a knife through her thin chest, a chest that would not be hard to pierce. Cherifa, an old woman now, still sat in the market, surrounded by young girls.... Cherifa had wished that Jane would die, and that had come true. Was the die cast by her spells? (8)

While Cherifa is represented as a hybrid figure, her hybridity is figured as a site of scandal and menace. The insistent mention of Cherifa's darkness is obviously symbolic (Jane shivers, "She is so dark, so wanton when we are together": 50). This stereotyped use of colour imagery calls to mind Chinua Achebe's comments about Conrad's obsessive and racist "fixation on blackness" in *Heart of Darkness* (1978:10). The representation of Cherifa further evokes Gayatri Spivak's analysis of the character Christophine in *Wide Sargasso Sea*:

... Christophine is tangential to this narrative. She cannot be contained by a novel which rewrites a canonical English text within the European novelistic tradition in the interests of the white Creole rather than the native. No perspective *critical* of imperialism can turn the other into a self, because the project of imperialism has always already historically refracted what might have been the absolutely other into a domesticated other that consolidates the imperialist self. (1989:186)

While Cherifa shares certain attributes with Christophine, such as their intimate knowledge of indigenous magic systems, there are also significant differences. Spivak examines the speech of Christophine and her disappearance off the scene as highly germane to her argument. In contrast, Cherifa is given barely any voice in *In Tangier We Killed the Blue Parrot*, a lacuna in the text made more apparent in light of her structural juxtapositioning with the articulate (and domesticated) Belquassim. The text unfolds against the backdrop of Belquassim's nostalgic memories of Paul, Jane, and the days of the International Zone. The frame narrative ends with a drunk Belquassim being led home by his son, whom he has not recognised. The last word of the novel, "home", thus attains an ironic significance, emphasising that Belquassim, as representative of natives of Tangier who came into intimate contact with the expatriates in various liminal zones, has been forever changed, and estranged, by the experience.

Adair allowed herself the latitude to create the character of Belquassim, while she apparently felt more constrained by the historical record detailing Cherifa's relationship with Jane Bowles. This record, told from the outside, is a hostile one. In Adair's novel she represents Cherifa as a hybrid presence through her dress code-switching, yet her subjectivity remains outside the imaginative scope of the text. Unlike Belquassim, who adapts to the Bowleses' domestic space and finally needs reminding of his own domestic space, Cherifa belongs in the market-place, where she fends for herself, and in her own domestic space, where she sets her own rules, and makes a home for a number of Moroccan women, who function as a harem. She does not "consolidate the imperialist self", in Spivak's term, but occupies an unimaginable space, a space of surprise, fascination and speculation. As Richard F. Patteson comments: "Surprise is inimical to domestication, whose aim is to make the strange seem familiar and predictable" (1987:21). Cherifa cannot be domesticated or appropriated. In fact, her great desire is to be given the house which Jane and Paul own. Her wish is thus to dispossess the expatriates and appropriate the home which they have established in Tangier. However, despite her strength of character, remarkable for a Moroccan woman of her class and time, she is accorded no textual space of her own in the text. Adair's inability to give a voice to Cherifa marks both a nagging, problematic absence in the novel, and an awareness of the impossibility of making a plausible imaginative leap into the psyche of the other woman. As Adair comments, it is easier to give a male character a voice, as men have traditionally been given disproportionate space in narrative (2004b). This skewed focus on the male characters in the text has the effect of perpetuating androcentrism; at the same time, however, power dynamics with relation to gender and sexuality are exposed. Terry Castle points out that lesbians in literature are 'apparitional', as desire between women destabilises traditional narratives (1993). Even more than the male-female-male triangle analysed by Eve Kosofsky Sedgwick (1985), the triangle including two women is profoundly destabilising and unsettling, as Adair's reticence reveals. In addition, an enigmatic, silent, indecipherable character like Cherifa may be invested with imaginative force by a receptive reader, allowing her to figure even more anarchically than her surface representation would suggest.

Although Cherifa is given virtually no direct voice in the text, and has motives and actions which are open-ended, Adair does give Cherifa's mystical and evil powers an interesting twist. In the novel Belquassim and Paul 'know' that Cherifa has killed Paul's beloved pet, a blue parrot. Yet the title of the novel is *In Tangier We Killed the Blue Parrot*. This is a surprising title: it forces the reader to assume both a position of identification with Cherifa and confront an implied collective responsibility for the death of the parrot, symbolising wildness, difference and creativity. Adair responded to my question about her usage of the word "we" in the title that it points to a wider sense of culpability: that experienced by "the expatriates in Morocco, Moroccans, colonialists and us in South Africa; we are destructive in many senses" (2004b). This blanket responsibility does, however, elide the different degrees of culpability and destructiveness displayed by different groups, both in Morocco and South Africa, in different periods.

* * *

In South Africa, the reception of *In Tangier We Killed the Blue Parrot* has been positive, although there has been some mystification about positioning the novel. In a review of the text Chris Dunton comments:

> In the end I'm not quite sure what it intends to achieve. One possible way beyond that uncertainty is to read it in the context of South African fiction,

post-*Disgrace*: to see it, in other words, as an exploration of notions of choice, distancing and home that reflects, very obliquely, on patterns of social consciousness in the author's own environment. (2004:18)

This analogy is apt and suggestive. The shorthand term "post-*Disgrace*" evokes a watershed in South African literary and public culture.[2] A full analysis of J.M. Coetzee's *Disgrace* takes into account its representations of the intersections of race, gender and sexuality as they play out both on the intimate sphere of the home and the wider domain of the nation. The body of the lesbian, Lucy, becomes a fecund site where power, force, choice (the specific motivations of which are unknowable), and a future-directed life-force coalesce. Like *In Tangier We Killed the Blue Parrot*, *Disgrace* provides an investigation of sexuality in a changing society with a racially over-determined history.

In Tangier We Killed the Blue Parrot is an anomalous text, difficult to classify, but comprehensible primarily within a South African context. The text raises important questions with regard to colonialism and its effects, voice, and the validity and responsibility of representing another culture, as a traveller, in a postcolonial context. It is a lyrically written, hybrid text which in a brief space does justice to the lives of Jane and Paul Bowles. Beyond the specifics of this representation of individual lives, however, the novel is a text set in the Interzone which raises questions about individual postcolonial societies and transcultural connections within the continent of Africa. In Interzone literature, "the indeterminacy and fluidity of interzone sexuality was counterbalanced by the rigidity of conventional colonial relations" (Mullins 2002:8). Similarly, while Adair uses the current cultural and literary climate to explore more fully the trope of bisexuality in South African fiction, thus expanding the boundaries of queer writing in this country, she is less successful in explicitly dealing with the consequences of racial privilege; however, the text itself reveals its limits in this regard. *In Tangier We Killed the Blue Parrot* is a polyvocal text which functions to critique homophobia and heteronormativity. It destabilises accepted binarist narrative conventions and broadens notions of sexuality, commitment, love, marriage and ethics beyond rigid orthodoxies. While it is situated in the Interzone of Tangier, it also allows for productive and progressive reflection on the contemporary South African social landscape, as well as on South Africa's position within the continent of Africa.

Notes

1. Fascinatingly, even Garber falls prey to an essentialising impulse when she ponders the relationship between the Bowleses in these terms: "What is a marriage? In this case a marriage between a bisexual man and a *lesbian* was reinvented so as to last a lifetime" (1995:407, my emphasis). In other texts Paul Bowles is referenced as gay, and claims of asexuality with regard to him also occur (Levin 2004). These usages point to the difficulties associated with accurately naming bisexuality in contexts of hegemonic, binarised hetero-/homosexuality.

2. My thanks to Dr Kai Easton for discussing this with me.

References

Achebe, Chinua. 1978. "An Image of Africa." *Research in African Literatures* 9:1-15.

Adair, Barbara. 2004a. *In Tangier We Killed the Blue Parrot*. Cape Town: Jacana Media.

_____. 2004b. Personal communication, 14 September.

Alderson, David and Linda Anderson (eds). 2000. *Territories of Desire in Queer Culture: Refiguring Contemporary Boundaries*. Manchester and New York: Manchester University Press.

Bacchetta, Paola. 1999. "When the Hindu Nation Exiles its Queers." *Social Text* 17(4): 141-66.

Barnard, Ian. 2001. "The United States in South Africa: Post Colonial Queer Theory." In: J.C. Hawley (ed.). *Postcolonial and Queer Theories: Intersections and Essays*. Westport, Connecticut; London: Greenwood Press: 129-38.

Barthes, Roland. 1975. *Roland Barthes by Roland Barthes*. London: Papermac.

Bell, David, and Gill Valentine (eds). 1995. *Mapping Desire: Geographies of Sexualities*. London and New York: Routledge.

Bhabha, Homi K. 1994. *The Location of Culture*. London: Routledge.

Binnie, Jon. 2004. *The Globalization of Sexuality*. London and New Delhi: SAGE Publications.

Bowles, Jane. 1979 [1943]. *Two Serious Ladies*. London: Virago.

Bowles, Paul. 1990 [1949]. *The Sheltering Sky*. London: Paladin.

Castle, Terry. 1993. *The Apparitional Lesbian: Female Homosexuality and Modern Culture*. New York: Columbia University Press.

Coetzee, J.M. 1999. *Disgrace*. London: Secker and Warburg.

Dillon, Millicent. 1988 [1981]. *A Little Original Sin: The Life and Work of Jane*

Bowles. London: Virago.

Dunton, Chris. 2004. "Vicarious Reconstruction of an Uneasy Existence in the Interzone." Review of *In Tangier We Killed the Blue Parrot*. *The Sunday Independent* (29 August): 18.

Eadie, Jo. 1997. "'That's Why She Is Bisexual': Contexts for Bisexual Visibility." In: *The Bisexual Imaginary: Representation, Identity and Desire*. Ed. Bi Academic Interventions. London and Washington: Cassell: 142-60.

Elder, Glen. 1995. "Of Moffies, Kaffirs and Perverts: Male Homosexuality and the Discourse of Moral Order in the Apartheid State." In: David Bell and Gill Valentine (eds). *Mapping Desire: Geographies of Sexualities*. London and New York: Routledge: 56-65.

Ellingham, Mark, Don Grisbrook, and Shaun McVeigh. 2001. *The Rough Guide to Morocco*. London: Rough Guides Ltd.

Epprecht, Marc. 2004. *Hungochani: The History of a Dissident Sexuality in Southern Africa*. Montreal: McGill-Queen's University Press.

Garber, Marjorie. 1992. *Vested Interests: Cross Dressing and Cultural Anxiety*. New York: Routledge.

_____. 1995. *Vice Versa: Bisexuality and the Eroticism of Everyday Life*. New York: Touchstone.

Hawley, John C. (ed.). 2001. *Postcolonial and Queer Theories: Intersections and Essays*. Westport, Connecticut; and London: Greenwood Press.

Hoad, Neville. 1999. "Between the White Man's Burden and the White Man's Disease: Tracking Lesbian and Gay Human Rights in Southern Africa." *GLQ: A Journal of Lesbian and Gay Studies* 5(4):559-84.

Hogeland, Lisa Maria. 1994. "Fear of Feminism." *Ms.* 5(3):18-21.

James, Christopher. 1996. "Denying Complexity: The Dismissal and Appropriation of Bisexuality in Queer, Lesbian, and Gay Theory." In: Brett Beemyn and Mickey Eliason (eds). *Queer Studies: A Lesbian, Gay, Bisexual, and Transgender Anthology*. New York and London: New York University Press: 217-40.

Knopf, Marcy Jane. 1996. "Bi-nary Bi-sexuality: Jane Bowles's *Two Serious Ladies*." In: Donald E. Hall and Maria Pramaggiore (eds). *RePresenting Bisexualities: Subjects and Cultures of Fluid Desire*. New York and London: New York University Press: 142-64.

Lambevski, Sasho A. 1999. "Suck My Nation—Masculinity, Ethnicity and the Politics of Homo Sex." *Sexualities* 2(4):397-419.

Levin, Adam. 2004. "Paul, Jane and Barbara." Review of *In Tangier We Killed the Blue Parrot*. *This Day* (10 June): 7.

Mullins, Greg. 2002. *Colonial Affairs: Bowles, Burroughs and Chester Write Tangier*. Madison: University of Wisconsin Press.

Patteson, Richard F. 1987. *A World Outside: The Fiction of Paul Bowles*. Austin: University of Texas Press.

Patton, Cindy, and Benigno Sánchez-Eppler (eds). 2000. *Queer Diasporas*. Durham and London: Duke University Press.

Pickford, Lucas. 2004. "Williams Burroughs: Tangiers." <http://www.lucaspickford.com/burrtangiers.htm> (15 August).

Povinelli, Elizabeth A. and George Chauncey (eds). 1999. *GLQ: A Journal of Lesbian and Gay Studies* 5(4). Special issue: *Thinking Sexuality Transnationally*.

Sawyer-Lauçanno, Christopher. 1989. *An Invisible Spectator: A Biography of Paul Bowles*. New York: Weidenfield and Nicolson.

Sedgwick, Eve Kosofsky. 1985. *Between Men: English Literature and Male Homosocial Desire*. New York: Columbia University Press.

Spivak, Gayatri Chakravorty. 1989 [1985]. "Three Women's Texts and a Critique of Imperialism." In: Catherine Belsey and Jane Moore (eds). *The Feminist Reader: Essays in Gender and the Politics of Literary Criticism*. London: Macmillan.

The Rocky Horror Picture Show. 1975. Dir. Sharman, Jim. Great Britain.

LIVING IN THE WORLD OF 'OTHERS'

INTERVIEW WITH ROBERT J.C. YOUNG IN SOUTH AFRICA

MICHAEL CHAPMAN

MC: During your brief visit to South Africa [July 2003]—first to Pretoria to the conference of the Association of University English Teachers of Southern Africa (AUETSA), and now in Durban in a workshop linked to the research project "Postcolonialism: A South/African Perspective"— you'll have picked up both a questioning—is South Africa postcolonial?— and a certain scepticism: is the postcolonial another Western regime of truth imposed upon 'Others'.

Two books by ex-South Africans—Elleke Boehmer (1995) and Dennis Walder (1998)—end up questioning the category, postcolonial. Boehmer ponders whether the postcolonial, if tied to models of literary representation, is not also tied to forms of postmodern style. For the terms hybrid or creolisation read, by analogy, experimentalism or artistic imagination. She points to a possible split in 'post' debate, in which northern literary study returns to postmodernism as a textual marker while in the South postcolonial serves as a political marker: the condition of society (223-50). Or to quote Walder, even if Caribbean or black British writers are willing to assert both "the centrality of the colonial experience and their own emancipatory agenda", the position for South African writers is less clear, "suggesting that although their particular vision of the colonial experience is unquestionably lasting, a dramatic, even revolutionary process of transformation is taking place which throws open once again the question of what we mean by 'post-colonial'" (189).

Whereas Boehmer and Walder focus on literature that might be termed postcolonial and whereas you—in your study *Postcolonialism: An Historical Introduction* (2001)—focus on the politics, you too have reservations about the term postcolonialism, preferring "tricontinental" (5).

RY: I begin with the premise and the actuality that the postcolonial perspective has developed the idea that the expansion of Europe, the move of Europeans out to the world from the 15th/16th century onwards is a fundamental part of modernity. If this involves texts, then the textual is a discursive act: an enunciation that both creates and circumscribes events or actions in the material world. I said modernity, but the European expansion guaranteed different kinds of modernities including the modernities that countered Western epistemological and political power: 'Third World' resistance movements, for example. The countermodernities of local needs: countermodernities which are aspects of modernity.

So, all sorts of different knowledges have developed, often—since the intervention of Edward Said's *Orientalism* (1978)—developed by scholars with diasporic affiliations. The way I see postcolonialism as a subject, an academic subject, is to pit countermodernities against the dominant Western paradigm. Many live in a world of 'Others'. How can we find a way to talk about this, to understand the condition? Since the early 1980s postcolonialism has developed a body of writing that attempts to shift the dominant ways in which the relations between Western and non-Western people and their worlds are viewed. What does that mean? It means turning the world upside down. If you are someone who does not identify yourself as Western, or is somehow not completely Western even though you live in a Western country, or someone who is part of a culture yet excluded by its dominant voices, inside yet outside, then postcolonialism offers you a way of seeing things, a language and a politics in which your interests come first, not last.

Why, then, tricontinental? Well, postcolonialism involves the argument that the nations of the three non-Western continents (Africa, Asia, Latin America) are largely in a situation of insubordination to Europe and North America, and in a position of economic inequality. At the Bandung Conference of 1955, twenty-nine mostly newly independent African and Asian countries initiated what became known as the Non-Aligned Movement. They saw themselves as an independent power bloc with a new Third World perspective.

The Bandung Conference—in important ways—marks the origin of postcolonialism as a selfconscious political philosophy. A more militant version came eleven years later at the great Tricontinental Conference, held in Havana in 1966. This brought Latin America, including the Caribbean, together with Africa and Asia. The conference established a journal, simply called *Tricontinental*, which brought together the writings of 'postcolonial' theorists and activists including Amilcar Cabral, Frantz

Fanon, Che Guevara, Ho Chi Minh, and Jean-Paul Sartre, elaborated not as a single political and theoretical position, but as a transnational body of work with a common aim of popular liberation.

The term tricontinental reminds us that postcolonial theory is not a theory in the scientific sense: that is, a coherently elaborated set of principles that can predict the outcome of a given set of phenomena. It comprises, instead, a related set of perspectives, which are juxtaposed against one another, on occasion contradictorily. It involves issues that are often the preoccupation of other disciplines and activities, particularly to do with the position of women, of development, of ecology, of social justice, of socialism in the broadest sense. The term tricontinental retains its power to suggest an alternative culture, an alternative 'epistemology', or system of knowledge. Also, it suggests that Third World problems have an internationalist reach and consequence. The journal, *Tricontinental*, appeared every month in four European languages.

MC: I hadn't encountered the journal.

RY: The journal came as a revelation to me. What I thought of as postcolonialism was all there, from the 1960s, in the *Tricontinental*. Because of the United States blockade of Cuba, the journal wasn't easily distributed. There's only one copy in the US, which is in the Library of Congress. I'm sure it wasn't allowed into South Africa...

MC: What you've said—indeed, your book *Postcolonialism*—suggests your materialist sympathies: a Marxist approach modified by particular Third World conditions and challenges. At the same time, in your earlier book, *White Mythologies* (1990), you locate within the political purpose of postcolonialism several critics who have sometimes been attacked as transferring politics to a realm of textuality: Bhabha, Spivak, for example.

Of Bhabha you say that he "demonstrates how dissonant, non-syncretic theory can shift control away from the dominant Western paradigm of historicist narrative....The problem of history becomes indissociable from the role of the investigator in the formation of knowledge and the traces of the historian as writing-subject" (156).

This is not the same division between the materialist and the textualist that we encounter in several other Marxist critics. I think of Benita Parry, who believes that the postcolonial project has gone wrong: that the politics of a symbolic order—in people like Bhabha—has displaced the theory and practice of politics; that politics has been sidelined by an attachment to styles of textuality. She concludes her argument by referring to a shift from social context to art text as a scandal! (2004).

RY: I'm not sure about Benita's argument. It's true that in terms of textual analysis postcolonial ideas and perspectives would mean that some texts are regarded as more significant than others. Even interventions in the Western canon favour interventions in some texts and not in other texts. But the import is not, I think, to be found in styles of representation. It is the knowledge conveyed, the extensions of our knowledge. Benita—in her own criticism—tends to re-read mainstream British fiction of the imperial era—Kipling, Conrad, Forster. But these writers don't necessarily help us extend our experience, our knowledge of worlds outside the British sphere of influence. Whatever the style—fictive or realist—in, say, Chinua Achebe or, from South Africa, Bloke Modisane, we encounter a load of African experience that we don't encounter in Conrad.

Benita is quite restricted in terms of what her method allows her to look at. To return to your reference to Homi Bhabha, when I read Bhabha, for example, I don't recognise a dichotomy between textuality and materiality. Rather, I agree with Foucault's analysis of the text not as a representation but as a discourse, in which discourse is never a disembodied imaginative representation prior to any interaction with the real. Discourse always forms at the cusp of knowledge acting in and on the material world. Discourse is language that has already been made history.

So it is with Bhabha's discourse. I mean, sometimes his prose is irritating in terms of intelligibility. But it's also oddly powerful. His hybridity shouldn't be divorced from his own material experience—his growing up in Bombay, a city of many cultures in many juxtapositions. Then his living in London, which, in a different way, is a city of many cultures in various stages of transformation. Such indissoluble strands of the textual and the material seem to me to be relevant to a country like South Africa—as far as I have been able to sense in my few days here—a country where you also have many cultures, many languages, all in the same national space. Issues of identity arise – another aspect of analysis that postcolonial studies can offer.

MC: Yes, there is something too binary about the text/context debate, even in postcolonial studies, the aim of which is to question spatial and geographical metaphors: position, displacement, interstices. I found suggestive your chapter in *Postcolonialism* on Foucault in Tunisia, in which you point to Foucault's apparent silence on colonial Tunisia, where he wrote *Archaeology of Knowledge,* as a silence of significant displacement: his distance from France as a site from which to develop an ethnological perspective on French culture; ethnology not as in anthropology for the study of the other culture, but—as in discourse theory—ethnology for the study of one's own culture.

RY: Discourse theory is a key concept in the politics of the postcolonial. Just as Foucault ties materiality to words, so did Fanon, in whose writing language is a formative event. More so than in Foucault, a Fanon text has a powerful material impact: the writing creates almost a bodily reaction in you as you read it. A great deal of Fanon's writing was part of a propaganda war, in which text as discourse entered the politics of struggle. What I find important about the possibilities of the postcolonial is its breaking out of narrow paradigms of what is considered to be 'literary'.

MC: The question of what is literary—high art or popular expression, or forms of testimony or reportage—was central to attacks in South Africa in the 1970s on what were then the predominant Arnoldian-Levisian assumptions of literary studies: the Africanist challenge, poststructuralism, neo-Marxism, extensions of the concept of text. What continues to be a challenge in a society of 'difference'—different cultures, different languages, different religions—is the challenge of unequal power relations, unequal resource distribution, within a single though heterogeneous space. How to translate or not translate difference?

RY: What I noticed at AUETSA was a group of people who share the desire to make some sort of cross-cultural, intercultural connections, to develop forms of understanding and to recognise value across cultures, across different cultural spaces without any sense of hierarchy, which is obviously one of the things you're fighting against in relation to the apartheid past. I do think that postcolonialism facilitates such communication because it is anti-hierarchical in its principles and, I hope, in its practice.

But looking across cultures is both challenging and painful. Painful, especially if you're living in South Africa where the language situation is painful—English as the predominant academic discourse in a country of several languages, all marked by their own histories of contestation, of dominance and subservience.

The academics that you mentioned earlier on—Boehmer, Walder, Parry—are perhaps significantly all South Africans who live abroad. This raises its own questions of 'us' and 'them', even within the academic discourse. It is true that postcolonialism with a South African perspective is dominated, internationally—at least in publishing opportunity and outlet—by diasporic South Africans who probably have priorities somewhat different from those who live in the country itself.

But this is not necessarily a bad thing. As I said, postcolonialism is not a single theory, but more like a cluster of interrelated ideas. It is not a prescriptive paradigm, and you are free to say: this is particularly relevant to this situation, but not to that. There remains a degree of common purpose, however, in the objective of social justice.

At the workshop (in Durban) you offered several columns of description—Canada, Australia, as white settler colonies, at the one extreme; Nigeria as a non-settler state at the other—and you posed the question as to where on such a continuum one might place South Africa. Not easy. I would add to the complication. Australia, for example, wishes to regard itself as free of politics. Any theme—private relationships, suburban life—is regarded as the legitimate field of interest for the Australian writer. But don't forget—and several Australian writers do not forget—that until 1972 Australia was a kind of apartheid state. It didn't allow immigrants to arrive unless they were white. And, of course, Australia perceived itself to have an Aboriginal problem: it had the practice of Abo hunting! So Australia—no less than South Africa—has to be re-imagined.

MC: And Canada, which until recently began its literary history in the 1860s with the arrival of white settlement. No Inuit oral past. Separate studies of Canadian-English and Canadian-French literature, and little mention of contemporary Asian or Chinese immigration.

RY: Or to slot onto your continuum somewhere near South Africa, the case of Brazil. Though not identical, South Africa and Brazil have certain similarities of structure. You've both got a history of colonisation, a history of slavery, a passage to independence linked to internal colonialism; you're both countries of vast discrepancies in wealth distribution; countries of different races and languages. São Paulo, for example, is a heavily industrialised, highly polluted modern city, while indigenous people, in the Amazon forests, fight for survival against gold prospecting, and so on. A situation reminiscent of the cultural experience we encountered yesterday...

MC: On the Inanda heritage route (outside Durban), a visit to the Gandhi settlement at Phoenix, after which the guide took us to John L. Dube's Ohlange Institute, and then to the Shembe holy village of Ekuphakameni. A syncretic African-Christian dance ritual by hundreds of worshippers—twenty minutes away from the drinks patio, beside the swimming pool, at the Oyster Box Hotel in Umhlanga Rocks. Admittedly, the whites suntanning at the pool didn't speak with local accents, but that's not the point—except for the waiters, not a black person in sight. To attach context to text, or to regard the entire space here as postcolonial, then a Gordimer novel, say, and a Shembe religious ritual may be interpreted as both marked by the postcolonial, at least from the South African perspective.

Whatever the ramifications, the perspective is not entirely encompassed within Dennis Walder's view of postcolonial in relation to literature as a celebration of new literatures in other englishes (1998:6). Clearly there is value to such a claim. But then the Shembe experience—an oral-based, isiZulu experience—falls outside of the field.

RY: Yes, postcolonial studies in the West has a location in English departments. So it is anglophone. But I don't think we can blame these people. They do a certain kind of work which many English departments—in Britain and the United States—still refuse to take up.

MC: Most of us in English departments in South Africa are also monolingual. The difficulty is that the Shembe voice impinges—or should impinge—on the multicultural experience. English may be the language of commerce, higher education and, now, government, but the Shembe voice is part of majority African-oral speech. Also, any study of postcolonialism that ignored the shaping power of Afrikaans in its forty years of power would be seriously limited in its political as well as literary knowledge.

RY: What the Shembe experience brought sharply home to me is that outside the issue of linguistic translation, there are issues of cultural translation that hardly feature in Western forms of postcolonial studies. Let me mention two: the power of spirituality, and, in a country in which modernisation contains within its processes living traditional practices, the issue of chieftaincy or, more broadly, patriarchy. Patriarchy, of course, is a significant aspect of postcoloniality in most parts of the world, but the role of the chief in a modern constitutional state must present unique challenges.

Postcolonial studies have emerged from the Left, and the Left has never been very interested at looking at religious views. There is some work on the spiritual dimension in Indian cultures. But a potent force of our times is Islam, which offers a kind of popular form of expression that is far broader in its appeal than most political movements have ever been. So it's something that needs to be addressed, but I don't think it's being addressed, at least not in postcolonial studies.

We've talked of the Shembe experience. I was reminded yesterday also of Gandhi's influence. And South Africa has, as well, its Islamic influence. Your discursive field of cultural politics is complex. Postcolonial studies in South Africa obviously has important work to do.

References

Boehmer, Elleke. 1995. *Colonial and Postcolonial Literature*. Oxford: Oxford University Press.

Parry, Benita. 2004. *Postcolonial Studies: A Materialist Critique*. London and New York: Routledge.

Walder, Dennis. 1998. *Post-colonial Literatures in English: History, Language, Theory*. Oxford: Blackwell.

Young, Robert J.C. 1990. *White Mythologies: Writing History and the West*. London and New York: Routledge.

_____. 2001. *Postcolonialism: An Historical Introduction*. Oxford: Blackwell.

Contributors

Michael Chapman is a professor of English at the University of KwaZulu-Natal in Durban, South Africa. His publications include *Soweto Poetry* (1982; 2007), *South African English Poetry: A Modern Perspective* (1984), *The "Drum" Decade: Stories of the 1950s* (1989; 2001), and the literary history *Southern African Literatures* (1996; 2003). His collection of essays, titled *Art Talk, Politics Talk: A Consideration of Categories,* appeared in 2006.

M.J. Daymond is an emeritus professor of the University of KwaZulu-Natal. Her numerous publications include the landmark compilation, *Women Writing Africa: The Southern Region* (2003).

Ileana Dimitriu is an associate professor of English at the University of KwaZulu-Natal in Durban. Her publications include the monograph, *Art of Conscience: Re-reading Nadine Gordimer* (2000).

Michael Green is a professor of English at the University of KwaZulu-Natal in Durban. His publications include *Novel Histories: Past, Present and Future in South African Fiction* (1997), *Sinking: A Verse Novella* (1997) and *For the Sake of Silence* (2008).

Sally-Ann Murray is an associate professor of English at the University of KwaZulu-Natal in Durban. She is also an award-winning poet whose second volume, *open season*, appeared in 2007.

Monica Popescu is assistant professor of English at McGill University, Montreal. Her book, *The Politics of Violence in Post-communist Films* appeared in 1999.

Corinne Sandwith lectures in English at the University of KwaZulu-Natal in Durban. She edited for *English in Africa* (29.2.2002) a collection of the work of the political activist and writer, Dora Taylor.

Matthew Shum lectures in English at the University of KwaZulu-Natal in Durban. He has published articles on the colonial/metropolitan interface in South Africa.

Cheryl Stobie lectures in English at the University of KwaZulu-Natal in Pietermaritzburg. Her study, *Somewhere in the Double Rainbow: Representations of Bisexuality in Post-apartheid Novels,* appeared in 2007.

Robert J.C. Young is professor of English at New York University. His publications include *White Mythologies: Writing History and the West* (1990), *Colonial Desire: Hybridity in Theory, Culture and Race* (1995) and *Postcolonialism: An Historical Introduction* (2001).

INDEX

Achebe, Chinua 6
Adair, Barbara
    In Tangier We Killed the Blue Parrot 171-84
        Bequassim 178, 181, 182, 183
        Cherifa 182-4
        city in 178-82
        class 182
        gender 183-4
        hybridity 174
        Interzone 173, 176-7, 185
        liminality 174, 180
        race 174, 182
Age of Iron (J.M. Coetzee) 115
ANC (African National Congress) 64, 68-9
ANC Youth League 64, 68-9, 76
Appiah, Kwame Anthony 3
Ashforth, Adam 100-1
Attridge, Derek 12, 115
Attwell, David 130, 141, 144
autobiographical writing 88, 89, 90, 91-6, 99, 102
    agency 95, 96
    as cultural resistance 84
    in post-apartheid period 84-5

Bantu World 61-3, 70-1
Barrell, John 26-7
Bhabha, Homi K. 4, 5, 6, 52, 60, 118, 157, 174-5, 191
bisexuality 173-4, 175-6, 177
Boehmer, Elleke 189, 193
Bowles, Jane 171, 176, 178
Bowles, Paul 171, 176, 178
Boyhood (J.M. Coetzee) 120-1
Brathwaite, E.K. 6

Bryant, A.T. 139-40
Bunn, David 17, 30, 53
Burke, Edmund 25-6
Burroughs, William 173

Carter, Paul 27
Childs, Peter 155
Coetzee, J.M. *Age of Iron* 115
Coetzee, J.M. *Boyhood* 120-1
Coetzee, J.M. *Disgrace* 185
Coetzee, J.M. *Elizabeth Costello* 125-48
    allegory 132, 135
    embeddedness 130, 141
    embodiment 130,141,145
    Lesson on 'The Humanities in Africa' 11, 133, 140-2
    Marianhill (J.M.Coetzee's) 126,133, 135, 139
    Mariannhill (Mission) 126, 127, 134, 135, 136-140, 145
        Trappist order 136, 138-9
    national identity and universality 133
    realism 126, 127-8, 130
    textuality and reference 129-30, 134, 144, 145
    as a work of fiction 126
Coetzee, J.M. *Life & Times of Michael K* 41
Coetzee, J.M. *The Master of Petersburg* 11, 106-24
    as historiographic metafiction 109-110
    impersonation in 114
    inter-generational conflict and authority 113-15, 116, 117
    and late postcolonialism 118
    plot 107-8
    as political *roman á clef* 109
    relevance to South Africa 108, 109, 111, 112, 113, 116, 118, 120
    Russian theme in 106, 120-1
Coetzee, J.M. *White Writing* 17, 52
colonial landscape 16, 31
Comaroff, Jean and John L. 46-7, 112
community of awareness 8
Cooppan, Vilashini 153

Derrida, Jacques 3, 6, 107, 112, 143
Dharwadker, Vinay 153

difference 3, 6, 8, 162, 193
discourse 5
Disgrace (J.M. Coetzee) 185
Dollimore, Jonathan 8-9
Dostoevsky and dialogism 11-12
Dostoevsky, Fyodor in *The Master of Petersburg* (J.M. Coetzee) 108, 109, 110, 113, 115
Dostoevsky, Fyodor *The Possessed* 111, 119

Eagleton, Terry 5
Elizabeth Costello (J.M. Coetzee) 125-48
    allegory 132, 135
    embeddedness 130, 141
    embodiment 130,141,145
    Lesson on 'The Humanities in Africa' 11, 133, 140-2
    Marianhill (J.M. Coetzee's) 126,133, 135, 139
    Mariannhill (Mission) 126, 127, 134, 135, 136-140, 145
        Trappist order 136, 138-9
    national identity and universality 133
    realism 126, 127-8, 130
    textuality and reference 129-30, 134, 144, 145
    as a work of fiction 126
'Evening Rambles' (Thomas Pringle) 16, 28-38
exotic species 44-5, 46

Fanon, Frantz 8, 72, 79, 193
fiction and history 109-110, 134
Foucault, Michel 2, 6, 143, 192-3
Frank, Joseph 109, 111

Garber, Marjorie 175
gardening 10, 41, 42
    in Durban 43-4
    and literary-cultural analysis 40-1
    for middle-class black South Africans 51-2
    in Nadine Gordimer's review of J.M.Coetzee's *Life & Times of Michael K* 41
    see also indigenous gardening
Gordimer, Nadine
    cultural globalisation 149, 151-4

freedom of expression 152
Jump 163
Loot 149, 162-8
Living in Hope and History 150
'Living on a Frontierless Land' 149-50
local and global 153-4,162, 167
None to Accompany Me 149
and peripheries 150, 154, 155, 156
and postcolonialism 154-6,168-9
Telling Tales 153, 169
The House Gun 149
The Pickup 149, 156-62, 166
and world literature 152-4

Harris, Wilson 6, 9
Heyns, Michiel 113
hybridity 6, 174,

In Tangier We Killed the Blue Parrot (Barbara Adair) 171-84
Bequassim 178, 181, 182, 183
Cherifa 182-4
city in 178-82
class 182
gender 183-4
hybridity 174
Interzone 173, 176-7, 185
liminality 174, 180
race 174, 182
indigeneity 49-53, 78
indigenous gardening 40, 46, 47-52, 53, 54
and identity 52-3, 55-8
landscaping styles 48
as a 'phenomenon' 50-1
and postcolonialism 40
settlers and 42, 53-4
significance for white South Africans 51, 54-5
in South Africa 42, 47-58
intercultural translation 85, 86, 87, 96-8, 99
Interzone 173, 176-7, 185
invasive alien species 45-8

Jacobs, J.U. 88
Jeyifo, Biodun 131-2
Jump (Nadine Gordimer) 163

Kendall, 'Limakatso' 90
Kossew, Sue 157
Kureishi, Hanif 9

landscape
        in Thomas Pringle 18-38, *see also* colonial landscape
Lee, Dennis 167
Lenta, Margaret 133
Life & Times of Michael K (J.M. Coetzee) 41
liminality 174, 180
Living in Hope and History (Nadine Gordimer) 150
Loomba, Ania 12
Loot (Nadine Gordimer) 149, 162-8
Lottering, Agnes
        family history 87, 93
        and mother 93, 100
        translation, inability 95-6, 99
        translation, refusal, 95-6, 99
        translation 93,102
        use of language (English and isiZulu) 86, 87, 89, 92, 93
        Winnefred and Agnes 85-9, 92-8, 101-2

McCleod, Ellen 43
Magona, Sindiwe 88
Mamdani, Mahmood 79
Marianhill (J.M.Coetzee's) 126,133, 135, 139
Mariannhill (Mission) 126, 127, 134, 135, 136-40, 145
        Sisters of the Precious Blood 138
        Trappist order 136, 138-9
Matlare, Isaac 63
Mda, Zakes *The Heart of Redness* 106
Mnganga, (Father) Edward Muller Kece 140
Mngoma, Khabi 63, 64
Moore-Gilbert, Bart 6
Mothopeng, Zeph 64, 71
Mphahlele, Es'kia 6, 63, 64, 71, 88

Narrative of a Residence in South Africa (Thomas Pringle) 17-27
Ndebele, Njabulo S. 110
Negritude 6, 79
Ngakane, Barney 63
Ngũgĩ wa Thiong'o 6
Nhlapho, Walter M.B. 61-2, 63, 64
Non-Aligned Movement 190
None to Accompany Me (Nadine Gordimer) 149
Nthunya, Mpho
    mother of 91-2
    printed book and reading 91, 92
    Singing Away the Hunger 85-7, 88, 90-2, 98-9,100-102
        bewitchment 98-9
    as storyteller 90, 91
    translation, inability 95-6, 99
    translation, refusal, 95-6, 99
    use of language (Sesotho and English) 86-8, 89, 90-1

Orlando 70
Orlando Study Circle 63, 64

Papini, Robert 92
Parry, Benita 191, 192, 193
Pfanner, Franz 136-7, 138, 139
picturesque 27, 28, 29, 30, 34, 35
Pieterse, Nederveen 151
political 'complicity' 61, 78
post- debate 4-6, 7
postcolonial 189
    and discourse theory 193
    periodisation 118
    and spirituality 195-6
    theory 8, 10, 173, 191, 194
postcolonialism 1-2, 190, 191
    cross- or inter-cultural communication 193-4
    language 195
    late 118-19, 120
    literature 1-9, 10, 12 154-6, 195
    materialism191, 192
    as process 154-6

textuality 192
utopian model 3
see also tricontinental
postcolonialising 11, 154-5, 169
Pringle, Thomas
    and colonial labour 35-6
    'Evening Rambles' 16, 28-38
    landscape 10, 18-38
        historical imprint in 22-3
        picturesque 28, 29, 30, 34, 35
        sexualisation of 34
        sublime in 22-6, 33
    Narrative of a Residence in South Africa 17-27
    'The Autumnal Excursion' 30-1, 33
Punter, David 9

Quayson, Ato 6, 154-5, 156, 159
queer theory 173-4

Ricards (Bishop) 136
Robbins, Bruce 153
Rushdie, Salman 4

Sachs, Albie 110
Said, Edward W. 2, 5, 6, 7, 8
San Juan Jnr, E. 3, 12
self-translation 88, 91, 92, 93
Shembe 195
Singing Away the Hunger (Mpho Nthunya) 85-7, 88, 90-2, 98-9,100-102
Slemon, Stephen 85
Sole, Kelwyn 7-8
Sommer, Doris 101, 102
Spivak, Gayatri 4, 5, 6, 182-3
sublime 24-6, 33, *see also* Pringle, Thomas
Sun 63

Tangier 177, 179
Telling Tales (Nadine Gordimer) 153, 169
'The Autumnal Excursion' (Thomas Pringle) 30-1, 33
The Heart of Redness (Zakes Mda) 106

The House Gun (Nadine Gordimer) 149
The Master of Petersburg (J.M. Coetzee) 11, 106-124
    as historiographic metafiction 109-110
    impersonation in 114
    inter-generational conflict and authority 113-15, 116, 117
    and late postcolonialism 118
    plot 107-8
    as political *roman á clef* 109
    relevance to South Africa 108, 109, 111, 112, 113, 116, 118, 120
    Russian theme in 106, 120-1
The Pickup (Nadine Gordimer) 149, 156-62, 166
The Voice of Africa 61-83
    and African nationalism 64, 68, 72, 80
    circulation 65
    and European/Western culture 60, 72-7, 79, 80
    and indigenous cultural forms 61, 74, 78
    origins and character 63-4, 65, 66, 67-71
    political views 64-5, 66, 68-9
    and resistance 61, 72, 79-80
Third Space 174-5, 177
tricontinental 5, 190, 191
Tricontinental 191
Tricontinental Conference (1966) 190

Umteteli wa Bantu 63

Van Wyk Smith, Malvern 17
Vladislavić, Ivan 55, 58

Walder, Dennis 189, 193, 195
Watson, Patrick 48
Watson, Stephen 53, 54
Western culture, attitudes towards 60, 62, 72-7, 79, 80
White Writing (J.M. Coetzee) 17, 52
Wicomb, Zöe 91
Williams, Patrick 155
Williams, Raymond 159, 168
Winnefred and Agnes (Agnes Lottering) 85-9, 92-8, 101-2

Young, Robert J.C. 2, 5, 8, 189-96